# Visible and Apostolic

# Visible and Apostolic

## The Constitution of the Church in High Church Anglican and Non-Juror Thought

Robert D. Cornwall

**DELAWARE**

Newark: University of Delaware Press
London and Toronto: Associated University Presses

BV
598
.C66
1993

Associated University Presses
440 Forsgate Drive
Cranbury, NJ 08512

Associated University Presses
25 Sicilian Avenue
London WC1A 2QH, England

Associated University Presses
P.O. Box 338, Port Credit
Mississauga, Ontario
Canada L5G 4L8

**Library of Congress Cataloging-in-Publication Data**

Cornwall, Robert D., 1958–
    Visible and apostolic : the constitution of the Church in High
Church Anglican and Non-juror thought / Robert D. Cornwall.
        p.   cm.
    Includes bibliographical references and index.
    ISBN 0-87413-466-8 (alk. paper)
    1. Church—History of doctrines—18th century.  2. High Church
movement—England—History—18th century.  3. Nonjurors.
4. Apostolic succession—History of doctrines—18th century.
5. Church polity—History—18th century.  6. Church of England—
Doctrines—History—18th century.  7. Anglican Communion—
Doctrines—History—18th century.  8. Sacraments—Church of
England—History of doctrines—18th century.  I. Title.
BV598.C66   1993
262'.0342—dc20
                                                        92-56626
                                                        CIP

PRINTED IN THE UNITED STATES OF AMERICA

# Contents

# Preface

As a former Episcopalian with ancestral roots in the Anglican church, it was not difficult for me to decide to make Anglicanism the focus of my doctoral studies. Those studies took up the better part of the past five years. The work that stands before you is a revision of my dissertation undertaken at Fuller Theological Seminary in Pasadena, California. This topic has provided me the opportunity to indulge my interests in ecclesiology, pastoral theology, and sacramental theology. Not only were early eighteenth-century high-church Anglicans intriguing individuals, but modern scholarship has largely neglected the movement, making it a fertile area in which to work.

While the beliefs and teachings of high-church Anglicans may not be attractive to many modern Christians, most high churchmen were sincere defenders of what they believed was orthodox Christianity. Their zeal may have crossed the boundaries of good judgment from time to time, but in the light of their context it is understandable. Eighteenth-century high churchmen provide the scholar with a study of contrasts, as there were very few shades of gray in their doctrinal formulations. Their intolerance of other Christians and their narrow limitation of Christianity to those who embraced and maintained the doctrines of apostolic succession and episcopacy might seem odd, but it was at the heart of their belief system.

Special gratitude is due my mentor, colleague, and friend, Dr. James E. Bradley, Professor of Church History at Fuller Theological Seminary. He introduced me to eighteenth-century English history and theology, a region I had rarely traversed prior to beginning my doctoral studies. The resulting adventure has been extremely rewarding. His encouragement and willingness to devote his time and energy to my work helped immeasurably in turning a doctoral dissertation into a published book. Jim not only guided my scholarly endeavors, but he provided an example of what a teacher should be and for that I am forever grateful.

Dr. Richard Muller, Professor of Historical Theology at Calvin Theological Seminary, who served as my second reader, helped me clarify the theological aspects of my studies, pointing out the historical precedents to the views expressed by the objects of this study. Dr. Gerald M. Straka, Professor of History at the University of Delaware, served as the outside reader on my dissertation committee, and his gracious comments provided contextual depth to the work. On a more personal level, Dr. Straka strongly encouraged me to publish the manuscript and then helped guide me along the path to that end. Along the way several other scholars read all or part of the manuscript. The comments of Dr. Colin Brown, Professor of Systematic Theology and Associate Dean of the Center for Advanced Theological Studies, Dr. John Thompson, Assistant Professor of Historical Theology, both of Fuller, and Dr. A. M. C. Waterman, Professor of Economics at St. John's College, The University of Manitoba, raised important issues of context and style that enabled me to improve the quality of the work before you. Each of these scholars has contributed greatly to the success of this study and I am greatly indebted to them.

I also would like to express my appreciation to the faculty and staff of Fuller Theological Seminary, especially Shelly Theisen, Deborah Dail, and Gretchen Immen, Program Assistants for the Center for Advanced Theological Studies. The staffs at the McAllister Library of Fuller Theological Seminary, the Huntington Library in San Marino, California, and the William Andrews Clark Library of the University of California, Los Angeles, all provided gracious assistance to this project and deserve a word of acknowledgment and thanks. I also would like to express my appreciation to the University of Delaware Press and the Associated University Presses for agreeing to publish this book.

My greatest debt is owed to my wife Cheryl, and to our son, Brett. Cheryl has endured hardship and uncertainty, and her willingness to undertake the financial burden of our family enabled me to move through the doctoral program at great speed. Her love and support have been my strength. Brett was born as I began revising the dissertation, and—though he slowed my progress on occasion—he has brought great joy to my life. Therefore, it is to Cheryl and Brett that I dedicate this project.

# Visible and Apostolic

# Introduction

The political and social consequences that followed in the wake of the Glorious Revolution of 1688–1689, together with the increasing authority of human reason in religious dialogue, provoked considerable debate concerning the nature of the church and its place in society. The flight of James II and the coronation of William and Mary ushered in a new age in English political and religious history. S. C. Carpenter, calling attention to the alleged change from Tory to Whig domination in church and state and the ascendancy of the Latitudinarians as the dominant religious party in the Church of England, declared that the "Church in 1688 turned over a leaf and began again."[1] These years were full of transition and conflict, being bracketed by the deposition of James II in 1688 and the failure of the last Jacobite Rebellion in 1745.

In the face of political, social, and cultural change, High Churchmen[2] and Non-Jurors, those high churchmen forced out of the church because of their refusal to endorse the change of government, sought to retain the traditions of the past. They were the successors of the Caroline divines, men such as Henry Hammond, John Pearson, and Jeremy Taylor. Politically, many high churchmen, only three decades removed from the end of the Civil War, continued to espouse the doctrines of divine-right monarchy, along with the corollaries of that doctrine: indefeasible hereditary right of the monarchy, nonresistance, and passive obedience. Believing that the monarchy was divinely ordained, they considered resistance to the king's authority to be a sin. Paul Monod, however, has demonstrated that they did not follow the lead of Robert Filmer's patriarchalism and acquiesce to arbitrary rule.[3]

The flexibility of divine-right thought is evident in the actions of William Sancroft, the Archbishop of Canterbury. Sancroft and six of his suffragans were imprisoned in 1688 for refusing to read James II's Declaration of Indulgence from their pulpits. Yet Sancroft and the majority of those imprisoned with him would eventually become Non-Jurors for refusing to break their oaths of allegiance to James II. Still, the events of 1688–1689 would appear to have caused these ideals to lose their cogency. Nevertheless, the "cult of divine-right monarchy" continued long into the eighteenth century. The most conspicuous example of divine-right thought was the persistence of the cult of Charles I, the royal martyr. The anniversary of his execution remained a key fast day in the established church, a day that occasioned sermons calling for submission to the government and all in authority.[4]

The doctrines and the practices of the Restoration church persisted among elements of the English church into this new political age. In part, this was a reaction to the uncertainties cast upon the church by the new government of William and Mary, leading churchmen to hold on to revered and safe traditions. Still, as Owen Chadwick has stated in his introduction to the Oxford Movement, one cannot understand the high-church suspicion of the Dutch Calvinist, William III, and the German Lutheran, George I, both of whom would have had a natural proclivity for their own Presbyterian and Lutheran traditions, on the basis of political churchmanship alone. He writes: "It is explicable only as a doctrine, as a conviction based upon principles of religious authority, and grounded not in political need but in theological thought."[5]

High Churchmen and Non-Jurors did espouse a theological position that focused on the centrality of the church to salvation, the equality of church and state, whether they believed church and state to be one or two societies, and on a divinely ordained hierarchy of bishops, priests, and deacons, authorized to administer the means of grace: baptism, and the eucharist. While low churchmen sought to downplay the necessity of episcopacy in their effort to find a point of unity with English Nonconformists, high churchmen made apostolic succession the heart of their ecclesiology. These theological issues underlie the high-church response to changes accompanying what some have called the age of reason or the Enlightenment, a response that sought to return the church to the structures and beliefs of the first four centuries of the Christian era.[6]

English men and women of this period witnessed the impact, if not the triumph, of the Enlightenment on their nation. There are questions about the nature and even existence of the Enlightenment in England, but Roy Porter notes that England became renowned throughout Europe for being the "pure crystal of the Enlightenment." In contrast to the rest of Europe, seventeenth- and eighteenth-century England was noted for its openness, freedom, and religious toleration. The English Enlightenment emerged from within a different milieu than did its counterparts in Scotland and on the continent, for the Erastian nature of English protestantism as well as the existence of an anti-clerical attitude among large elements of the populace limited the need for the existence of philosophes who would protest the problems of religious authority. Still, despite the moderation of the English Enlightenment, the origins of this movement are rooted in Britain. Though some historians, such as Peter Gay, find the quintessence of the Enlightenment in the France of Voltaire and Diderot, Porter notes that the benchmarks of the Enlightenment, the Declaration of Rights, the Toleration Act, the Act of Union, Locke, Newton, Defoe, Shaftesbury, and Toland are English and all predated the French Enlightenment of the 1740s.[7]

In the light of the religious and social disturbances of the seventeenth century, English religion after 1688 came to be influenced by writers such as John Locke and others who sought to prove the "reasonableness of Christianity." Locke's rational religion was tolerant but moderate, and it found its adherents among liberal Anglicans such as Benjamin Hoadly and the Deists. Deism and Arianism predated both Locke and the Revolution of 1688, but they had begun to make inroads into the established church by that time. This development caused great concern among many conservative or orthodox members of the established church. Additional pressure came from the politically dominant latitudinarian Anglicanism, which pushed orthodoxy to its accepted limits even if it did not move beyond them. The Erastianism that dominated the Church of England found institutional expression in the deprival of the Non-Juror bishops in 1691 and the prorogation of the Convocation of Canterbury in 1717. The general tone of the church appeared to be pragmatic, leaning more toward moralism than toward intense spirituality. High churchmen, and especially the Non-Jurors, stood in the midst of this sea of change as the last bastions of traditional belief and practice. Some High Churchmen fashioned an alliance with the Tory party in Parliament, hoping to find security and protection for the church. Many of these High Churchmen saw the state as the last hope of confronting both the heresy that existed within the established church and the threats of Roman Catholicism and Nonconformity outside it. Tory politicians raised the battle cry "the Church in danger" in order to distinguish themselves from the Whig party, whom they deemed to be the enemies of the church's privileged place in society. The Non-Jurors, on the other hand, found themselves disillusioned with the political process and declared that the church was independent of the state and in control of its own destiny.[8]

The ensuing study seeks to fill a void in contemporary historical scholarship by providing an analysis of the theological basis of high-church Anglican ecclesiology. Although there is currently a revival of interest in high-church Anglicanism, historians continue to neglect the theological basis for the high-church response to the events and issues of the day. Scholars have tended to concentrate on the politics of the period, the practical activities of the church leadership, and the ecclesiologies of the dominant Latitudinarian party.

An additional question that must be addressed concerns the foundation of the Non-Juror schism. This schism is usually attributed to political motivations, making the Non-Jurors little more than the religious side of the Jacobite movement. Yet the strongly theological rationale given in defense of the schism militates against this view.[9]

That church and state in England were considerably intertwined during the seventeenth and eighteenth centuries must not be denied. But, questions relating to the alliance between church and state were determined by theological concerns that were only derivatively political. Theological arguments are especially evident in the debates concerning the integrity of the church as a society independent of the state. The state's deprival of the Non-Juror bishops, the proposals for comprehension and the toleration of the Dissenters, and the Convocation Controversy all raised theological concerns. Theological issues also were components in the disputes over the Test Act and the corresponding practice of occasional conformity. We will seek to examine the constitution of the church in England from 1688 to 1745 from the theological perspectives of High Churchmen and Non-Jurors.

The term "constitution" was used in the seventeenth and eighteenth centuries to refer to both the nature and the government of the church. This usage is exemplified by the title of George Hickes' tract, *The Constitution of the Catholic Church and the Nature and Consequences of Schism* (1716).[10] Consequently, "constitution of the church" is broader in meaning than "doctrine," and this study will attempt to examine theologically both the relationship of church and state and questions regarding the nature of the church as a religious society. An analysis of the nature of the church also must deal with related issues, such as the sources of authority, the ministry, and the sacraments.

High-church Anglicanism conceived of the church as a visible, episcopal, and catholic institution, in which membership was required for salvation. George Every states that the title "High Church Party" did not come into use until the latter part of the seventeenth century, and that the party could not be distinguished from the rest of the church to warrant the name until 1689. The dividing line, according to Every, was the election of the Prolocutor of the Convocation of Canterbury in 1689; the term applied to those who opposed the largely latitudinarian policies of the majority of the bishops.[11]

High Churchmen and Non-Jurors were, for the most part, of the same theological persuasion. However, the Non-Juror refusal to change their allegiance from James II to William and Mary led to their separation from the established church. This allowed them to push many of their theological emphases to their logical conclusion, including ecclesiastical autonomy and the liturgical embodiment of high church eucharistic doctrine. We also will attempt to demonstrate that the theological position of these men often preceded their political engagements. Therefore, theology contributed directly to several major political debates. Although Francis Atterbury[12] grounded his defense of convocation in the English constitution, he joined other writers, including Thomas Brett, Henry Dodwell, and Samuel Hill,[13] in seeking to give a theological basis to the right of Convocation to meet regularly to discuss the business of the church. Support for political issues, such as the Test Act and the ban on occasional conformity, was rooted in the high-church belief in the necessity of episcopal government. Tories and High Churchmen perceived these measures to be the proper means of protecting the established church from the encroachment of a Parliament that might become dominated by dissenters if severe measures were not taken to prevent it from occurring.[14]

We will endeavor to provide, in the subsequent chapters of this study, a comprehensive analysis of the ecclesiology of high-church Anglicans. In order to be comprehensive, the term "high churchman" must be construed broadly to include both Non-Jurors and more moderate churchmen who affirmed both the proper ordering of society and the centrality of the church and the episcopate to Christian life. The inclusion of a wide spectrum of writers allows one to see both the unity and the diversity of belief among theologically conservative Anglicans. The tension that existed between Catholic and Protestant tendencies can be perceived in each of the fifty-one writers studied here. No previous systematic examination of their thought on the church has been undertaken. A number of the authors studied were among the principal disputants in the political and ecclesiastical debates of the period. Francis Atterbury was the leading figure in the Convocation Controversy, and William

Law and Andrew Snape played a major role[15] in the Bangorian Controversy.

Besides making use of the works of prominent High Church and Non-Juror divines, such as Atterbury, William Beveridge, John Potter, Henry Sacheverell,[16] George Hickes, Thomas Brett, and Henry Dodwell, we also will refer to several minor figures who contributed a tract or sermon to the various conflicts and discussions. More obscure authors, such as Joseph Betty, William Roberts, and Matthias Symson, can be associated with high church movement themes by their public stance on key ecclesiological issues, including the primitive authority of the episcopal hierarchy and sacramental theology.[17] In a few instances, there were figures, such as Edmund Gibson and William Wake, whose political alliances and theological moderation distinguished them from the more rigid high churchmen, but who also demonstrated high-church proclivities on key issues, including the centrality of the episcopal hierarchy, the integrity of the church as a visible society, and sacramental theology.

An objective of this study is the consideration of the usefulness of viewing the high-church movement as a coherent and unified group. We will find that in the interplay with political events, theological consensus diverged dramatically, resulting in irreconcilable differences and disunity, particularly with respect to episcopal jurisdiction and the sacraments. Despite this diversity, High Churchmen and Non-Jurors do reflect a sufficiently coherent perspective on the authority, independence, and the necessity of the church and its episcopal order. It is important to stress that for these two movements not only doctrine but the visible practices of the church were deemed essential to salvation. Thus, the specific ecclesiological concerns of the high churchmen require detailed attention. Yet it also is important that the points on which Anglicans agreed are clarified.

In interpreting eighteenth-century Anglicanism, scholars have disagreed concerning the state of the church and the influence of theological and political parties on the church. Nineteenth-century scholarship, influenced by Methodist and Non-Juror criticisms of the established church, charged that latitudinarians dominated the church, causing eighteenth-century religion to become lethargic, worldly, self-seeking, and pragmatic.[18] Twentieth-century scholarship, dominated by the works of Norman Sykes, has attempted to refurbish the reputations of the Latitudinarian party, and with it the Church of England. Although Sykes acknowledged the practical nature of eighteenth-century churchmanship, he noted, non-pejoratively, that the tone of religion was moderate, rational, and ethical. Sykes' emphasis on the Latitudinarians paralleled the focus on the Whig Party in political historiography, with its attending focus on social and economic progress. On the other hand, twentieth-century scholars have tended to exclude the importance of the contributions made by Tories, High Churchmen, and Non-Jurors to the history of eighteenth-century England.[19]

This concentration on latitudinarianism and whiggism recently has been challenged, both in political and religious historiography. Jonathan Clark believes that Jacobite[20] scholarship is one of the "few expanding areas within the contracting circumference of historical enquiry." He attributes this increased attention to Jacobitism to the demise of the "Whig Consensus" in historical scholarship during the 1980s. Although many Non-Jurors were Jacobites, their separation from the established church was not based solely on their adherence to James II, for they also were advanced high churchmen, whose advocacy of episcopal government colored the defenses of their effort. J. H. Overton has denied that Non-Juror and Jacobite were interchangeable terms, as some Non-Jurors, he claims, were not Jacobites, at least in the active sense. Paul Monod agrees that not all Non-Jurors were Jacobite agents, yet he states that the refusal to take the oaths, in an age that took oaths seriously, was a "very strong political statement." He concludes that whether or not they were active in the Jacobite cause, they were still "Jacobite by definition." Whether or not the Non-Jurors were Jacobites, Clark also challenges the idea that Non-Juror writings were "ephemera, like the political pamphlets of the 1760s, buzzing noisily for a few hours before sinking into oblivion." He states that both their political and their theological works were substantial and "powerful and complex in their argument." John Morrill on the other hand, has challenged Clark's revisionism and embraces the Whiggism of G. M. Trevelyan. He complains that the revisionists fail to use the "historical filter" to focus on the events and values that in the end prove to be the winners. Thus, Clark has written what he calls "horizontal history," in which "every event, every idea is over-contextualized and over-particularized." Despite this danger of over-contextualization, it is important to indulge in the study of all contributors to the historical process. Still, it is in the spirit, if not the specifics, of Clark's thesis that this inquiry has been undertaken.[21]

Though we are concentrating on neither Jacobitism nor Anglican political theology, the importance of both the High Church and the Non-Juror theological perspectives, which developed in the context of political change and debate, need to be affirmed and developed more fully than they have in the past. Important recent works, including those of G. V. Bennett, George Every, Mark Goldie, and F. C. Mather, and the dissertations of John Findon and G. M. Yould on the Non-Jurors, develop aspects of the high-church position. No major study exists, however, that attempts to understand high-church ecclesiology, with its attendant theological and political ramifications. Though Norman Sykes has provided a masterful analysis of eighteenth-century religious practices, his effort does not extend to the theological underpinnings of those practices.[22]

We will, therefore, seek to fill this void in contemporary scholarship by examining in detail the ecclesiastical thought and practice of the High Churchmen and Non-Jurors. The purpose of the following study is to illuminate the theological foundations of the high-church movement in order to understand better the reasons why these men stood fast against what they perceived was the encroachment of a secular and utilitarian age, one that gave little room for traditional religious authority.

The sources for this study are published works, including: printed sermons, tracts, theological tomes, catechisms, and devotional manuals. High churchmen took advantage of their opportunities to enter the theological and political debates of the age and left a substantial record of their thoughts and beliefs. Many of the works are apologetic or polemical in nature, since they often were written in the midst of religious conflict. Moderation and tolerance were virtues that were often lacking. Although the tone is often sharp, the polemic has enabled the issues to be drawn out much more clearly.

The study begins with a discussion of the contextual issues, noting the various competing views of the church and the ecclesiastical controversies of the period (chapter 1). Because of the primary place given to reason by the Latitudinarians and Deists, the high-church attempt to balance Scripture, tradition, and reason must be considered (chapter 2) before their doctrine of the church is analyzed. On the basis of the discussions of the key contextual issues as well as the sources of authority in the church, our examination of the nature of the church will commence, beginning with a study of the high-church understandings of the visibility of the church and the historical marks *(notae)* of the church (chapter 3). Chapter 4 continues the investigation of the nature of the church by examining the theological rationale for the independence of the church from the state. Belief in the church's independence from the state played a crucial role in the Non-Juror defense of their separation from the established church. We will proceed from this foundation with discussions of the doctrine of the ministry (chapter 5) and the sacraments (chapter 6). These final two chapters enable the reader to observe the essential components of the "true church" in England. Each chapter demonstrates that the church played a central role in the religious consciousness of the high-church movement. Without the church one would not have access to the means of salvation, leaving the church without a purpose, other than as a support to the political and social orders.

# 1

# High Church Ecclesiology in the Context of Religious Liberalism and Nonconformity

The eighteenth century was a period of great conflict and transition in ecclesiological thought and practice. New philosophies and ideologies challenged long-held beliefs. Lines were drawn between traditional and nontraditional, liberal and conservative, orthodox and heterodox positions. Anglicans were as divided among themselves as the Dissenters. High Churchmen and Non-Jurors stood in the midst of these competing theologies and polities as the guardians of orthodoxy.[1]

Popular religious piety in the late seventeenth and early eighteenth centuries, though it appears somewhat lackluster and moralistic, still played a primary role in the lives of the English people. There were numerous signs of secularization, including the spiritualizing of religion in popular religious works and the ramifications of toleration for the Anglican ideal of a nation unified by religious considerations. Yet popular religion continued to dominate the popular press. The literacy rate during the middle of the seventeenth century approached a third of all adult males in England, with the numbers approaching one-half of the adult male population in London. Though book prices rose in this period, most popular books remained affordable. In addition, numerous lending libraries began to appear during the later stages of the seventeenth century. Thus, there seems to have been a wide audience for reading materials. One half of all books that went through at least six editions between 1660 and 1700 were religious, while two thirds that went through more than twelve editions were religious books. The devotional classic, *The Whole Duty of Man,* went through forty-five editions between 1660 and 1745. A ready audience continued to exist for the myriad of religious tracts produced in the era following the Glorious Revolution. The lapsing of the Licensing Act in 1695 removed the state's power to censor published literature, giving even wider latitude to printed matter. And though means of suppressing radical materials remained, Deists, such as John Toland, and heterodox writers, such as William Whiston, continued to publish freely. This atmosphere enabled religious conflicts to be aired and understood not only by the intellectual elite, but also by the popular masses.[2] Conflict centered on the proper sources of authority in the church. While Latitudinarians, Deists, and many Nonconformists were voices for the new age of reason, which included openness to biblical criticism, high chuchmen continued to give a prominent place to tradition.[3] Therefore, High Church and Non-Juror thought must be understood in the context of the leading philosophies and ecclesiologies of the day. This chapter sets forth some of the philosophical challenges to traditional ecclesiology, examines the ecclesiologies of the major contending parties, and concludes with an appraisal of the major ecclesiastical controversies of the day.

## The Influence of John Locke and the Primary Place of Reason in Religious Discourse

The whole fabric of ecclesiastical thought in the late seventeenth and early eighteenth centuries was torn by the exaltation of reason as the primary source of ecclesiastical authority. Though reason was elevated above tradition, this did not mean a wholesale rejection of divine revelation. John Locke, Isaac Newton, Latitudinarian divines such as John Tillotson and Edward Stillingfleet, who had been influenced by the Cambridge Platonists, all appealed to the authority of reason. Latitudinarians desired a religion in which revelation was in accord with human reason and natural religion.[4] Thomas Hobbes also remained influential through the early years of the eighteenth century, though even Latitudinarians opposed his views. Still Hobbes, who considered the church to be a corporation needing the oversight of a single head, proved to be an important contributor to the Erastian feel of established religion in England. Church and state, in his opinion, should have the same head, and that person was the king.[5]

Locke's writings, though not the first to appeal to reason's authority, revolutionized its influence in England. Although his treatises on government and toleration, which provided an apology for William and Mary's claim to the throne of England and a philosophical basis for the toleration of the Dissenters, have been the focus of historical inquiry, his religious works also proved to be very influential.[6] His attempts to ground the Christian faith in reason led to accusations of heterodoxy, including charges that he held Arian and Socinian views. Whether or not he held heterodox beliefs, his writings served as fuel for the fire among Deists, Arians, and Socinians. More importantly, while the writings of a Deist such as John Toland might prove to be distasteful to moderate Anglicans, Locke's more temperate views could be seen as more acceptable and in the end more influential.[7]

Locke believed that religion should be marked by simplicity; therefore, he turned from theological systems to the Bible in search of a simple creed. Having taken Scripture at face value, Locke, according to Gerard Reedy, was a "severe and simple inductionist." Locke believed that one could discover the true meaning of Scripture only after all preconceptions were wiped away. Reedy notes that Locke perceived even the chapter and verse divisions of the Pauline letters to be a hindrance to fully comprehending the meaning of the letters. Though reason was insufficient to discover the truth of revelation, it was needed to ascertain whether it derived from God. He reduced the requirements for salvation to acceptance of Jesus as Messiah. Assent to Jesus' claim to be Messiah, evidenced by his miracles, marked believers from unbelievers. For Locke, the miracles of Jesus were not contrary to reason, since the Jews were waiting for a miracle-working Messiah, and Jesus fulfilled those expectations. Locke's reasonable Christianity retained a measure of mystery, and he did not press his arguments to the point of denying the validity of faith. Those who followed in his wake, including Deists John Toland and Matthew Tindal, did not feel as constrained by orthodoxy, and they went much further in demystifying religion. After Locke, however, revelation served to confirm the faith established by reason, rather than reason supporting revelation.[8]

The exaltation of reason and the establishment of a noncreedal faith led to a moralistic emphasis in religious formularies, a trait Locke shared with Latitudinarians such as John Tillotson. Reasonable Christianity required moral obedience to God's law. This law, in turn, served as the standard of judgment for everyone. Yet, since perfect obedience to the law was impossible, Christ required only sincere obedience. Assent to the messiahship of Jesus and sincere obedience to God's laws were perceived to be the only reasonable requirements for salvation. But because common people did not have the leisure of reflecting on the truths of natural religion, ecclesiastical authority was needed to help them discover their proper duties and morality.[9]

Locke defined the church as a voluntary society gathered for the worship of God in a manner pleasing to God. The contractual understandings that permeated Locke's political thought also surfaced in his ecclesiology. The church's foundation consisted in the free assembly of like-minded men and women who contracted together to form a church. Faith could not be passed on from one generation to the next; rather, it had to be appropriated by each individual. Locke cast the meaning of faith in terms of assent to propositions, not to a person.[10]

Toleration was the "chief characteristical mark of the true church," and acts of "charity, meekness, and goodwill in general towards all mankind" were perceived to be superior to religious rites and ceremonies, orthodoxy, or ecclesiastical discipline. Locke believed that free choice, not coercion, led to acceptance of Christianity. An involuntarily chosen form of religion was more of a hindrance than a furtherance to salvation. Unlike Thomas Hobbes, Locke did not blur the lines that divided church and state. He considered them to be two separate societies with different purposes. A national church was allowable only if it was broad enough to include all Christians. The churches, not the civil magistrate, were responsible for the care of souls; therefore, the state was called on to tolerate all belief systems, with certain limitations.[11]

The government and laws of the church flowed out of society itself. Locke found no scriptural support for the necessity of episcopacy or an uninterrupted apostolic succession. The only requirements for establishing a church were those found in Christ's teachings: the gathering of two or three in the name of Jesus, (Matthew 18:20). He did not reject episcopacy out of hand, but he did maintain that each person had the right to join the church or society that he or she believed taught the necessary truths for salvation. The only conditions for communion were those laid out in Scripture as essential for salvation. To require more than this was not reasonable. Foreshadowing the position of Benjamin Hoadly, Locke stated that faith and inward sincerity were the sole criteria for one's acceptance by God. The choice of a religion by the supreme magistrate did not determine the rightness of that religion. Although Jonathan Clark has asserted that Locke's primary influence was felt by Arians and Socinians, a more important and wide-ranging legacy may have been with regard to his challenge to episcopacy and the doctrine of apostolic succession, which was the primary obstacle, for high churchmen, to the full comprehension and toleration of the English Nonconformists. This can be seen in Hoadly's efforts to challenge the position and authority of the episcopate from within the established church. Questions also were raised concerning episcopacy in the early work of Peter King, Locke's cousin and later Lord Chancellor of England, who wrote in defense of the primitive nature of presbyterian ordination. King, in turn, influenced John Wesley, who attributed his reversal on the question of episcopal ordination to his reading of King's, *An Enquiry into the Constitution, Discipline, Unity and Worship of the Primitive Church,* (1691, with a second edition published in 1713).[12]

Although the parameters for toleration were broadly defined (they were, in fact, much broader than what was finally enacted in 1689), Locke excluded all societies whose moral rules and opinions were contrary to the preservation of society, however rare. Anyone who would make use of toleration to gain power and deprive others of their civil rights was to be proscribed. Those who claimed allegiance to another prince were also excluded from the enjoyment of toleration; Moslems of the Ottoman Empire were his primary example of groups to be excepted from toleration, although, in the wake of James II, Roman Catholics must have been in his mind as well. He felt that toleration of these groups posed a threat to the English state. Finally, those who denied the existence of God were not to be tolerated.[13]

A whole generation of religious thinkers followed Locke in making reason preeminent, including A. A. Sykes, Benjamin Hoadly, Peter King, William Warburton, Samuel Clarke, as well as Deists Matthew Tindal and John Toland. Reliance on reason led many of Locke's disciples into heterodoxy, especially with regard to the Trinity. Yet Latitudinarian divines, such as John Tillotson, Gilbert Burnet, and Edward Stillingfleet, while embracing reason, remained, for the most part, orthodox. These latter divines, however, were influenced more by the Cambridge Platonists of the mid seventeenth century than by Locke. Thus, the advocacy of reason might lead one to either orthodoxy or heterodoxy, but it also led to change in the church's self-perception. The ecclesiologies of Locke's proteges, such as Hoadly, would come much closer to Nonconformity than to traditional Anglicanism.[14]

## Competing Views of the Church

The Reformation was the first step in the breakdown of a monolithic concept of the church in the West. In its wash a variety of polities emerged. While the Church of England resembled the Roman Church more closely than any other Protestant group did, the two churches were not identical. The Church of England was not the only religious society in Britain. Religiously, England had embraced religious pluralism. If England was not pluralistic in a legal sense, it was so in reality.[15]

High Churchmen and Non-Jurors linked the visible and invisible manifestations of the church. Their church was well-ordered and regulated and not a voluntary society. God had appointed the "true church" for the salvation of all people, and those who chose to remain outside were separated from God. Temporally, Christ's vicegerents, the bishops and priests, whose authority descended uninterrupted through apostolic succession, governed the church. The clergy, when properly ordained by the bishops, had sole authority to dispense the means of grace, baptism and the eucharist. In the final analysis, it was the relative authority of the bishops that distinguished the high church ecclesiology from its competitors.[16]

THE LATITUDINARIAN ECCLESIOLOGIES

The Latitudinarians, at least politically, were the dominant party in the Church of England. William and Mary drew from this group to fill the vacancies on the episcopal bench, including John Tillotson, who replaced William Sancroft, a deprived Non-Juror, as Archbishop of Canterbury in 1691. While Latitudinarians were loyal to the traditions of the church, they did not stress the external trappings. The roots of this movement can be found in the philosophical teachings of the Cambridge Platonists, a movement that arose during the middle of the seventeenth century at Cambridge University. It was marked by the veneration of Plato and Plotinus, opposition to religious fanaticism, and preaching of a reasonable religion of holiness. Religious authority was based not on an appeal to the religious institutions but to the human mind. Unlike Locke's empiricism, the Cambridge Platonists insisted on the existence of innate ideas and self-evident ideas. The leading figures of the latitudinarian movement in the seventeenth century all conformed during the Interregnum to Presbyterianism and then returned to the episcopal church following the Restoration. Perhaps one half of the clergy who had served during the period of the Civil War conformed to the reestablished episcopal church. This made for a strong foundation for a moderate party in late seventeenth-century England.

The moderation with which the latitudinarians approached ecclesiological questions led Gilbert Burnet to define the church as a:

> [S]ociety that preserves the essentials and fundamentals of Christianity . . . so when we acknowledge that any society is a true church, we ought to be supposed to mean no other, than that the covenant of grace in its essential constituent parts is preserved entire in that body; and not that it is true in all its doctrines and decisions.[18]

By putting the emphasis on the essential doctrines of the faith, the Latitudinarians had more freedom to support schemes for comprehension and toleration in the context of an established state church. The advocacy of a strong state church included the provision that the final decisions concerning the nature and functions of church government were to be left to the state. For some Latitudinarians, state power over the church was designed to protect the state from encroachment by the church. It was on this basis that Benjamin Hoadly defended the deprival of the Non-juror bishops and clergy after the Glorious Revolution.[19]

Concern for protecting the state was coupled with a desire to provide religious freedom. Hoadly, influenced more by Locke than by the Cambridge Platonists, insisted that the free exercise of religion was "necessary to the happiness of a *governed society*." He believed that as long as religious freedom did not compromise public safety it should be indulged. Therefore he proposed the creation of a comprehensive state church, broad enough to assuage the scruples of the Dissenters. While Edward Stillingfleet was less open to extending legal rights to the Dissenters, Hoadly and his ally, A. A. Sykes, who also saw sincerity as the hallmark of religious devotion, sought protection and political rights for them. Hoadly and Sykes encouraged the practice of occasional conformity, as well as the repeal of the Test and Corporation Acts. The latter two statutes prevented Dissenters from holding national and municipal offices.[20] Latitudinarians, though they might differ as to the role of the state in religion, were moderates, not radicals. They sought to provide a reasonable, biblical, and comprehensive Christianity that would be inclusive of all Christians in England.[21]

### THE DEIST ECCLESIOLOGIES

Deists such as Matthew Tindal and John Toland, in their attempt to return to natural religion, were the most radical of all. The influence of John Locke is evident in their contractarian views of the church, but Deism has its origins much earlier than Locke's emergence on the scene, and unlike Locke, the Deists diverged into more radical manifestations of religion. Deism in England goes back to Edward Herbert, Lord Cherbury, and Charles Blount, with the latter being the more direct founder of Deism. Lord Herbert, like later Deists, affirmed a brief creed that would be inclusive of Socinians, Arians, Jews, and Muslims. John Toland held to an atheistic world view in line with his espousal of a religion of nature, thus worship of nature replaced the worship of God. Lord Herbert shared a second important concern with the Deists and that was opposition to "priestcraft," or the dominance of a priestly caste over religious and political life.[22]

Deist ecclesiology was marked by its rejection of priestcraft, and this is seen in Matthew Tindal's ecclesiological formulations. He wrote that "all ecclesiastical power has no other foundation than the consent of society."[23] The consent of society may have been the basis of the church's existence, but dictates of human reason formed the essence of the church's identity. Christianity became equated with life lived according to reason. The Deists pushed this view so far that atheists could be considered a part of the church if they lived in agreement with the dictates of reason. Putting their trust in the reasonableness of humanity, Tindal and Toland rejected the necessity of episcopal government. With Christ as its sole head, and with its establishment based on the consent of its members, the church did not require a particular polity. Willingness to serve formed the basis of ministry; while overseers could emerge from inside or outside the congregation, Toland and Tindal rejected a priestly caste, believing that it would lead to superstition. They would allow for bishops, but these officers were not to be imposed on a congregation. Religious rites and cultic celebrations were perceived to be antithetical to the vision of reasonable and simple religion, one marked by voluntarism and sincerity, not orthodoxy. Uniformity was rejected as impractical, and possible only in a nation of ignorance and stupidity. Liberty of conscience was in the best interest of everyone, as long as it did not infringe on the rights of the community and the government.[24]

Despite their espousal of natural religion and freedom of belief, Deists did not refrain from embracing an Erastian view of church and state. Tindal, like Hoadly, appealed to the good of society as a rationale for government involvement in religion; he affirmed the right of the magistrate to cut both clergy and laity off from church communion. The church was to be subordinate to the state in everything. Tindal concluded that an independent church would generate an *imperium in imperio,* for "all independent power must be supreme, because what is not so must be dependent; and no power can be supreme, which does not necessarily carry legislation with it." This was, for Tindal, the creation of a monster. But within this "state church" great diversity was to be allowed, even to the extent of permitting a variety of sects. Dissenters, who out of conscience refused to take the sacrament in the established church, were to be allowed to receive it in their own churches. Thus, like Locke and Hoadly, the Deists reduced episcopacy to a functional role in the church, stripping the episcopate of its authority and power to affect the course of church, ministry, sacraments, and paramountly, of personal salvation.[25] The Deists sought to combine freedom of conscience with social stability under the rubric of their trust in the reasonableness of the people. Ultimately, the church, as an institution, was not that important to them.

## THE NONCONFORMIST ECCLESIOLOGIES

Presbyterians were the successors of the Elizabethan Puritans. In 1569 Thomas Cartwright discovered and proclaimed that presbyterianism, not episcopacy, was the true scriptural polity. Despite their rejection of an episcopal hierarchy, Presbyterians remained in the established church until their expulsion for refusing episcopal orders after the Restoration. Even then Richard Baxter and Edmund Calamy were offered bishoprics, but the two Puritan leaders refused the sees. In the end those who refused to conform to the Act of Uniformity issued in 1662 were ejected. Though Presbyterians were similar to the Separatists in their claims to derive their polity from the New Testament, they differed with them by seeking to bring reform and proper discipline to an established church. Presbyterianism, as a polity, was defined by the authority vested in the lay eldership, and therefore, it stood in opposition to episcopal authority.[26]

The Presbyterian view of the church was exemplified in the work of Richard Baxter, who believed that the Reformed churches had the soundest polity in Christendom. The church was, first, catholic, with Christ as the head and all Christians as his body. The catholic church was both invisible in terms of individual faith, and visible in terms of one's baptism and profession of faith. Broad and comprehensive, the church included within its bounds any Christian who did not deny the essentials of the Christian faith. This definition, therefore, did not exclude members of the Roman Church. Second, the church was holy and separate from the world, set apart for God. The membership of the visible church was composed only of the saints, those who had separated themselves from the world. The maintenance of this holy church required Godly discipline; thus discipline became a major element of Presbyterianism. Third, the church was apostolic. Apostolicity was derived not from apostolic succession or episcopacy, but rather from holding to the apostolic faith, as it was taught by Scripture. These three foundational points formed the basis of the universal church.[27]

The local Presbyterian congregation was distinguished by the authority given to the pastor, exemplified by the pastor's right to determine one's membership in the church. The congregation also made a strong distinction between clergy and laity, which they traced back to Clement of Rome.[28] Presbyterians did not limit the definition of the church to local congregations, for beyond them lay the presbyteries, synods, and general assemblies, each of which provided guidance and oversight to the manifestation of the church that lay below it. Baxter spoke of councils or associations that God had required to enable churches to cooperatively promote "the common ends of Christianity." These extra congregational associations could be called churches, but such a designation was not necessary. Michael Watts has pointed out that the Presbyterians had a three-fold, extra-congregational government. A conference consisted of one minister and one elder, elected by a group of twelve churches, who met every six weeks. The half-yearly provincial synod was composed of the representatives of twenty-four conferences (two pastors and two elders from each). Finally, the national assembly met annually and consisted of three elders and three pastors, elected from each synod.[29]

The Congregationalists, like the Presbyterians, affirmed the existence of the gathered church of the saints, but the congregation, not the pastors or elders, was the locus of church authority. Congregationalists traced their roots to the Elizabethan Separatists, whose scruples forced them to leave the established church. A second movement emerged in the 1640s, which repudiated the terms separatist and independent in favor of congregationalist, thereby distinguishing themselves from both the Separatists and the Presbyterians. Michael Watts states that an independent might be either a Separatist or a Congregationalist, with both "asserting the independence of the local congregation from any higher ecclesiastical authority."[30]

The local congregation was the church in the strictest sense of the word. It was a voluntaristic or covenanted assembly gathered together to fulfill the duties appointed by Christ. Philip Doddridge defined the church as a "society, consisting of all those who profess to believe in him as a teacher sent from God, and form their worship and conduct according to what they apprehend to be his institutions."[31] The congregation came into existence on the basis of lay initiative, and thus it was not clergy oriented. This was also seen in the way in which ministers were called and ordained. Unlike the Presbyterians, who placed stress on learning and lengthy preparation, the Congregationalists usually required only a day of fasting and prayer, a congregational vote, and prayers by other ministers. They believed that a congregation organized upon these principles would experience the presence of Christ in a special way. Yet, as James E. Bradley has pointed out, the distinctions between the dissenting denominations became less important after toleration was granted in 1689. For their part the Presbyterians became a congregational church, the only difference being their name.[32]

The church was separate from the world, a gathered society of the saints. Regeneration, though determined by God, was symbolized by baptism. While election was in God's hands, the church had the responsibility to exercise discipline to keep itself pure. The requirements for church membership included an adequate knowledge of the doctrines of the faith, submission to Christ, self-denial, and fulfillment of all moral and religious duties. After the pastor, along with one or two deacons, interviewed the applicant, the candidate for membership faced a congregational vote. Great care was taken so that the applicant could give account of his or her faith and Christian experience.[33]

Despite the separatist tendencies and concern for purity of conduct, theology, and worship, a tolerant spirit marked the religious outlook of many eighteenth-century Congregationalists, except perhaps with regard to Roman Catholics. Though maintaining a Calvinist theology, they advocated religious freedom and toleration. Doddridge, unlike his Separatist forbearers, did not reject the established church out of hand, though he would allow that "in proportion to numbers, there is generally more practical religion to be found in our assemblies than in theirs." The Congregationalists cooperated in numerous ventures with both the Presbyterians and the Baptists, and intercommunion, including the practice of occasional conformity, and efforts at comprehension with the established church continued throughout the century.[34]

Believer's baptism, usually by immersion, distinguished Baptists from other Dissenters. Michael Watts notes, however, that among some of the Calvinist Baptists, believer's baptism became an open question with advocates of both believer's baptism and pedobaptism residing in the same congregations. James Bradley points out that, despite their emphasis on believer's baptism, the Baptists met with other dissenting denominations on occasion.[35] The Baptists divided into two groups: the General Baptists, who were Arminian and connectionalist; and the Particular (Calvinist) Baptists, who had their origins among the Separatists and were marked by ecclesiastical independence to the point of making a fetish out of local autonomy.[36]

The churches discovered in Scripture a three-fold form of ministry, comprised of messengers, elders, and deacons. Messengers were extra-congregational officers and, at least among the General Baptists, they had a supervisorial role over the local congregations. Nonetheless, their primary work was evangelistic. Elders, chosen from among the church members, were the local pastors, having responsibility for preaching, baptisms, and presiding at the Lord's Table. The deacons, also chosen from within the church, had responsibility for congregational finances. District associations and the General Assembly linked the General Baptist congregations with each other. The General Assembly was composed of all messengers and elders, as well as representatives from the local congregations. Although the Particular Baptists affirmed local autonomy, they too had assemblies, beginning in 1689. These assemblies, however, were not considered to be superior to the local congregations, and their decisions were not binding.[37]

The Quakers, or the Society of Friends, grew out of George Fox's hunger for God, a hunger that was not satisfied by contacts with ministers of either the established or Nonconformist churches. Led by a vision of Christ, Fox began calling the people to leave their existing ecclesiastical structures and join him in promoting a pure religion. The radical nature of his message led to the persecution of his followers. Fox was imprisoned and beaten by his opponents, and some of his followers faced martyrdom. Yet persecution failed to deter them.[38]

Quakers, like other Dissenters, defined the church as a gathered assembly. This assembly was marked by similar beliefs, principles, and doctrines. The heart of the early Quaker corporate life was the cell, which met on the first day of the week. Corporate worship consisted of "waiting on the Lord," in which the people waited in silence for the movement of God to lead someone to speak. They also rejected the visible sacraments of baptism and eucharist. This led to suspicion and outright opposition from the rest of the Christian community. The early openness of the Quakers to the direct inspiration of the Holy Spirit ironically later led to the creation of a complex and centralized organization. Fox devised a hierarchical system of meetings to govern the denomination. At the bottom of the pyramid structure were the particular meetings for worship, and above them were the monthly meetings for discipline, the county quarterly meetings, and finally the yearly meeting. Michael Watts suggests that the structure paralleled the Scottish kirk in polity more than it did any of the other English dissenting churches. At the head of the entire denomination was an executive committee, which no other denomination would have until the nineteenth century.[39]

These competing views of the church led to a series of controversies, and then brought both strife and division to the Anglican communion. The inability of the different churches to come to terms with their divergent ecclesiologies prevented a semblance of unity from being established in the Christian community of England. The controversies, however, brought the festering ecclesiological issues to the public's attention.

## The Ecclesiological Controversies

Four major controversies rocked the English establishment during the Augustan age. These led to the cry "the Church in Danger," on the part of High Churchmen and Tories. Proposals concerning comprehension and toleration, occasional conformity, convocation, and Benjamin Hoadly's sermon on the nature of church authority, served to highlight the divergent concepts of the church.

### COMPREHENSION AND TOLERATION

The Restoration in 1661 initiated a series of attempts at comprehending the majority of English Protestants into one church. In 1662 the authorities chose coercive methods, in the form of the Act of Uniformity and the Clarendon Code to unify the church. The Act of Uniformity led to the deprival of 1,700 clergy for refusing to subscribe to the Thirty-nine Articles, to accept the Book of Common Prayer, and to receive episcopal ordination. This left many moderate Puritans outside the established church. The Clarendon Code, enacted to give teeth to the Test Act, proscribed the religious activities of the Dissenters.[40]

The failure of coercion to achieve a unified church led the leaders of both church and state to turn to a grant of toleration. Two forms of toleration were considered: comprehension and indulgence. The former was to be employed within the national church, while the latter was offered outside it. The majority of Presbyterians and Episcopalians preferred comprehension, while Charles II and James II endorsed a declaration of indulgence, which would allow Roman Catholics, as well as Dissenters, to participate in the civil government. Indulgences were issued in 1673 by Charles, and in 1687 and 1688 by James, a practicing Roman Catholic. Anglicans, apprehensive about the possibility of Roman Catholic influence and domination in the civil government, leaned toward comprehension as a way of maintaining their domination of the moral and religious life of the nation. Several comprehension bills were introduced to Parliament, beginning in 1667–68, but each was rejected. Yet the threat posed by James II led Presbyterians and Anglicans to look again to comprehension as a means of retaining order in the church.[41] Other alternative attempts to accommodate the Dissenters, while continuing to proscribe Roman Catholics, included an indulgence that almost passed Parliament (1672), and the successfully enacted Test Act (1673). The Test Act required the reception of the eucharist in the Anglican Church to qualify for public office, and it was directed at Roman Catholics who would not commune with the Anglicans.[42]

Most moderate Dissenters and Anglicans preferred comprehension to an indulgence. The original comprehension bill limited the terms of subscription to the prayer book and to the Thirty-nine Articles for clergy and members of the universities. It eased the admission of Presbyterian clergy into the Church of England, and dealt with other issues, such as the surplice, kneeling at communion, and the sign of the cross at baptism. Many Anglicans, including Archbishop William Sancroft, saw comprehension as the safest means of bringing security to the Church of England. Norman Sykes believed that the bill was largely a high-church project, and that the suspension of Sancroft in 1689 removed the natural leadership to the project, allowing the members of the commission on comprehension to dissociate themselves from the plan. Nevertheless, comprehension was also very amenable to many Presbyterians, who were comfortable with a national church and preferred comprehension to an indulgence given by a Catholic monarch and shared with "papists." Richard Baxter was among the leading advocates of comprehension and a strong advocate of a national church, with his major concern being the provision of proper discipline within a comprehensive church.[43]

Baxter's concept of a national church combined a modified Erastianism with a theocratic ideal. He believed that a national church was the best means of exercising effective discipline over the reprobate majority of the population. Taking up apocalyptic themes, he envisioned the founding of a Protestant empire, with England as its base, ruled by a biblically and theologically informed magistrate. Although his frustration with the effectiveness of the diocesan system in providing proper discipline had led him into sectarianism, his apocalypticism induced him, in his later years, to embrace comprehension. The national church that Baxter envisioned would be broad in terms of polity and liturgy, but strict in its exercise of moral discipline, and it would incorporate a reduced episcopacy under the direction of the civil magistrate.[44]

Under the influence of Baxter's leadership, it appeared likely that the majority of the Presbyterians would return to the state church. The ascension of William and Mary, however, caused some Presbyterians to back away from comprehension, in hopes that the Calvinist monarch would grant a general toleration and repeal the Test and Corporation Acts. This would have allowed Nonconformists to hold public office without conforming to the Church of England.[45]

The comprehension bill was introduced into Parliament in February 1689; along with a bill granting limited toleration. The two measures were designed to be passed as a package. The comprehenion bill offered a broad platform on which the majority of Anglicans and Dissenters could agree, and toleration would be granted those Dissenters who still refused to enter the comprehensive state church. However, William's call for the repeal of the Test and Corporation Acts, only days after the second reading of the bills, led Parliament to reject the comprehension bill but pass the very limited toleration bill. Moderate Nonconformists, who were ready to enter a comprehensive church, were forced to submit to the provisions of an act designed to cover only the more radical Protestants. The failure to pass the Comprehension bill effectively cut the moderate Dissenters off from full participation in English society.[46]

The Act of Toleration granted freedom of worship and protection to the persons and property of orthodox Protestant Dissenters. Nevertheless it required the registration of the Dissenters meeting places, subscription to the doctrinal elements of the Thirty-nine Articles, an oath of allegiance to the monarch, and a declaration of opposition to the doctrine of transubstantiation. Quaker meetings were to be open for inspection. An affirmation of allegiance also could be substituted for the oath. Baptists, for their part, no longer needed to affirm the validity of article 27 on infant baptism.

Sunday church attendance remained mandatory for those who did not attend a meeting house, and non-Anglicans continued to be excluded from public office and the universities. The Schism Act of 1714 required the Dissenters' academies to obtain a license from the bishop, but to gain a license one would have to provide a certificate indicating that the applicant had received the sacrament from the Church of England within the previous year.[47]

The limitations on the activities of the Dissenters imposed by the Toleration Act were rarely enforced, though Philip Doddridge was prosecuted in 1733 for operating the Northampton Academy without an episcopal license and other dissenting ministers were harassed.[48] G. V. Bennett has suggested that a majority of the people had questions concerning the bill's intent. While the clergy took a strict view of its provisions, the church wardens and most Anglican lay people saw it as equivalent to the more general indulgence promulgated by James II. The laxity in ecclesiastical discipline led to a decrease in the number of Anglican communicants. Yet despite the worries of the Anglican hierarchy about the large numbers of licenses taken out by dissenting congregations, the Dissenters appear to have decreased numerically, losing a considerable number to the established church. An additional worry to the Anglican clergy was the expiration of the Licensing Act in 1695, which allowed the distribution of a plethora of heterodox pamphlets, such as those written by Deists John Toland, Matthew Tindal, and Anthony Collins.[49]

It is a mistake to believe that the passage of the Toleration bill marked a glorious new age of religious freedom. Any freedom granted to the Nonconformists by the establishment was done grudgingly, and it did not include the Roman Catholics, who were seen as a threat to the state. While the Toleration Act of 1689 made it easier for Dissenters to meet for worship, and strictures against publishing gradually disappeared, the Dissenters remained secoond-class citizens in the new English state.

OCCASIONAL CONFORMITY

The Test and Corporation Acts precluded dissenters from holding either royal or municipal offices. The two acts—the former relating to national government offices and the latter relating to corporation and municipal governments—required the reception of the sacrament according to the Anglican rite to qualify for office. The limitations were designed to disbar Roman Catholics, but they were also an effective deterrent to most Dissenters. Despite the limitations placed on them, the Dissenters were generally loyal Whigs, and they were able to form a political block with latitudinarian Anglicans in many of the boroughs. Ironically, the Anglican Whigs did not reciprocate the Dissenters' loyalty with political or religious equality.[50]

The Toleration Act of 1689 did not eliminate the Test and Corporation Acts, and Dissenters who wished to hold public office had to look for other alternatives to qualify for election. The most common means was the practice of occasional conformity. The roots of occasional conformity went deeper than simply being a way of qualifying for office, but it became a key means of getting around the Test and Corporation Acts. Henry Jacob, an Independent minster, had advocated occasional participation in the established church's eucharist as early as 1616. In the late seventeenth and early eighteenth centuries, Richard Baxter and Edmund Calamy periodically received the eucharist in the Church of England as a way of demonstrating their unity with all Christians. Thus, the practice emerged out of a concern for Christian unity. Despite the "ecumenical" roots of the practice, both separatist Dissenters and High Churchmen, most of whom were Tories, attacked the custom.[51]

Opponents of the practice among the Dissenters, including Daniel Defoe, were appalled by the fact that such a holy institution as the Holy Communion would be used as a political test. He referred to the requirements of the Test Act as a "vile prostitution of it, and contrary to the very nature and design of the Gospel institution." There were, however, many Dissenters who took advantage of occasional conformity to gain office. Two Presbyterians, Sir Humphrey Edwin (1697) and Sir Thomas Abney (1700), qualified for election as the Lord Mayor of London by partaking of the eucharist in an Anglican church. These events roused the ire of many High Churchmen, who saw this as a threat to the establishment of the church.[52]

The call to battle from the right was given in a sermon delivered in 1702, and in a tract entitled *Political Union* (1710), by Henry Sacheverell. Sacheverell charged that the Dissenters were using the Anglican sacraments to undermine the established Anglican church. For Sacheverell presbyterianism and republicanism went "hand in hand," and were "implacable enemies to monarchy and episcopacy; and if the government does not severely find this truth in their indulgence, 'tis not beholding to their tenets."[53] Shortly thereafter William Bromley and Arthur Annesely, both High Churchmen and Tories, submitted to parliament a bill to ban the practice of occasional conformity. Offenders were to be fined five hundred pounds for attending a Nonconformist meeting house after receiving the eucharist in an Anglican church to qualify for office; an additional five pound fine was to be imposed for every day that the offender remained in office. The Tory-sponsored bill received overwhelming support in the House of Commons, but several additional amendments caused its defeat by one vote in the House of Lords. The bill appeared again in 1703 and in 1704 but failed to pass, and then the issue died after the Whig triumph of 1705. Tory victories in the Parliamentary elections of 1710 and 1711 led to the passage of an Occasional Conformity Act, but some Dissenters were still able to circumvent the law and remain in office. Thomas Abney continued to hold office, but instead of attending Dissenter meeting houses, which was prohibited for office holders, he had services held in his home. Tory leaders next passed the Schism Act of 1714 to gain control over the Dissenters, this time focusing their attention on the Dissenters' academies.[54] The two Tory-sponsored bills emerged from the fear that the Anglican church would lose its privileged position if the Dissenters were given any latitude.

The ascension of George I in 1714, accompanied by the eclipse of Tory prominence, eased the Dissenters' situation to some extent. The Riot Act of 1715 outlawed the destruction of meetinghouses and compensated Dissenters for previous losses. In 1719 the Occasional Conformity and Schism Acts were repealed. The periodic passage by Parliament of indemnity bills enabled government officials to satisfy the sacramental test of the Test Act after taking office, rather than prior to taking office, as the Act specified. The indemnity bills were designed to facilitate the participation in elections of those who had been aboard ships, or abroad, attending to royal service, but many Dissenters also took advantage of the bill's allowances.[55]

CONVOCATION CONTROVERSY

The Convocation Controversy erupted in the last decade of the seventeenth century, as High Church leaders grew alarmed at the low state of the church and demanded that the Convocation of Canterbury be given the authority to bring order to the church. Francis Atterbury became the most prominent Tory advocate for the supremacy of the Convocation of Canterbury in English ecclesiastical affairs. He initiated the controversy with his anonymous *Letter to a Convocation Man* (1697), written at the behest of the

Tory lawyer, Sir Bartholomew Shower, an ardent supporter of the rights of Convocation. Atterbury believed that a sitting Convocation was the only remedy for the spread of heresy and for addressing grievances of the church. Thomas Tenison, the Archbishop of Canterbury, gathered three of the leading medieval scholars of the day, William Wake, Edmund Gibson, and White Kennett, to answer Atterbury. The three scholars sought to demonstrate, from historical precedent, that Convocation could be convened only when the monarch specifically summoned it. Although, as G. V. Bennett has pointed out, Atterbury's scholarship was weaker than the three divines, his perspective prevailed with the majority of the people.[56]

The Convocation Controversy went beyond simply a pamphlet war. Under Atterbury's leadership, Convocation became a forum for airing competing views of the church. William had filled the episcopal bench with low-church Whig bishops, who comprised the upper house of Convocation. The lower house, composed of the deans and other clergy, was largely High Church and Tory in orientation.[57] Tension between the two houses was inevitable on both theological and political grounds, with Atterbury serving as the point man for much of the debate.

Convocation met briefly in 1689, in preparation for the vote on Comprehension by Parliament, and again in 1701, after Tory political gains compelled William to convene it. The Convocation of 1701 saw the lower house defy and insult Archbishop Tenison, attack heretical books, and launch an attack on Gilbert Burnet's commentary on the Thirty-nine Articles. Atterbury and other Tory clergy, frustrated by the obstructionism of Tenison, demanded a direct confrontation with the upper house. They presented a petition to Tenison, calling for the condemnation of John Toland as a heretic. Tenison refused to receive the petition and forcefully reminded the petitioners that the presbyters were to subordinate themselves to the bishops. The extreme disorder of the assembly resulted in the dismissal of Convocation. Little of substance was accomplished, but it had become clear that the party of Atterbury intended to undermine the authority of the largely Whig episcopate. Ironically, Atterbury's attempt to use the alliance between the lower house of Convocation and the House of Commons to override the bishops in the upper house appears to have run counter to the high-church elevation of episcopal authority.[58]

After Henry Sacheverell's infamous trial and the landslide Tory victory in 1710, Convocation was convened, with Atterbury as Prolocutor of the Lower House. Tory control of the House of Commons allowed the leaders of the two legislatures to forge an alliance to forward their common causes in both church and state. Yet, in spite of their hopes that Convocation would engender great changes in the fabric of the Church of England, their opponents were able to limit their success to the passing of a bill to build fifty churches, of which twelve were actually built. In the end the enthusiasm of the High Church party died out, and Atterbury was able to accomplish only a small portion of his intended counter-revolution against Latitudinarian dominance. The end came, as Bennett demonstrates, because Atterbury did not have sufficient support from the Queen, and because his vision of a "union of Church and State in a single authoritarian regime was itself a thing of the past."[59] Atterbury had a vision that could not endure under the political, social, and ideological conditions of the day.

There would be other attempts to assert the authority of the Convocation, but its greatest opportunity to control the destiny of both church and state had passed. When Convocation attempted to attack the sermon of Benjamin Hoadly in 1717 it was prorogued by George I, and it did not meet again until the middle of the nineteenth century.[60]

## BANGORIAN CONTROVERSY

High-church passions were stirred up by Benjamin Hoadly's sermon, "The Nature of the Kingdom, or the Church of Christ" (1717), preached before George I, and Hoadly's response to George Hickes, *A Preservative against the Principles and Practices of Non-jurors both in Church and State* (1716). The two works challenged conventional Anglican understandings of the church, which resulted in a plethora of heated responses from Anglican and Non-juror divines.[61]

Hoadly exposed himself to criticism on several fronts. The use of sincerity as a sufficient measure of the favor of God was first developed in response to Hickes' contention that the episcopal deprivations of 1691 were acts of schism and that communion with a schismatic church imperiled one's soul. Hickes had made communion with a particular part of the universal church the determining factor for salvation, for he believed that salvation was to be found in the church that was the true repository of apostolic succession in England. Hoadly, on the other hand, appealed to the sincerity of the believer as the sole basis of salvation. Sincerity also figured prominently in Hoadly's sermon before the King, where he described the church of Christ as those "who are *sincerely,* and willingly subjects to him, as law-giver and judge, in all matters truly relating to conscience, or eternal salvation."[62] Hoadly believed that no one could be coerced into professing what they did not believe in. Coercion removed authority from Christ and forced the people to "prostitute their consciences at the feet of others." Peace in the kingdom came not as a result of uniformity, but out of "charity, and love, and mutual forbearance, and receiving one another, as God receives us."[63]

William Law concluded that Hoadly's position on sincerity meant that anyone who was not a hypocrite received God's favor.

> Not only sincere Quakers, Ranters, Muggletonians, and Fifth Monarch-Men, are as much in the favour of God, as any of the Apostles; but likewise sincere Jews, Turks and Deists, are upon as good a bottom, and as secure of the favour of God, as the sincerest Christian.[64]

Hoadly answered the charge by qualifying himself. He claimed that he did not mean all sincere people, but only sincere believers in Jesus Christ. The position he had taken in his *Preservative against the Principles and Practices of the Non-jurors* was meant to show the Non-Jurors that salvation did not lay in their communion alone.[65]

The most important accusation concerned his purported denial of any temporal authority in the church and the continuance of Christ's activity in the church. The sermon asserted that Christ had not left vicegerents to rule in his place.

> He hath, in those points, left behind Him, no visible, humane authority; no vicegerents, who can be said properly to supply his place; no interpreters, upon whom his subjects are absolutely to depend; no judges over the consciences or religion of his people.[66]

Andrew Snape agreed with Hoadly that ecclesiastical authorities were not infallible; yet Christ had in fact authorized a succession of vicegerents, who were to be obeyed unless they contradicted Christ's explicit laws. He believed that without an authoritative hierarchy the church would fall into confusion.[67] Hoadly insisted that his opponents had misunderstood him; rather than denying that Christ no longer was active in his kingdom or that Christ had not appointed anyone to represent him in the world, he claimed that Christ had not, since proclaiming his law, given anyone the authority to interpret infallibly that law. In qualifying his statements on church authority he insisted that concerning salvation and the conscience the church did not have absolute authority.

Christ alone could determine the requirements of salvation, and to add to them was to usurp his authority.[68] In addition, Christ had not authorized church leaders to rule with absolute power; rather, they were to serve as guides to the people. Their business was "to point out to the people, not their own opinions and decrees, but the laws of their great and common master."[69]

William Law was not satisfied with Hoadly's response. Law claimed that Hoadly's denial of absolute authority entailed the denial of all ecclesiastical authority. He believed that what Hoadly had stated in specific cases must logically hold in the general cases as well.

> "For if the authority of others is inconsistent with Christ's being King of his own Kingdom, then every degree of authority, so far as it extends, is an invasion of so much of Christ's authority and usurping upon his right."[70]

While Hoadly never directly responded to Law, he believed that the ability of a Christian to relate to God according to his or her own conscience did not contradict the role of the church leaders to serve as guides to salvation.

Hoadly was roundly criticized for his description of the invisible church. He had stated clearly in his sermon that Christ's kingdom was not of this world. His critics felt that this undermined the authority of the church. Hoadly again qualified himself, insisting that he had spoken of the invisible, not the visible, church in the sermon. Whereas his opponents believed that if the church was a kingdom and that everything that comprised a kingdom should be in the Church, Hoadly stated that the kingdom was spiritual; therefore those things that made up a visible society did not necessarily have to be in the Church. Again Hoadly failed to defuse the tension with his qualifications. He was accused of being inconsistent and of altering the definition of the church. While he had attemped to distinguish between the visible and invisible churches, making the invisible church the true church, or kingdom of Christ, his opponents rejected his view, defining the church largely in visible terms. Thus, they believed that he had undermined church authority.[71]

Hoadly's vision of the church parallels that of John Locke in many respects. His concept of the church allowed for latitude and toleration. The authority of the church was limited by the appeal to private judgement. To make laws that added to the decrees of Christ was to usurp Christ's authority, though his critics denied that ecclesiastical law contradicted Christ's laws in any way. In addition, he had blurred the lines between church and state by speaking of an invisible church. He was vague, and Thomas Sherlock may be right when he suggested that the true aim of Hoadly's efforts was the repeal of the Test and Corporation Acts, for he was involved in that effort throughout his career.[72] Despite his ambiguity on the issue, Hoadly's views of the church were scarcely compatible with state establishment. He had been accused of Erastianism for suggesting that the crown had the right to deprive the bishops of their sees; he defended himself by stating that, since the right to operate in the diocese was given by the monarch, the monarch had the right to take it away. Yet, like Locke, he conceived of the church as nothing more than a voluntary society. Salvation came to Christians who sincerely desired to obey Christ, regardless of their ecclesiastical affiliation. This was strikingly different from the high-church insistence on episcopal government for the church. Hoadly had taken a radical turn from both Erastianism and the traditional view of the divine authority of a visible church. The fact that, in practice, Hoadly appeared to be a political bishop further clouded the issue. He was not the ideal bishop who devoted himself to his diocese; in fact, he never visited Bangor during his entire period of office.[73]

## Conclusion

The High Church and Non-Juror clergy and theologians stood as the beacons of the traditional view of the Church. The High Church and Non-Juror positions contrasted greatly with the voluntaristic and gathered church views put forth by both Dissenters and many liberal Anglicans. The High Church claim that the Church of England was the sole representative of Christ's church in England was a rejection of the arguments of Dissenters and low-church Anglicans for a more broadly construed definition of Christianity in England. As the eighteenth century wore on, the High Church party lost much of its prominence. For their part, the Non-Jurors' hopes for a restoration of the divinely appointed Stuart dynasty slipped away with the failure of the Jacobite revolts of 1715 and 1745.

The loss of prominence of the two groups does not mean that their views did not live on or that they lost all influence. Methodism had roots in the High Church movement, with William Law, a Non-Juror cleric, being an important influence upon John Wesley.[74] By the end of the century, high-church views were again espoused by clergymen such as Bishop George Horne of Norwich and William Jones, as well as by the lay leader, William Stephens. There also appears to be continuity between the opinions of the High Church party of the early eighteenth century and the Oxford Movement of the nineteenth century. Another point of impact can be seen in the fact that the first American bishop was consecrated by Scottish Non-Juror bishops. By the time of the reign of George III, the High Church party regained its prominence; the episcopal bench was filled from the High Church party, as opposed to the low-church Whigs who had been dominant during the reigns of the first two Georges.[75] Thus, a study of high-church ecclesiology and theology is warranted. John Morrill has suggested that the revisionists' attention to movements who in the end did not emerge victorious, is a form of historical nominalism, but history has shown that even minority positions hold on to color the way we perceive and embrace reality. Norman Sykes rehabilitated latitudinarian Anglicanism during the early part of this century, and now it is time that we attempt to do the same for the high-church movement.[76]

# 2

# Sources of Authority: Scripture, Tradition, and Reason

The faith and practice of the Church of England traditionally rested on a three-fold authority: Scripture, tradition, and reason. The faith witnessed to by these authorities embraced the central and abiding beliefs of the church through the ages. Although one must recognize the important role played by the state in determining church practices and doctrine, theoretically, authority was based on this three-fold cord. This understanding, which found its greatest exponent in Richard Hooker at the end of the sixteenth century, still had currency at the end of the seventeenth century among most Anglicans, but especially among high churchmen. The theological method of divines such as William Beveridge and William Sherlock[1] made use of all three elements of the formula. Beveridge, in evaluating the value and orthodoxy of the Thirty-nine Articles, desired to show that each article was "grounded in Scripture," either expressly or implicitly, was "consonant with right reason," and was confirmed by the practices of the primitive church. The justification for the latter was to show how the Church of England differed from Rome, and yet did not differ from the "primitive and more unspotted church of Christ."[2]

The late seventeenth century and early eighteenth century saw the development of new challenges to traditional authority. The trust of earlier theologians in Scripture and tradition was either replaced by, or forced by the primacy of reason to take a more limited role in theology. In philosophy, the rational empiricism of John Locke was the dominant force. Biblical criticism further undermined the authority of Scripture and tradition. Reason replaced Scripture as the final court of appeal, and even among those who accepted the authority of Scripture, reason served as the means of validating its trustworthiness. Challenges to traditional understandings of authority emerged both from inside and outside the Church of England.[3]

High churchmen stood in the midst of this crisis, defending orthodoxy by appeals to Scripture and primitive tradition. Many of the debates and discussions of the era were rooted in questions about the church, ministry, and sacraments. Occasionally, as with the Usages controversy that divided the Non-Jurors, the polemics were somewhat intramural. To understand how High Churchmen and Non-Jurors determined their doctrines, one must first look to their doctrine of religious authority.[4]

## The Primary Place of Scripture

Men as diverse as the Latitudinarian Bishop of Salisbury, Gilbert Burnet, and the Non-Juror mystic, William Law, agreed that Scripture contained all that was necessary for salvation.[5] This was orthodox Anglican doctrine, proclaimed clearly in Article VI of the Thirty-nine Articles. In his commentary on this Article, William Beveridge affirmed that Scripture contained the "whole will of God; so that there is nothing necessary to be believed by us, but what is here revealed to us."[6] Few Anglicans would have debated the point, except perhaps Non-Jurors such as Thomas Brett, who challenged the idea that Scripture contained *all* that was required for salvation.[7] The divinity of Scripture was rarely questioned, even by the heretical, the exception being the Deists. John Locke, Benjamin Hoadly, and A. A. Sykes all appealed to the sole authority of Scripture at the expense of traditional theology, whereas High Churchmen, such as Thomas Stackhouse, affirmed the authority of both.[8]

For most High Churchmen and Non-Jurors, Scripture was the very "Word of God." It substituted for "an immediate *Divine Revelation*," being to them what the "personal preaching of Christ and his Apostles" had been to their audience.[9] Scripture, as the definitive revelation of God, could not be amended or added to. It was not defective in any way, and it would unfailingly fulfill its purpose, namely, the salvation of the people of God. If it was not sufficient, the writer of the book of Revelation would not have declared that it was a sin to add to or subtract from the words of Scripture (Revelation 22:18–19). The sufficiency of Scripture and the subordinate authority of reason and tradition were questioned, especially concerning the need to elicit an understanding of texts that were either unclear or whose doctrinal implications needed to be drawn out more fully.[10]

The external testimony of God—prophecy and miracles—was

the first line of defense of Scripture. These were the material witnesses to its authenticity. Miracles helped validate the truth of Scripture because they testified to the credibility of the revealer. The denial of their truth served to undermine all of Scripture. Although John Locke affirmed the reality of miracles, Deists, including Matthew Tindal, Thomas Woolston, and Thomas Chubb, in their attempt to undermine traditional religion, attacked both Scripture and miracles. Therefore, not only the authority of Scripture, but also that of the miracle stories had to be buttressed.[11]

A second line of defense was the intrinsic witness of Scripture, as seen in Jesus' refutation of the Jews and in the verification of his doctrine. Paul's assertion concerning the inspiration of Scripture (II Timothy 3:16) and the approval given by the author of the book of Acts to the Bereans for searching the Scriptures to discern the truth of Paul's preaching (Acts 17:11) also provided intrinsic verification to the integrity of Scripture.[12] Not everyone, however, found the testimony of Scripture to be sufficient to establish its own authority. Some high churchmen raised questions concerning the ability of the still-incomplete New Testament to authenticate itself. Therefore, the statements concerning Scripture would apply only to the Old Testament. Thomas Brett epitomized those who doubted whether Jesus had prescribed the Bible as the only rule of faith.

> If this be true, I am afraid it will very much sink the credit of the New Testament. For if Scripture is prescribed by our Lord to his Disciples as the only rule they are to walk by, it must be such Scripture as was in being at the time when he gave that direction; consequently the Scripture of the Old Testament, for the New could be no part of that rule, because not only any one book of it was wrote till several years after our Lord was ascended to the right hand of his Father, and had ended his conversation with his Disciples upon earth.[13]

Though Brett did not question the authority of Scripture, he believed that the New Testament could not verify its own truthfulness. This required a further form of attestation to Scripture's authority.

The authority of Scripture was further buttressed by an appeal to history, more precisely to the writings of the Fathers and the universal assent of the Christian Church to the authenticity of the biblical record. The most important element of the historical corroboration of Scripture was the formation of the canon. High-church divines believed that the process of canonization used by the early church leadership placed the New Testament on the same plane of authority as the Old Testament. The initial verification of Scripture bestowed through canonization was further enhanced by the "providential" preservation of Scripture over the centuries, despite the great number of wars, revolutions, persecutions, and tremendous amount of change that the church had endured.[14]

Finally there was the ontological necessity of revelation. John Locke had recognized that while true religion could not contradict reason, there were matters that lay above and beyond the realm of reason. It was here that revelation found its place, though many Deists, in their advocacy of reasonable religion, found revelation to be redundant.[15] Locke approached the need for revelation from a philosophical perspective, but many High Churchmen and Non-Jurors found a more compelling reason in the reality of sin and the darkness of the world. Yet, even without the problems of sin and ignorance, the need for God's revelation existed. Like Locke, and Hooker before him, they recognized that there were limits to reason that only divine revelation could overcome. Reason could point to the existence of deity and the need to worship the deity, but it could not provide the specific means of reconciliation with God.[16]

Belief in the primacy of Scripture as the normative and infallible authority for the church was not unique to high-church thought. High-church affirmations of the authority of Scripture differed little from those of Protestantism in general, but they also stood squarely in line with earlier Anglican theologians, such as Lancelot Andrewes and William Laud, who balanced Scripture's primary role with the confirmation of tradition and reason in their theological method.[17]

## The Interpretation of Scripture by Tradition

The authority of tradition was not affirmed by all eighteenth-century Anglicans. Tradition and the study of patristics were not appreciated by liberals such as Samuel Clarke, Benjamin Hoadly, and John Toland. Liberals rejected tradition in favor of reason and experience. Deists, such as Toland, even derided the works of the Fathers as silly and superstitious. Though he did not go as far as Clarke or Hoadly, Gilbert Burnet denied that the Apostles had passed on an oral tradition that could supplement Scripture. He asserted that the church had laid aside anything that could not be found in Scripture, as a corruption of true Christianity. This prohibition excluded from orthodox faith and practice such items as belief in Christ's thousand-year reign on earth and infant communion. This left little room for tradition. For Burnet, Scripture was sufficiently clear so that no interpreter was needed.[18]

The high-church movement, beginning at the Restoration, had considered the patristic writings to be the foundation of orthodox Christianity. Eamon Duffy has stated that divines such as John Pearson, John Fell, and George Bull, had found in antiquity "not merely its origins, but occasionally and increasingly, a mirror image of itself."[19] Those who followed Pearson, Fell, and Henry Hammond, in the late seventeenth and early eighteenth centuries, perceived the need to refer to the teachings of the early church to interpret Scripture properly and to determine doctrinal disputes. The earliest ages of the church were seen as providing the clearest and most acceptable interpretation of Scripture.[20]

Evidence of the High Church and Non-Juror adherence to primitive tradition is found in the significant body of patristic scholarship that they produced. John Henry Newman credited George Bull with introducing him to the principle that "antiquity was the true exponent of doctrines of Christianity and the basis of the Church of England."[21] Jeremy Collier, Nathaniel Marshall, and William Wake were among the High Church and Non-Juror scholars who either translated or produced critical editions of patristic works. Thomas Brett compiled and translated several important liturgies from the first centuries of the church. Henry Dodwell was a well-recognized patristic scholar, whose published studies included introductions to the works of Cyprian and Irenaeus.[22]

Two groups of high churchmen emerged; the first, representing the majority, perceived the writings and practices of the early church as the definitive interpretation of Scripture. For a smaller group, primarily the Non-Juror Usages party, the early church provided additional authoritative truth that supplemented the biblical record.

### TRADITION AS INTERPRETER OF SCRIPTURE

Protestants, as a general rule, view tradition with caution. They consider tradition to be an aid in interpreting Scripture, but they do not regard it to be normative. Instead, authentic tradition is judged according to a biblical standard. Richard Bauckham has designated this the "ancillary" view of tradition.[23] Many high churchmen affirmed the concept of *Sola Scriptura,* a fact well-illustrated by the perspective of the Restoration divine Jeremy Taylor. Taylor grounded his defense of episcopacy in the biblical evidence, and only secondarily in the patristic record. The latter served solely as corroboration and not as the determining factor.[24] In spite of the caution with which the patristic traditions were approached, most High Churchmen and Non-Jurors saw them as essential elements in an accurate interpretation of Scripture.

High churchmen established the first four to six centuries of the Christian era as the parameters of trustworthy tradition. The theological works of later writers needed to be read with caution, since high churchmen believed that the errors of the Roman church began to develop in the seventh century. Generally, the first four centuries were considered to be the standard boundary for tradition, although some were less specific, appealing to the "first and purest ages." Chronological distance from the apostolic period progressively reduced the authority of tradition in the interpretation of Scripture.[25] In addition to the matter of trustworthiness, the limitation of tradition to the first four centuries allowed one to distinguish between the Church of England and the Church of Rome, since the latter accorded the ongoing traditions of the church a decisive voice in the interpretation of Scripture. This method of apologetics was firmly within the Protestant framework, having been used by John Calvin in his debate with his Roman Catholic opponents. Calvin, however, desired to show the selectivity of his opponents, who chose to follow the Fathers when they erred rather than when they taught the truth. Calvin hedged more on the trustworthiness of the Fathers than did high churchmen such as Charles Leslie and John Johnson of Cranbrook.[26]

Central to the high-church Anglican view was the perception that the Church Fathers had the clearest understanding of the original apostolic message. William Lowth wrote that it was a "received maxim, *that every Law is best explain'd by the subsequent practice,*" and this led him to conclude that the primitive Christians had the clearest knowledge of the beliefs of the Apostles, since they had lived nearest the apostolic age.[27] The testimony of the Fathers was respected because the Fathers had a clearer window on the manners and customs of the apostolic period than did the medieval or Reformation divines. This made the Fathers an invaluable asset in determining the proper interpretation of Scripture, and by implication this usage raised their authority above that of contemporary human reasoning.[28]

Checks were placed on even the earliest traditions. First, a line was drawn whenever Scripture and tradition disagreed. Secondly, the writings of a single Father were not to be taken in isolation. While one writer taken alone might err, there was a much smaller chance of error when there was agreement among a number of writers. High Churchmen and Non-Jurors accepted the validity of the fifth-century Vincentian Canon of "antiquity, universality, and consent," and as a result, they collected numerous quotations from the Fathers in defense of their doctrinal positions.[29] The appeals to the Fathers by theologians, such as Thomas Brett, led to charges of "Romanism," since many institutions that had parallels in the Roman Catholic Church were based on primitive precedents. The apologetic against these charges was based on a comparison made between the two churches. Brett, in his apology, attempted to demonstrate the ways in which the Church of Rome diverged from the Vincentian Canon, thereby falling into error. The key to the use of the Vincentian Canon was the belief that error varied, but truth remained constant. It was this universally approved tradition that was authoritative.[30]

Brett raised the issue of private interpretation of Scripture, reacting strongly to those who interpreted Scripture without regard for the patristic testimony. He accused them of making the "Scriptures to be a waxen rule to be bent as the expositor pleases."[31] To buttress his position, Brett appealed to a rule passed by the Convocation of 1571 that declared that nothing was to be preached that was not agreeable to Scripture and the teachings of the Fathers. He concluded that the rule required preachers to interpret Scripture "according to the consentient Tradition of the Primitive and Catholick Fathers in the first Ages of the Christian Church."[32]

For some, the primitive church was seen as the final court of appeal in matters dividing the universal church. William Lowth believed that the "practice and judgment of the primitive church" was the "only visible means that is left to heal the breaches which distract the Catholick Church."[33] The majority of high churchmen were content to use the traditions of the primitive church to interpret Scripture. Scripture remained primary and tradition took a subordinate, though important, role in the defense of orthodox Christianity, and in the structuring of the Church of England.

### TRADITION AS AN INDEPENDENT AUTHORITY

Was Scripture, by itself, the only rule and authority for the church? Puritans had argued that whatever was not explicitly found in Scripture was unacceptable. Roman Catholics, in the aftermath of Trent, believed that tradition was a supplementary authority equal to Scripture. Anglicans, as a rule, found themselves between these two poles. Most believed that where Scripture was silent there was freedom for the church to make a determination.

Often the state had taken this prerogative on the basis of royal supremacy; this was especially true with regard to matters of worship and church government.[34] Not everyone, however, was content to leave matters of *adiaphora* to either the contemporary church or to the state to decide.

The necessity of observing all that was explicitly revealed in Scripture was a given, yet there were many issues that were found in Scripture only implicitly, including the authority of the New Testament, episcopacy, infant baptism, and the Lord's day. There were some who believed that doctrines implicitly revealed in the Bible, but confirmed by the later universal practice of the primitive church, were not only allowable, but were to be accepted as essential doctrines. Infant baptism, for example, was an ordinance accepted by most Protestants, including the Puritans, as a central element of faith, although it was not mentioned explicitly in the New Testament. It could only be defended, therefore, from the universal practice of the primitive church. The foundation for this viewpoint was the presupposition that error varied and truth remained constant, which gave credibility to the inductive method used to search the patristic writings for confirmation of church practices and doctrines such as infant baptism.[35] Another example would be the patristic authorization of episcopacy. Francis Brokesby attributed the absence of an explicit description of episcopacy in Scripture to the lack of a settled episcopate until approximately thirty years after the birth of the church. Thus, the epistles of Paul and the book of Acts were written prior to the establishment of the monarchical episcopate. He explained further that the fact that several Apostles continued to live after the writing of the extant New Testament books meant that there was still an opening for God to provide new revelations to them.[36] In each of these cases, Scripture remained the sole basis of authority, but the practice of the church was used to draw out and confirm added meanings and implications from the Biblical text.

Though several High Churchmen and Non-Jurors went beyond the explicit statements of Scripture, they refrained from setting up the Fathers as an independent authority. In going beyond the confines of the biblical record, they resembled what Richard Bauckham has termed the "coincidence" view of tradition. In this perspective, the teachings of Scripture and tradition are seen as coinciding; thus, the purpose of tradition is to provide an authorized interpretation of Scripture. This view, according to Bauckham, dominated the church from Irenaeus until the late medieval period, when the "supplementary view" eclipsed it. The origins of the "supplementary" view can be traced to the patristic period, but it became dominant during the medieval period and triumphed at Trent. It proposed that Scripture and tradition were independent authorities, with tradition able to fill the gaps left by the silence of Scripture and interpret obscure passages of Scripture.[37]

Although Thomas Brett probably would deny following the Tridentine understanding of Scripture and tradition, his perspective on the independent authority of tradition appears to fall in line with Bauckham's categories. He was concerned that Scripture, although it was the infallible Word of God, might not have revealed all that was necessary for salvation. Following this line, Brett contended that the Apostles had set up tradition as the "next authority to Scripture; an authority that is to be obeyed where the Scripture is silent or not clear." Brett differed from Trent by not according to tradition "equal reverence" to Scripture. It had supplementary authority, but it remained secondary.[38]

While Brett would have felt comfortable with the "coincidence" view and would have denied taking the "supplementary" perspective, he had clearly deviated from the traditional Anglican position. Nathaniel Spinckes, a rival Non-Juror bishop, responded to Brett, making it clear that Brett had moved beyond the Protestant doctrine of Scripture that made Scripture the sufficient revelation of the means of salvation. Brett, however, denied going outside orthodox Anglicanism. In defense of himself, he referred to Henry Hammond's *Of Heresy* (1656), which noted two means of conveying revelation, written and oral tradition. He appealed to Herbert Thorndike's *Epilogue* (1659) as well, contending that Thorndike had allowed oral tradition a definitive place in deciding church doctrine. Unlike the Roman Catholics, the area of Brett's concern was small. He and a number of the Non-Jurors had found themselves in a debate over several eucharistic practices that they believed were essential to the valid celebration of the sacrament, and therefore, necessary for salvation. Brett believed that the so-called "Usages" were primitive and apostolic, and therefore they were necessary elements. Spinckes and the Non-Usagers, on the other hand, denied that the Usages had patristic precedent; they asserted that the Scripture had revealed all necessary elements of church life.[39]

Brett's position rested on the belief that the Apostles had passed on oral traditions that were to supplement the written traditions (Scripture). Oral tradition, because of its apostolic origin, was perceived to have the same authority as Scripture in matters of faith and practice.

It is sufficient for my present purpose if it can be shewed that there is anything which can be proved to have been taught by the Apostles as of Universal and perpetual obligation, though they did not put it in writing in some part or other of the New Testament, it is to be observed as the revealed will of God.[40]

Although this perspective appears to conflict with Article VI of the Thirty-nine Articles, Brett denied that he had strayed from the article's intent. He appealed again to Henry Hammond; he maintained that Hammond also denied that one could find every essential doctrine of the Christian faith contained in the New Testament. Although he disavowed any resemblance to Roman Catholic understandings, he stood clearly within the "supplementary" circle.[41]

Church practices such as the liturgy, infant baptism, and the celebration of the Lord's Day were not *adiaphora*. Although they might lack an explicit biblical injunction, they were grounded in primitive tradition. Brett and Thomas Wagstaffe, the younger, theorized that the Apostles had passed on a *depositum* of oral instructions to their successors, such as Timothy (II Timothy 1:1); they speculated that the liturgies and directions for celebrating the eucharist were among those instructions. Wagstaffe could not conceive of the early church deviating from apostolic practice, and therefore the Church of England was required to return to the usages of the primitive liturgies.[42] Brett appealed to Tertullian, who provided the rationale for making primitive precedent obligatory for the contemporary church: "Tradition authorizes it to you," wrote Tertullian, "custom confirms it and faith teaches you to observe it." Brett concluded that Scripture alone was not sufficient to instruct Christians on the "discharge of Christian duties," and thus, he became a vocal champion of the authority of the primitive church. Jeremy Collier took this a step further, asserting that where the Scripture did not condemn a practice, such as prayers for the dead, then the practice of the early church was sufficient authority for its continuance.[43] In the end, where Scripture was silent, the customs of the early church held preeminence.

The use of the Fathers and early-church practice to determine contemporary faith and practice, whether as a normative interpreter of Scripture or as a supplementary authority, put some high churchmen, and more specifically the Non-Jurors, in a place of divergence from the majority of their colleagues, who had shifted the weight of authority to the alliance of Scripture and reason, or as was true of the Deists, to reason alone.

## The Proper Place of Reason

The eighteenth century is often called the age of reason, a period of history when human reason was seen as the highest authority in every field and endeavor. In religious and theological matters, reason often became either the equivalent or the superior of revelation. Gerald Cragg states that the early eighteenth century leaders did not question the authority of reason, only its sufficiency. Both heretic and orthodox saw themselves as "loyal disciples of John Locke." John Tillotson represents well the Latitudinarians, who placed strong emphasis on the use of reason, believing Christianity to be the most reasonable of all religions. The advocacy of the authority of reason was not unique to the followers of Locke or to the eighteenth century. Richard Hooker, according to Cragg, attempted to balance reason with revelation, realizing that there were matters discussed in Scripture that went beyond reason, and yet the truth that Scripture was the "Word of God" was discerned by reason. William Laud was also willing to submit his arguments for Christian faith to the "test of reason." Therefore, there was nothing in the appeal to reason that ran contrary to traditional Anglican theology or was unique to eighteenth-century Anglicanism.[44]

High-church Anglicans did not oppose the use of reason, as the radical attacks on Scripture by David Hume still lay in the future. John Sharp, the Archbishop of York, is representative of High Churchmen who readily affirmed both the place and authority of reason. He asserted that although religion was to be guided by revelation, the divine nature of that revelation was to be determined by reason, and faith could never be in conflict with reason. Yet Gerald Cragg and John Hunt have both noted that there was little difference in the position of Sharp and that of the Latitudinarian divine, John Tillotson.[45] Though he was a High Churchman, Sharp appears to have given greater credence to reason than many others did.

Every theological party found it advantageous to establish itself as being reasonable and comprehensible. Although elements of the faith might not be clear to the common person, it was agreed that at its foundation Christian faith was in accord with reason. An element of private judgement was allowed, but unlike the Deists, and even some more liberal and Latitudinarian Anglicans such as Tillotson or Hoadly, there was a sense of limitation placed on the authority of reason.[46] The authority of reason was linked in the minds of most with that of Scripture and tradition. Daniel Waterland affirmed Scripture's place as the only "complete rule of faith" and sought the understanding of the ancient Fathers, but he also saw the necessity of checking with common human reason. For Waterland this did not necessarily mean private judgment, but rather checking with a variety of interpreters.[47]

Biblical religion was seen as building on the foundation of natural religion. Robert Nelson spoke encouragingly of the place of reason and natural religion, but in a way that differed from the perspective of the Deists.

> It discovers to us the principles of natural religion; and justifies the wisdom and prudence of acting according to them. It shows the conveniency of those things to our natures and the tendency of them to our happiness and interest; that as we are thereby convinced, that piety towards God, that justice, gratitude and mercy towards men, are agreeable to our natures; so reason discovers to us that these duties are good, because they bring benefit and advantage to us.[48]

Biblical religion was reasonable because it brought benefits to its adherents. It did not run counter to human self-interest to believe in the God of Christianity. In spite of the great trust placed in Scripture and tradition, Scripture still needed to be put to the test of reason. Nelson believed that there must be evidence to sustain the belief that a revelation came from God. Though he recognized the weaknesses and fallibility of human reason, he still thought that reason held an important place in theological discourse.[49]

Reason had the same value as tradition in the attempt to uncover implicit truth in Scripture. The people of God were encouraged to search Scripture and discover truth that was not taught there explicitly. George Smalridge believed that an implicit reference had the same authority as an explicit one.

> For Nothing can be more unreasonable, than to allow the Scriptures to be true and divine, and at the same time to question the truth and divinity of those doctrines, which are evidently deduc'd from the Scriptures. For since it is agreed on all hands, that from truth nothing can follow but what is truth, he who denies the truth of what is rightly inferr'd, doth at the same time impeach the truth of those Scriptures, from whence it is inferr'd.[50]

Reason was not so weak that it could not be used to discern the truth taught in Scripture and to explain it. Yet high churchmen did not give license to the authority of opinion; rather, they bid interpreters to explicate the meaning of Scripture using, what Henry Stebbing called, the "ordinary rules of criticism." Stebbing guarded the rightful interpretation by limiting those who determined doctrinal truth to ecclesiastical authorities, and more specifically the bishops.[51]

Given these uses of human reason, boundaries were placed around the legitimate utilization of reason. High-church Anglican apologists wrote tracts in response to challenges to orthodox doctrine, including those by Arians, Socinians, Deists, and even liberal Anglicans, such as Benjamin Hoadly. George Smalridge, who gave such an important place to reason, laid down the line over which one could not cross. A doctrine was not true simply because it was "agreeable to right reason" without also being scriptural. Such a doctrine was to be condemned as "invading the prerogative of God."[52]

The primary limit placed on reason by high-church Anglicans was its insufficiency. By itself it had no authority, as there was nothing to back up its claims, and in the end it was only a human precept. Reason or natural religion also had a limitation with regard to the general populace, who could not, without help, move beyond instinct and conscience. Most people would not be able to methodically deduce the truth from "clear and self-evident principles." Reason could determine the existence of something only *a posteriori*. It could, though observation, determine that there was a cause of everything, but reason by itself could not decide the nature of the cause.[53]

Overall, the bulk of religious truth lay outside the realm of unaided reason. William Lowth noted that even the greatest of the philosophers, though they were able to agree on the need for moral duty, could not "settle the great foundation of religion." He saw reason as a "blind guide in heavenly things, even to those who had made the best improvement of their natural talent." William Law took a similar position, stating that reason conceived of God imperfectly, being able to discover only a few of the divine attributes. Even the best attempts at discerning the attributes of God left much unclear concerning God's true nature.[54] Law made it plain that it was not reason that he opposed, nor those who used reason, but only those who reasoned wrongly. Law said that revelation was given, not to take away the right of judgment, but to free it from false judgments.[55]

The primary limitation on the use of reason was its relationship to Scripture. Although it was called on to interpret Scripture, and even to judge its truthfulness, it did not have independent authority. To give human reason an authority equal to or above Scripture was seen as blasphemous and as a usurpation of God's rights. Reason had value and an important place in theology. High churchmen did not fear that the appeal to reason would undermine the Christian faith—they questioned its sufficiency and use. When reason was used with Scripture and tradition, it was considered safe.[56]

## Conclusion

Scripture, tradition, and reason together stood as firm and definitive authorities among High Church and Non-Juror divines. Each authority had its place, with Scripture having the first place. Even those who would have elevated the authority of tradition to a place just beneath Scripture, would not place them in opposition. Scripture, as the Church of England had taught since the Reformation, stood as the judge of all Christian doctrine. Although high churchmen held Scripture in high regard, like Richard Hooker and William Laud before them, they affirmed the important and even necessary place of reason and tradition (early Christianity) in properly interpreting and understanding the meaning of Scripture. Reason and tradition served to enable interpreters of Scripture to deduce, and then confirm, truths that were not expressly revealed, and therefore they could fill out the picture of Christian faith. The three elements when in balance provided a proficient defense for orthodox faith and practice.

The question of authority was key to the debates concerning the church, sacraments, and the ministry. Where one stood on those issues depended largely on how one used these three sources of authority. High-church defenses of episcopacy were rooted largely in patristic practice, and the episcopate often served as the major point of contention in the important controversies of the period. The outcome of the period's debates frequently rested on how the three elements were kept in balance. The more liberal the position, the greater the weight that was placed on reason, and the more conservative, the greater the weight placed on tradition. High churchmen, as a rule, were found at the conservative end of the spectrum, and therefore, they made the greatest use of patristic sources. Consequently, high churchmen constructed their doctrine of the church on the foundations of patristic theology. Conformity to "primitive" precedent was the criteria for judging the value of the episcopacy, priesthood, sacraments, and liturgy. Where Scripture was silent, as it often was, tradition, guided by reason, provided direction.

# 3

# The Nature of the Church

High-church ecclesiology was forged not in systematic dissertations, but in the midst of controversy. The rallying cry of High
Churchmen and their Tory allies was the "Church in danger." They
did not espouse a new vision of the church, but provided a defense
of traditional doctrine. The challenges of the Enlightenment provide the context for examining the High Church and Non-Juror
doctrines of the church. Their ecclesiologies were found not in
theoretical treatises, but in sermons, catechisms, and in apolo-
getical and polemical works.[1] The only true ecclesiological treatise
written in this period was John Rogers' *A Discourse of the Visible
and Invisible Church of Christ* (1719), which was not a distinctively
high-church work.[2]

Although contemporary scholarship has examined the key ecclesiological issues that confronted seventeenth-and eighteenth-century Anglicans, including questions of church and state, church
practices, and liturgical developments, no work has examined the
theological underpinnings of these issues. This chapter seeks to
fill that void by examining three pivotal aspects of ecclesiology
addressed by high-church writers: the debate over the visible nature of the church, the definition of the traditional marks of a true
church, and the relationship of church to salvation. The third as-
pect of their ecclesiology, the necessity of the church to salvation,
is the natural consequence of their theological position with regard
to the church, ministry, and the sacraments.[3]

## Visible and Invisible Churches

Two important events fostered the discussion of the visible
church in the late seventeenth and early eighteenth centuries: the
deprivation of the Non-Juror bishops in 1691, and Benjamin
Hoadly's sermon, "The Nature of the Kingdom, or Church of
Christ" (1717). The deprivations of the bishops raised questions

concerning the integrity of the church as an independent society, while Hoadly's sermon dealt with the nature of ecclesiastical authority.[4]

Hoadly's radical position, which appeared to relegate the visible church to a minor role in history, drew spirited responses from high churchmen eager to defend the honor of the Church of England. John Potter charged that Hoadly and his supporters had defined the church:

> as a number of persons disunited from, and independent on one another, than as an orderly society under lawful governours of divine or necessary appointment; and thus root up, as far as in them lieth, the very foundation of all ecclesiastical authority at once.[5]

Whereas Hoadly couched his discussion of the church in terms of the invisible kingdom of God, or universal church, High Churchmen and Non-Jurors tended to blur the distinctions between the visible and invisible churches. The issues of ecclesiastical authority and church government raised by the Bangorian Controversy could not, at least for high churchmen, be dealt with by defining the essence of the church in terms of the invisible church.[6]

Article XIX of the Thirty-nine Articles summarized the Anglican doctrine of the church, and it describes two manifestations of the church: the church triumphant in heaven, and the church militant on earth. Anglicans believed in both forms of the church, but high churchmen, in their attempt to establish an ordered church, focused on the church as a visible society. They perceived the church to be a society of people who professed faith in God; as a society, it possessed a particular form of government with precise rules and guidelines for Christian living. Gilbert Burnet, a Latitudinarian, made the same distinctions in terms of the nature of the church, but Burnet's focus was on the covenant of grace and not on the truth of the visible church's doctrines and practices. This enabled Burnet to be an advocate of religious toleration.[7]

The earthly, or militant, church held the attention of High Churchmen and Non-Jurors, who dedicated themselves to preserving the rights of the English church in the face of challenges from Rome, liberal Anglicanism, Deism, and Nonconformity. High

Churchmen, from within the established body, were joined by Non-Jurors, such as Thomas Brett and John Hughes, in emphasizing the definition of the church as a visible society, the importance of church government, and the necessity of church membership.[8]

The distinction between the invisible and the visible churches was foundational for the Reformed doctrine of the church. The Reformers' emphasis on justification by faith, the authority of Scripture, and private judgment, led them to accentuate the invisible church of the elect over the visible and institutional church. This did not lead to a denial of the visible church's existence, but it did relativize it. Richard Hooker, whose influence on later developments of Anglican ecclesiology is immeasurable, distinguished between the mystical body, known only to God, and the visible body politic existing on earth. The focus of the latter manifestation of the church was on the performance of Christian duty and human fellowship rather than the spiritual relationship with God. Hooker believed that the visible church might include idolaters (perhaps referring to Roman Catholics), heretics, those who were excommunicated, and even "imps and limmes of Satan." On the other hand, the "true Israelites, true sonnes of Abraham, true servantes and saints of God" comprised the mystical body of Christ.[9]

High Churchmen and Non-Jurors were uneasy with a strict distinction between the visible and invisible dimensions; they were concerned that differentiating them too explicitly might diminish the value of the visible communion of Christians on earth. John Potter recognized that external wickedness, on the part of some church members, had led to the claim that the true church was invisible, consisting only of those who possessed the inner qualifications, which might never be associated with the visible church. Nevertheless, though external ordinances were of little value without faith and obedience, outward and visible communion was still an obligation.[10]

Although they were willing to recognize that the visible church was a mixture of good and evil, high churchmen would not limit the composition of the true church to the invisibly virtuous. They rejected, as a modern invention, any definition of the invisible church that denied that the universal church had a perceptible existence. High churchmen feared that the views of Hoadly and other liberals would diminish the authority of the church and the necessity of the sacraments and ministry of the church. Emphasis on the visible church also provided a rationale for opposing the repeal of the Test and Corporation Acts, for the sacramental test called for in the Act served to keep Nonconformists and Roman Catholics out of Parliament; thus, the church and its ministry were protected, at least partially, from outside interference.[11]

Charles Leslie dealt with the problem of distinguishing between the heavenly and earthly churches by conceiving of the church as one body, with two parts. Whereas Hoadly had limited the kingdom of God to the invisible church, Leslie asserted that the church on earth was also part of the kingdom of God, and Christians on earth were fellow citizens with those in heaven. Whether in heaven or on earth, the church had one head: Christ. The government of the church was hierarchical, with the earthly portion mirroring the heavenly.[12]

Although most High Churchmen and Non-jurors affirmed, to some extent, the invisible nature of the church, they accentuated the importance of communion with the visible church. They emphasized the signs, symbols, sacraments, rites, and government of the church that were discernible on earth. Though one might speak of the invisible church, it was the visible church with which the world had to contend.

Belief in the visible church was rooted, according to High Churchmen, in Scripture (Matthew 28:9; Acts 15:3–4; 20:28; III John 10) and in the Thirty-nine Articles (Article XIX). They defined the church of Christ as a visible society of Christians, marked by the faithful preaching of the word of God and the proper administering of the sacraments. Although they were thoroughly Protestant, most High Churchmen believed that the established Church of England was the only true visible expression of the church in England. They rejected the concept, advocated by Hoadly, Locke, and the Dissenters, of the church as a voluntary society, asserting that Christians were obliged to be members of the one true church. Though another congregation or denomination might appear to be better than one's own, the fact that the established church had all necessary foundations for a true church prevented one from leaving to join another church. To leave the church was schism, and schism was a sin.[13]

Although the church might be invisible as well as visible, the invisible church was not more than the visible. More importantly, Christians on earth had to concern themselves with what lay before them, the visible church. Definitions of the true church had to address matters of authority, sacraments, ministry, preaching, and polity. These emphases did not, however, prevent high churchmen from recognizing the relationship of their church to the universal church as it existed on earth; thus they affirmed with all

Protestants, and the church throughout history, that the true church could be recognized because of particular marks or notes.

## The Marks of the True Church

Article XIX, in line with the Reformed foundations of the Church of England, decreed that the true church was marked by the pure preaching of the Word of God and the proper administration of the sacraments. The English Church also embraced four universal notes of the church: unity, holiness, catholicity, and apostolicity. These marks, defined by the creeds and the Fathers, were accepted by the Church of England as valid descriptions of the church. All six marks found a prominent place in the high-church defenses of the church, but two marks were stressed above the others: the proper administration of the sacraments and the apostolicity of the church.[14]

### PREACHING AND ADMINISTRATION OF THE SACRAMENTS

High churchmen affirmed that preaching and the proper administering of the sacraments were essential elements of the definition of the visible church. Indeed, they were a prerequisite for the existence of the church, for without them the church would cease to exist. Thus, the public worship of God defined the church's essence, and high churchmen insisted that true Christian worship had to be authorized by apostolicly commissioned bishops.[15]

Although sacraments and preaching were signs of the true church, in and of themselves they were not sufficient. Both preaching and the sacraments required properly qualified ministers for validation. High churchmen differed markedly from Latitudinarians in their interpretations of Article XIX. Gilbert Burnet, a Latitudinarian, recognized the need for properly ordained ministers to guide the church, but he did not believe that they were essential to the efficacy of the sacraments. In contrast to Burnet, High Churchmen and Non-Jurors insisted that episcopal ordination was essential to the validity of the sacraments and to preaching, and therefore, to the existence of the church as the visible body of Christ on earth. To a great extent they affirmed the Cyprianic principle: "the Church rests on the bishops and every act of the Church is governed by these same prelates."[16] Regarding the necessity of a divine commission, William Beveridge wrote:

In so much that if I did not think, or rather was not fully assured, that I had such a commission to be an ambassador for Christ, and to act in his name, I should never think it worth the while to preach or execute any ministerial office. For I am sure, that all I did would be null and void of itself, according to God's ordinary way of working; and we have no ground to expect miracles. But blessed be God, we in our church, by a successive imposition of hands, continued all along from the Apostles themselves, receive the same Spirit that was conferred upon them for the administration of the Word and Sacraments ordained by our Lord and Master, and therefore may do it as effectually to the salvation of Mankind as they did.[17]

The basic definitions of the church demonstrated the importance of the episcopate and the clergy to the nature of the church. The key was the proper administration and pure preaching, both of which required a proper commission.[18]

### APOSTOLICITY OF THE CHURCH

The historic Christianity of the creeds, which the Church of England claimed to reflect, affirmed the existence of the one, holy, catholic, and apostolic church. High Churchmen and Non-Jurors insisted that this church was visibly present in the myriad of particular or national churches extending across the world. The high-church definition of apostolicity differed markedly from the position of the Reformers. Unlike the Reformers, who defined the church's apostolicity in terms of its adherence to Scripture, High Churchmen and Non-Jurors saw apostolicity in terms of unbroken apostolic succession. For them the sign of apostolicity was the episcopate. Though Anglicans had attempted, since the Reformation, to hold both definitions in tension, high churchmen believed that apostolic succession was the more salient element. They thought it was imperative to vigorously defend the doctrine of apostolic succession. Non-Jurors found apostolic succession to be especially pertinent, for they saw the apostolicity of the Church of England threatened by the "unlawful" episcopal deprivations following the Glorious Revolution.[19]

Most high churchmen were primitivists, turning to Scripture and the Church Fathers for guidance in matters of doctrine, biblical interpretation, sacraments, liturgy, and church government. Scripture was foundational, for in it one could find the teachings of Jesus and the Apostles, the basis of the Christian faith from the beginning (Acts 2:42).[20] Still, the lure of the primitive church was deeply felt.

Henry Dodwell deemed it necessary to call the Church of England back to its primitive roots.

> So that, indeed, for modern churches to be determined by antiquity, is really no other than to make themselves in their purest incorruptest condition, judges of their own case, when they have not the like security against impurities and corruptions. I cannot understand therefore how, even on account of authority, our late brethren can excuse their pretended zeal for even our common mother the Church of England, when they presume to oppose her authority to that of the Catholic Church, and of the Catholick Church of the first and purest ages.[21]

Although the New Testament and the Church Fathers formed an essential element of the church's apostolicity, the continuance of apostolic government, embodied in the episcopate, guaranteed it. The bishops represented the apostles as the earthly rulers of the church. They received their authority from the apostles through an unbroken succession of orthodox and catholic bishops. Apostolic authority was derived from Christ, who had been sent by the Father. The people's adherence to their bishops symbolized the modern church's apostolicity. Uninterrupted apostolic succession guaranteed the validity of the ordinations of the church's ministers, the sacraments, and the right preaching of the Word of God, thus insuring the efficacy of the means of salvation.[22]

The importance of the high-church, especially the Non-Juror, defense of apostolic succession, was related to attacks on the Church of England's apostolicity by Dissenters, Roman Catholics, and the Anglican left, particularly Benjamin Hoadly. This became a key issue of the Bangorian Controversy, wherein Hoadly effectively denied that Christ had authorized vicegerents for the visible church. In each case the most sustained defenses of apostolic succession and the Anglican episcopate came from high churchmen. The Dissenters were rebutted by coupling the right to baptize with apostolic succession, and since the Church of England was the only church in England that had preserved apostolic succession, it alone could offer effectual baptism. They answered the Roman Catholics by asserting that authentic succession did not require the overall headship of the Pope. The keys of the kingdom had not been limited to Peter, but had been given to all the apostles.[23]

A major threat to the authority of the episcopacy in the eighteenth century came from within the episcopal bench itself. Hoadly's attack on apostolic succession, which questioned the authority of the bishops over the church, provoked a flurry of responses. William Law attempted to refute the challenge that "the perpetual succession of the clergy" was not supported by Scripture. He denied that scriptural authority was necessary in every case, for if this were true, then not only was episcopacy at stake, but so was the necessity of scripture as "a fixed rule of faith for all ages." He made it clear that it was apostolic succession that differentiated the Church of England from the Dissenters.

> So that, my Lord, if Episcopal ordination, derived from Christ, hath been contended for by the Church of England, your Lordship hath in this point deserted her: And you not only give up Episcopal ordination, ridiculing a Succession; but likewise by the same argument exclude any ministers on earth from having Christ's authority.[24]

Hoadly's opponents believed that the consequence of his views was the relegation of the clergy, and especially the episcopate, to lay status. This reduction of the episcopate to the level of the laity was seen as an affront to the existence of the Church of England as a visible expression of the catholic church. Apostolic succession served to buttress the Anglican claim that it was an equal partner with other national churches, hence, the doctrine was resolutely defended.

### CATHOLICITY OF THE CHURCH

Apostolicity was closely linked to the catholicity of the church. High Churchmen and Non-Jurors recognized the need to see the church as larger than their own national church. Catholicity not only pertained to the invisible, as envisioned by Calvin or Hoadly, but it also included the visible institutional church. They denied that any particular church could claim to be *the* catholic church not even Rome. The catholic church, unlike the "Jewish church," was not confined to one nation, and it endured throughout history. The faith, sacraments, apostolic government, and head, Jesus Christ, defined the church's catholicity. The catholic church, demarcated by these specific elements, comprised all particular churches dispersed throughout the world.[25]

The possibility of communion between catholic churches that were sound in faith and doctrine, which included the Church of England, was affirmed. William Sherlock thought that the definition of the church should be narrow enough to exclude schismatics, but large enough to include all "true Catholick Churches."[26] One important indication of catholic communion was the universality of the sacrament of baptism. Wherever one went, baptism brought access to all Christian privileges, including admission to communion, without the need for rebaptism. There were other signs, such as the eucharist and excommunication, that united the various national churches.[27]

A further sign of catholicity was its indefectibility. The catholic church, high churchmen believed, was ultimately invincible. Particular churches might experience error and failure, but the church as a whole would never fail. This belief was grounded in Christ's promise never to allow the gates of hell to prevail against the church (Matthew 16:18). In fact, the church was Christ's chosen instrument to destroy the works of Satan. Without the church, William Beveridge declared, there would be no hope of salvation. The catholic church, which transcended national boundaries, was God's chosen means of evangelizing the world. Yet this church was visible and institutional, and not invisible.[28]

### UNITY OF THE CHURCH

The creeds, and the Church of England, affirmed that this apostolic and catholic church was one church. Unity, in part, derived from a belief in a visible church that was linked to the primitive church by a succession of properly consecrated bishops. This concern may explain why high churchmen affirmed the need for uniformity of belief and practice among Christians in England. Many Anglicans, from all theological parties, sought to unite English believers through comprehension, and others made overtures to foreign churches, including those of William Wake to the Gallican church of France and of the Non-Jurors to the Eastern Orthodox Church.[29]

High churchmen, like other Anglicans, found the unity of the church rooted in the headship of Christ, but unlike other Anglicans, they believed that this unity was only manifested by submission to the apostolicly commissioned authority. They affirmed that the one holy catholic church comprised all believers. George Hickes declared that Christians were members of the "same family, members of the same corporation, citizens of the same city." Although they had different polities, languages, and governments, the different national churches were like "apartments of the same house, as wards of the same city, as towns, hundreds, shires, provinces of the same spiritual kingdom, under one ecclesiastical economy and administration, whereof Christ is the author as well as sovereign Lord and Head."[30]

With Cyprian, high churchmen made the bishop the principle of unity. The church, cast in Cyprianic terms, was a "people united and cleaving to its bishop." Henry Dodwell wrote that communion with the Father and the Son occurred only in the visible church—to despise the one sent by God, the bishop, was to despise God.

> But there was none in the visible constitution of the Church that represented God and Christ under the notion of a head but the Bishop. And therefore he was taken for the principle of Unity, without union to whom there could be no pretensions to union with God and Christ.[31]

The unity of the catholic church was found not in a single, supreme temporal head, but in episcopal collegiality. Accountability was to be made to the bishops as a whole and not to the Pope, with an ecumenical council as the final arbiter in ecclesiastical matters. Thomas Brett maintained that the division of the catholic churches into smaller bodies, each locally separate from the others, did not prevent the church from being one body, "any more than the several cities or distinct commonwealths within the realm, who have their distinct governours and their distinct by-laws, hinder the whole nation of Great Britain from being one entire kingdom."[32] What Brett failed to realize was that this example could have left him open to rejoinders from Roman Catholics; for even as the political kingdom had one supreme ruler, one could argue that the catholic church also needed a supreme governor on earth.

Like Cyprian and Augustine, High Churchmen and Non-Jurors saw schism as the greatest sin against the church. Schism occurred when one rejected the principle of unity: the bishop. For high churchmen, as it was for Cyprian, even martyrdom could not atone for separation from one's bishop. Non-Jurors, in line with this thinking, accused the established church of schism for assenting to the state deprival of the bishops who refused to swear allegiance to William and Mary. Unity was a desired object, but it proved to be elusive.[33]

The unity of the church was embodied in the common sacraments of baptism and the eucharist. The two sacraments served as signs of agreement in matters of faith, without which visible communion was impossible.[34] Whereas Augustine had made love the basis of Christian unity, high-church divines, such as Henry Sacheverell, questioned the sufficiency of love, maintaining that there must be "nothing less than an external, visible communion in the same sacraments and prayers, and other religious offices,

which the church, by the authority of Christ and his Apostles en-
joins, can perfectly unite Christians in one visible body."[35]

## HOLINESS OF THE CHURCH

The "Apostles Creed" taught that the church was holy, and this
was affirmed by all Christians. Yet High Churchmen and Non-
Jurors, unlike Augustine and Calvin, did not seek to set the holiness of the church in an invisible church of the elect; nevertheless,
they confessed the holiness of the church. The high-church view
of the holiness of the church was expressed most poignantly in the
prayerful comments of Thomas Ken on this phrase of the "Apostles Creed."

> I believe, O holy Jesus, that thy Church is holy like thee its author;
> holy by the original design of its institution [II Timothy 1:9], holy by
> its baptismal dedication, holy in all its administrations which tend to
> produce holiness [II Timothy 2:19]; and though there will be always a
> mixture of good and bad in it in this world [Matthew 13:24], yet that it
> has always many real saints in it; and therefore all love, all glory be
> to thee.[36]

Holiness could be found not in the lives of the people but in the
institution itself, in the purity of its origins, rules, ordinances, and
ministry, all of which were derived from Christ. Its partisans com-
mended the Church of England for lacking nothing necessary for
the attainment of salvation. In addition, they placed complete trust
in the grace of the Holy Spirit to sanctify the people of God; if
they were not fully sanctified while they lived on earth, they would
in the next life. In the end, the holiness of the institution was
located in the holiness of its head, Jesus Christ.[37]

Holiness did not require the infallibility of the particular
churches. Nathaniel Marshall noted that although the Church of
England was the "bulwark and glory of the Reformation," it admitted its defects, unlike the "haughty and pretentious" Church of
Rome or the Quakers.[38] They did not equate holiness with infallibility, which neither William Beveridge now John Sharp believed was
prescribed by Scripture or patristic tradition. Though no primitive
church had ever pretended to be infallible, this did not preclude
the assertion of the holiness of the visible church. High churchmen
took care not to credit the church with more than they believed
it deserved.[39]

In spite of the emphasis on institutional, over personal holiness,

High Churchmen and Non-Jurors were not unconcerned about personal holiness. Nathaniel Marshall lamented the lack of penitential discipline in the contemporary church, stating that although "I never thought the purity and perfection of this discipine essential to the *being* of the Church, yet I could not but judge it highly conducive and expedient to her well-being."[40] Concern about the lax morals of the period led to numerous attempts, by both clergy and laity, to reassert discipline on the nation. One alternative was the Society for the Reformation of Manners, a largely lay-led organization. Although high churchmen, such as Robert Nelson, were members of the society, other high churchmen, including Henry Sacheverell, accused the society of being hypocritical, in part because it approved of toleration and included Dissenters among its members. High Churchmen and Non-Jurors tended to focus on the restoration of disciplinary authority to the bishops and church courts. George Hickes and Thomas Wilson were strong advocates of episcopal and clerical discipline, and Wilson was well-known for having imposed firm discipline on the diocese of Sodor and Man. Efforts also were made to make Convocation an effective means of discipline, though most of the issues taken up there were doctrinal. Ironically, J. P. Kenyon has criticized Convocation for focusing on the moral problems of society, rather than on the more important church-state issues. His perspective is illustrative of the lack of attention paid to the theological undergirding of the issues of the age.[41]

High Churchmen and Non-Jurors granted that the membership of the visible church was not perfect, but they believed that the imposition of discipline was the prerogative of the clergy, and the bishops in particular. The means chosen for the implementation of moral discipline exemplifies the distinctiveness of the high-church movement. Discipline was not to be left to societies or to the state; rather, authority for providing discipline was to be given to the bishops.

## The Church and Salvation

In an age when voluntarism had increasingly become a central element of definitions of the church, and when religious toleration was becoming more acceptable, high churchmen were distinguished from other Anglicans by their narrow coupling of church and salvation. William Beveridge reclaimed the patristic view of the relationship of the church to salvation, bringing to bear the insights of Cyprian, Ambrose, and Augustine, declaring that outside the church there was no salvation; rather, "that whosoever would be a member of the Church Triumphant in Heaven, must first be a member of the Church here Militant on earth."[42] To spurn membership in the church was to reject Christ, the Spirit, and, ultimately, salvation.[43]

The purpose of the church, according to Christ's institution, was to bring salvation to the world. Whereas Benjamin Hoadly and A. A. Sykes contended that sincerity alone, and therefore membership in the invisible church, was necessary to receive salvation, High Churchmen and Non-Jurors asserted that God ordained the visible church, with all of its sacred institutions, to be the sole repository of the means of salvation. Thus, church membership was obligatory for the true Christian for as long as the church continued to exist. Even as the book of Acts recorded that Christ had added to the church those who were being saved, William Beveridge found no evidence that Christ would ever change the established process of salvation.[44]

The relationship of the visible church to salvation was emphatically linked to two specific factors: the presence of the clergy (bishops, priests, and deacons), and therefore, apostolic succession; and the sacraments, which were administered by the clergy.[45] The church was the nurturing mother of the people of God, and its clergy were the authorized dispensers of the sacraments, the means of grace. The church was the forum where the Gospel was rightly proclaimed, the truth of God upheld and propagated, and the way of salvation made known. High Church divines perceived the Church of England to be the only suitable site in England for this to occur, and the Non-Jurors took an even narrower stand with regard to the necessity of communion in their church. It was not simply church membership, but membership in the one holy catholic and apostolic church, that provided a satisfactory location to receive salvation. Because the church was established by the state, High Churchmen defended the use of the sacrament as a political test,for if the Church of England was the only true Christian church in England, then a member of the government of this Christian nation would have to be a member of the true church. In short, as John Kettlewell maintained, outside the church, one depended, "at best only on presumptions, and uncovenanted mercies; the covenant which God seals with us, respecting his church, and being proposed and ratified in the word which it preaches, and the sacraments which it depends."[46]

## Conclusion

The doctrine of the church propagated by High Churchmen and Non-jurors was not new nor was it unique. They affirmed the continuity of their positions with the Caroline divines, the Laudians, and the primitive church. They held, with all Protestants, that preaching and the sacraments were marks of the church, but this was qualified by their emphasis on the place of the ministry. Whereas Latitudinarians found the Anglican forms of the church convenient and helpful, High Churchmen and Non-Jurors insisted on their necessity. With all Anglicans they affirmed that the true church was the one holy catholic and apostolic church, but they accented the apostolic basis of the Church of England. They not only found the church's apostolicity rooted in its doctrine, but they also insisted on the apostolicity of the church's government and liturgy. Apostolic succession was firmly espoused as the foundational mark of the church. Finally, unlike their Latitudinarian counterparts, High Churchmen and Non-Jurors affirmed that salvation could be found only in a church that was constituted through apostolic succession; thus, the Dissenters were outside the realm of salvation. In an age in which the role and place of the church in society was under constant attack, High Churchmen and Non-Jurors proved to be formidable defenders of traditional Christianity.

Although High Churchmen, such as Francis Atterbury and Henry Sacheverell, sought to ally church and state, there was also a strong concern for the autonomy of the church from the state. This doctrine of the church, that it is a visible society under the rule of bishops, who are God's vicegerents, formed the foundation of the assertion of ecclesiastical independence in the face of the Erastianism foisted on the church by low churchmen.

# 4

# The Independence of the Church from the State

The Anglican church-state union formed the foundation of English society. For most Anglicans the church was part of the constitution of the state. Yet, in spite of their active support of the idea of England being a Christian commonwealth, High Churchmen such as Francis Atterbury and Henry Sacheverell rejected any attempt to make the church subservient to the state. If a high churchman affirmed the need for a strong union he did not embrace the Erastianism that predominated among many Latitudinarian Anglicans at the end of the seventeenth century. The Glorious Revolution raised again the specter of Erastianism as bishops and clergy were deprived of their positions in the church because of their political allegiance to James II, an allegiance based on a conscientious adherence to the principles of divine-right monarchy, indefeasible hereditary monarchy, and passive obedience. This political boiling pot raised a further issue concerning the nature of the church. Was the church simply a creature of the state, or did it have an existence separate from the state? Non-Jurors answered the question by affirming the church's complete autonomy from the state. Yet even juring high churchmen, those willing to take the oaths to William and Mary, insisted that church and state were independent and equal partners.[1]

The scholarly consensus attributes the Non-Juror defection from the established church to political causes, but a closer look at the evidence will demonstrate that there were serious theological concerns underlying the Non-Jurors' political response.[2] One can find the key to the issue in the high-church ecclesiology, which even prior to the Revolution affirmed the spiritual independence of the church. Mark Goldie's recent article, "The Nonjurors, Episcopacy, and the Origins of the Convocation Controversy," has rightly attempted to correct this scholarly misunderstanding by positing high-church adherence to what he calls a "two societies" doctrine of church and state. He believes that this doctrine formed the basis of the High Church and Non-Juror ecclesiologies and political theologies.[3]

Although one cannot use this "two societies" doctrine as a blanket to cover all high churchmen, there was indeed a strong belief in the integrity of the church as a society independent of the state. High churchmen understood the Church of England to be a visible branch of the catholic church, not simply an extension of the national government. Fears that the perceived threats from Erastianism, Deism, Nonconformity, Roman Catholicism, and Latitudinarianism would undermine the structural integrity of the visible church, brought into question the traditional understanding of church and state as one commonwealth. The Glorious Revolution and the Whig dominance over the episcopal bench gave sufficient impetus to high-church divines to reassert the church's autonomy from state control. Nonjurors were compelled to espouse the doctrine of ecclesiastical autonomy by what they believed was the "unlawful" deprivation of those bishops and clergy who refused to take the oaths of allegiance to William and Mary. The Non-Juror bishops, and their supporters, insisted that the newly consecrated bishops had usurped the rights of the actual holders of those sees. They concluded that the actions of the government, and the acquiescence of the church's leadership to those actions, warranted their separation from the established church.

Though Mark Goldie's article is an important contribution to the discussion, the theological rationale for an independent and authoritative church, episcopate, and convocation, has not, as yet, received sufficient scholarly attention. This chapter will examine the manner in which the independence of the church from the state was understood and taught by High Church and Non-Juror divines. Chapter 3 demonstrated that high churchmen perceived the Church of England to be a visible society and a member of the one holy catholic and apostolic church, though they particularly emphasized the apostolicity of the church. Notwithstanding the political factors involved in the debates over the episcopate and the Convocation of Canterbury, the underlying theme was clearly theological. We will examine the defense of the church as an independent society, including discussions of the separation of church and state as well as the opportunities that existed for cooperation between the two entities. We will then examine the impact of high-church espousals of ecclesiastical independence on two important institutions, the episcopate and convocation.

## The Defense of Ecclesiastical Independence

High churchmen believed in the one holy catholic and apostolic church; thus, the church transcended all political structures. They believed that the church's roots as an independent society reached back to the apostolic church, predating by several centuries the Constantinian embrace of Christianity. Yet Anglicans had understood since the Reformation that the Church of England was part of a unified commonwealth, governed on the basis of royal supremacy. A series of political events, however, impinged on the integrity of the church and led to a rethinking of the existing relationship between church and state.[4]

The Non-Jurors, ejected from the established church because the political realities of the Glorious Revolution conflicted with their religious and political sensibilities, found the need to defend the legitimacy of an independent church. Although the Non-Jurors had been deprived, in part because of their adherence to the doctrines of divine right monarchy, passive obedience, and indefeasible hereditary right, they did not perceive royal supremacy to be an acceptable foundation for the church's long-term viability. Their political theology led to their refusal to swear allegiance to William and Mary, and to see the accession of the new rulers to the throne as an act of sinful rebellion against God. The Non-Jurors were not the only adherents of divine-right ideology, but many High Churchmen who transferred their loyalties to the new government either abandoned their earlier beliefs or redefined divine-right theory. While the majority of the population accepted William and Mary, either wholeheartedly or grudgingly, the relevance of the concept of church and state as a unified society was called into question by those who refused to acknowledge the new monarchs. The deprived leaders protested that they had been unjustly divested of their spiritual rights as leaders of the church, and that the independence of the church as a society had been undermined.[5]

The question of an independent church was not a novelty, unique to the post-revolution period. Although John Findon has shown that Non-Juror thinking about ecclesiastical independence evolved over time, with these views gaining cogency among Non-Jurors only after the episcopal deprivations in 1691, John Kettlewell had espoused the doctrine of church and state as two independent societies as early as 1681. Henry Dodwell and Simon Lowth[6] also held a "two societies" position prior to 1689. Findon acknowledges that Dodwell had affirmed the doctrine of ecclesiastical independence before 1689, but he denies that Dodwell's views precipitated the schism. While taking heed of Findon's cautions, it does appear that the theological rationale for ecclesiastical autonomy was in place prior to the Glorious Revolution, and it must have influenced their decision to place in jeopardy the unity of the Church of England. Although politics were involved, the Non-Juror movement cannot simply be defined as a political movement, for at heart it was clearly theological.[7]

Mark Goldie has argued that the independence of the church from the state was the definitive component of high-church ecclesiology, and of Non-Juror ecclesiology in particular. The "two societies" doctrine, which he develops, envisioned church and state as two distinct entities, subsisting separately under the sovereign rule of God. Non-Jurors denied the novelty of the doctrine and proclaimed the ancient lineage of the principle, finding its roots in both Scripture and the primitive church. Each of the two distinct spheres of government had particular duties within human society and in relationship to each other that demanded the allegiance of the people. The state had jurisdiction over civil matters, while the church had supremacy over spiritual affairs. Each society had its own governors, or vicegerents, who had been ordained by God, the ultimate ruler over both societies. Harmony between the two societies depended on the restraint of each government from meddling in the affairs of the other. The result served to undergird both divine-right monarchy and episcopacy.[8]

Defenses of an independent church were not, however, limited to the Non-Jurors. Besides the Nonconformists, many influential leaders of the established church, who were content to comply with the Revolution Settlement, affirmed the doctrine. Gerald Straka notes that High Churchmen such as William Sherlock affirmed that the sacredness of the king was in the office, not the person who held the throne; thus, residents of the country only were obliged to submit to the safely seated monarch. J. P. Kenyon, however, notes that Sherlock's view was less than satisfactory, since, on the foundation of providence, Oliver Cromwell would have been the legitimate divinely appointed ruler.[9]

Fears of Erastianism led John Potter to declare that the church was designed to be "distinct from all earthly kingdoms." In keeping with this, he maintained that Christ and the apostles had submitted themselves to the authority of the state in civil matters, while insisting that the church was an independent and spiritual kingdom. Edmund Gibson, the Bishop of London and ally of the Whig Prime Minister, Robert Walpole, maintained that the Church of England was governed by two separate authorities—religious and secular. Gibson's understanding of independence did not exclude royal supremacy, but placed boundaries on it. Like Potter, Gibson feared an Erastianism that would threaten the existence of the church as a society. He made it clear that the church derived its existence and authority from Christ, not from the state. William Beveridge did not deny the authority of the civil magistrate over ecclesiastical persons, but argued that church and state were two distinct powers, each of which descended from God.[10]

William Warburton, the Latitudinarian Bishop of Glouchester, later would use the concept of two societies to place the church under state domination. Although he believed that church and state were originally separate from one another, the alliance of the two societies required that one of them relinquish its independence. He felt that the needs of the church—a settled clergy, ecclesiastical jurisdiction with coactive power, and state protection—demanded the concession of power by the church to the state. State supremacy rested upon the state's need to protect itself from a hostile religion and preserve the essence and purity of religion.[11]

Although not all high churchmen affirmed the complete independence of the church from the state, neither did they affirm the church's subordination to the state. Henry Sacheverell and Francis Atterbury believed in the political union of church and state, asserting that they were two parts of the one body politic; yet they also considered church and state to be distinct in purpose and authority. The union was based on the need of both parties for mutual support; though linked, they were equal partners. The church was in no way subservient to the state. High Churchmen did ally themselves with the Tories in Parliament to protect the rights of the Church of England, but the church, as a religious society, remained self-governing. Atterbury appealed for the Convocation of Canterbury to be recognized as the principle legislative body of the church in place of Parliament. Atterbury appears to have ignored or discounted the existence and authority of the Convocation of York, which would have had jurisdiction over the church in northern England. For him, the Convocation at Canterbury, presided over by the Archbishop of Canterbury, provided a spiritual counterbalance to the political authority of Parliament.[12]

## Separation of Church and State

The Non-Jurors pressed for the recognition of the church's independent spiritual authority much more forcibly than High Churchmen in the established church did. The Non-Juror assertion of independence caused them to become, in essence, a nonconformist sect; yet unlike the Dissenters, the Non-Jurors saw themselves as the only legitimate heirs of primitive catholic tradition in

England. The ambiguity of the Non-Jurors' position has been noted by Paul Monod.

> Separated from the juring church by their uncompromising allegiance, their anti-erastianism, their religious 'purity' and even their liturgy, the Nonjurors transformed themselves into a Nonconformist sect. They would not have admitted it, but their strict loyalty alienated them further and further from the ecclesiastical establishment that they both loved and hated.[13]

The Non-Juror defense against charges of sectarianism was rooted in their belief that they were the sole heirs of apostolic succession in England. Apostolic authority, they claimed, was granted and held without the consent of the secular magistrates, and the Church of England had forfeited its right to apostolic authority by depriving bishops who refused to swear oaths to a usurping king and queen.[14]

The assertion of ecclesiastical independence in spiritual matters was coupled with the recognition of the independence of civil authority in secular matters. Proponents of the concept of two autonomous societies were forced to explain how separate sources of authority could exist simultaneously in the same nation. They rebutted the charges of creating an *imperium in imperio;* Matthew Tindal derisively labeled this duality of authority a "two-headed monster." They asserted in reply that God constructed the two societies to have parallel yet distinct authority. By a special grant, God had divided authority between spiritual and temporal authorities, but the purpose of both was to promote holiness and obedience to God. The power of the church was not held in opposition to the state, but, rather, the church taught the people to obey the government.[15]

High churchmen made a clear distinction between the spiritual and the temporal realms. The doctrines of passive obedience and nonresistance were designed to help keep the proper tension between church and state. The contemporary church, in emulation of the New Testament Church, was obliged to obey the proper authorities, even those hostile to the church (Romans 13:1–6; Titus 3:1–2; I Peter 2:13-17), unless the commands of the state ran counter to those of God (Acts 5:29). This critical principle of high-church political doctrine, therefore, was grounded in theology, and more specifically, in ecclesiological concerns.[16]

Every Anglican, and even non-Anglican, would have conceded that ecclesiastical independence would be warranted if the church faced a hostile, pagan government, but the current situation was markedly different. Here the Church of England confronted state infringement on its spiritual rights in a presumably Christian nation. The Non-Jurors asserted that the relationship of church and state was the same in the seventeenth century as it had been in the first century. George Hickes challenged the idea that church and state had been one society since the conversion of Constantine. He contended that the distinction between clergy and laity had existed since the beginning of the church, continuing unabated until the seventeenth century. Even Henry VIII, he charged, would have agreed with this assessment. Non-Jurors thought it incredulous to believe that the church had simply ceded authority over spiritual affairs to the monarch. This position did not take into account the possibility of a monarch reneging on agreements to enforce church membership, or that he or she might fall into either schism or heresy. They saw the deprivation of bishops and clergy, for matters of conscience, as an example of state persecution of the church, which proved that the state could not be trusted to protect the church.[17]

Separation of the church, as a visible expression of the kingdom of God, from the state required the church to have sufficient authority to act in religious matters without the assistance or interference of the state. The juridicial powers of the church included the right of excommunication. Some Non-Jurors went as far as asserting that the church could remove the temporal benefits attached to spiritual authority, such as episcopal revenues. Although high churchmen agreed that Christ's kingdom was spiritual and not temporal, this concession did not detract from the church's status as God's designated representative in the world. The authority of the church was equal to, yet distinct from, that of the state. They made it clear that Christ had distinguished between the two spheres of government, and that he had not rejected an authoritative government for the visible church. Christ, the Non-Jurors maintained, established a form of government, in the persons of the Apostles and their successors, that was to continue until the end of the age. The conversion of the state did not change this situation.[18]

Peace and cooperation between church and state, in the Non-Juror schema, required that each government recognize the sovereignty of the other within its own sphere of influence. Charles Leslie pointed to the possible implications of this position in distinguishing between the right of the state to pass judgment on criminals and the church's prerogative of excommunication. While the state might pardon the offending person, this did not automatically change the religious censure. There was no confusion of powers because each acted according to its own authority.[19] Confusion occurred only when one society meddled in the affairs of the other. One notorious example of such a problem was the series of wars between the popes and the emperors during the middle ages. Leslie wrote:

> The Emperors claim'd the investiture of Bishops; and the Popes, to be even with them assumed the power of deposing the Emperors from their temporal authority. Here was wrong on both sides: And what could follow but confusion?[20]

Such examples of irresponsibility could have been prevented if each sphere had seen fit to allow the other its rightful place in society. Citizens of the two societies were to "Give to Caesar what is Caesar's, and to God what is God's" (Matthew 22:21; Mark 12:17; Luke 20:25).

## Cooperation Between Church and State

The Non-Jurors believed that mutual respect for each society's boundaries would lead to peace and cooperation. The two governments were to work to support one another. The church would teach obedience to the state and the state would make laws favoring the church. Simon Lowth referred to the monarchs as "nursing fathers and mothers," ordained by God to nourish and protect the church. Cooperation resulted in civil and secular honors, including benefices for the bishops and clergy. Although the magistrates were allowed to nominate candidates for bishoprics, nomination, by itself, did not make one a bishop. The final decision concerning fitness for office lay with the bishops themselves. The magistrate's right to nominate bishops was linked to the bishops sitting in the House of Lords, but having a role in nominating bishops did not mean that the magistrate had the final choice.[21]

Cooperation did not require the merger of church and state into one society. Charles Leslie denied that the magistrate had a power over the church that was inherent in the crown; for if it were intrinsic to the state, then both Christian and heathen monarchs would have the same prerogatives. The conversion of the Roman Empire had not, Leslie insisted, led to the exchange of ecclesiastical autonomy for state protection and honors. The Erastian British magistrates, for their part, rejected that explanation in favor of an inherent authority of the state over the church. Leslie concluded, however, that the bishops did not have the authority to make such a compromise.[22]

The problem of cooperation and merger raised a further question. If the church did merge with the state, why would the church be in submission to the state, rather than the state submitting to the church? Henry Dodwell responded that the greater nobility of the church would have led to its supremacy over the state.

> This, I am sure, is against the general rule of subordinations, to make the more noble power subject to that which is less so; by reasons peculiar to this particular condition of two societies into one.[23]

The church's responsibility for humanity's eternal destiny gave it priority over state concerns. This, of course, had been the traditional Roman Catholic position, as seen in the post-tridentine writings of Robert Bellarmine and Cesare Baronious. George Hickes noted that these authors had asserted that civil power should be taken from the state if it abused the church. He stressed that this view was as damaging to the proper balance between church and state as was state supremacy.[24] Still, despite the Non-Jurors' rejection of the views of Bellarmine and Baronious, their opponents accused them of being "Romanists." The Non-Juror rebuttal to the charges maintained that ecclesiastical independence predated the rise of papal authority. "Popery" contrasted markedly with the Non-Juror understanding of ecclesiastical independence. The popes usurped the rights of the bishops over the churches and seized temporal authority; thus, they had attempted to control both church and state.[25]

The Non-Jurors, however, rejected the church's right to secular power. Instead, church and state were to work together, with the state giving the church protection and the church teaching the people to respect and obey the government. Neither government was to meddle in the affairs of the other. If the monarch should try to coerce the church into acting contrary to what was right, the church should refuse to comply with the request, but it should not foment rebellion. Thus, each governor should recognize that the other was competent to judge and rule in its own sphere.[26]

Passive obedience, evidenced by the Seven Bishops Case of 1688, provided the model for a Christian response to secular constraints on the church. In June of 1688, seven English bishops refused to authorize the reading of James II's Declaration of Indulgence in the churches. The bishops were charged with sedition and imprisoned in the Tower of London. It is ironic that this act, which finally led to James' downfall, was undertaken by many of the same men who would forfeit their offices to support his right to the throne a year later. The bishops, including Archbishop William Sancroft, refused to comply with measures that would jeopardize the integrity of the church. Still, they chose not to participate in or recognize a rebellion against what they considered to be the divinely ordained political authority.[27]

Henry Sacheverell conceived of church-state cooperation differently than the Non-Jurors. Whereas the Non-Jurors affirmed the complete separation of powers, Sacheverell perceived church and state to be in an alliance, with the health of each dependent on the health of the other. He did not, however, call for state domination of the church; rather, he affirmed the partnership of church and state that currently existed. A strong church would be the "surest and most infallible means to strengthen, support, and establish the civil power." In this scheme, religion, or the church, was the foundation of the state; therefore, the two were completely interdependent on one another. In essence, Sacheverell did not differ that much from the Non-Jurors, for the church remained a distinct entity; yet on the basis of strength, it had joined in a union with the state.[28]

Two issues illustrate the high-church concern with the independence of the church from the state, which we have heretofore outlined. The first was the authority of the episcopate as the primary and apostolic governors of the church. The second issue concerned the authority of the provincial synods, or Convocations, over the church. These two issues will be addressed presently.

## Episcopacy and Independence

The theological basis of the Non-Juror separation and the espousal of ecclesiastical independence was rooted, finally, in their understanding of the episcopate. The Non-Jurors left the established church because they believed the state had illegitimately deprived those bishops and clergy who had refused to take the oaths of allegiance to William and Mary. High-church ecclesiology was clearly episcopal in nature, and the Non-Jurors were earnest advocates of the divine origins of the episcopate. Attempts to displace the canonical bishops were perceived as threats to the very livelihood of the church. Yet the Non-Jurors had a two-fold problem: the king's privilege of episcopal nominations, and the fact that the civil government had attempted to deprive canonically consecrated and ordained bishops and clergy.[29]

The nomination of bishops was a difficult issue to handle. The Non-Jurors recognized the need of the government to protect itself against prejudicial church leadership and laws. Consequently, they recognized the right of the monarch to give consent to church activities, but their authority extended only to adding temporal sanctions to ecclesiastical decisions. Non-Jurors saw the problems of the late seventeenth century and early eighteenth century rooted in both the medieval period and in the Reformation. They charged Thomas Cranmer with teaching that the monarchs derived their privilege of nomination from the right of lay church members to nominate bishops during the patristic era.[30] Gilbert Burnet did, in fact, state that the prince, as the supreme power, should comprehend the "whole body of the People in him: Since according to the constitution of the civil government, the wills of the people are understood to be concluded by the supreme, and such are the subject of the legislative authority."[31] Thus for Burnet, as it had been for Cranmer, in a Christian nation, the church was under the rule of the prince. This may explain Burnet's espousal of William's cause against James II, which was rooted in Burnet's belief that James threatened England's national sovereignty, and therefore, the nation's church was also under attack.[32]

While the Non-Jurors recognized the delicate balance between the needs of church and state, they believed that the church could exist without the support of the state but not without bishops. So if the concession to the crown of episcopal nomination came into conflict with the canonical rights of the bishop, the church would be forced to choose the latter. Ultimately, all spiritual authority was derived from Christ, and he had not committed this power to the state, the people, or to common Christians. Instead, Christ had committed all spiritual authority to the Apostles (John 20:21), who in turn ordained elders for each church (Acts 14:23). The power of ordination was passed on by the apostles to bishops, through whom all ecclesiastical authority descended (Titus 1:5). Without a proper commission from Christ, no one had the right to preach the Gospel or perform ministerial functions.[33]

Though there might be disagreement as to when the problem of state nomination became acute, Anglicans, and even all Christians, agreed that church and state were distinctly separate entities for the first three centuries of the Christian era. Following the conversion of Constantine in the fourth century, the boundaries between the two societies became increasingly blurred. As time passed, the bishops acquired civil privileges and the emperors commenced nominating candidates to fill bishoprics. Yet for Non-Jurors, and for some High Churchmen, this did not give civil magistrates the right to create bishops, nor did it mean that nomination by a magistrate was necessary. Even in the fourth century, they claimed, state intervention was restrained. In general, ecclesiastical matters were left to the bishops and ecumenical councils. When magistrates nominated candidates for holy office, the bishops retained the right to decide if the candidate was fit for office. Thus, the bishops had the ultimate authority to decide the makeup of the episcopate.[34]

The consecration of bishops, by the laying on of hands, conferred to the recipient spiritual authority and jurisdiction. High churchmen believed that spiritual or episcopal powers were derived from Christ, through apostolic succession. Since these powers were given by Christ through the bishops, only bishops could remove episcopal authority. The Non-Jurors protested that the removal of the bishops from their sees, and the consecration of other bishops to replace them, was a violation of ecclesiastical authority. Nathaniel Bisbie[35] lamented the "ill news" that a *new primate, and a new bishop*" had replaced those unlawfully deposed by the state. He stated that this was a "project utterly dissonant to all primitive *practice*, to the *antient constitutions and canons* of the Church; and which, if not timely compromised, must necessarily beget, and perhaps unavoidably propagate a lasting *schism* among us."[36]

The Non-Jurors contended that the magistrates' right of deprival was limited to temporal benefits, such as civil jurisdictions, benefices, revenues, and the right to sit in the House of Lords. These powers and benefits were over and above those conferred by Christ through the episcopal college. While Christian magistrates could revoke the civil backing given to the "spiritual ministrations" of the church, they could not keep the church from exercising its proper spiritual authority. There were some, including John Kettlewell, who agreed that some church powers had been yielded in exchange for incorporation. These powers included the right of synods to make canon law without the consent of the magistrate. Yet he affirmed that obedience to Christ had priority over obedience to the magistrate. Norman Skyes' contention that the debate over the deprival of the Non-Juror bishops and clergy revolved around the question of which monarch could lawfully deprive a bishop rests on the position of John Kettlewell. Kettlewell, however, represented only one position among the Non-Jurors. For

Dodwell, Brett, Leslie, and Hickes, it was not a question of which king had the authority to remove bishops from their sees, but whether the state had authority to remove bishops at all. Ultimately, magistrates had civil but not spiritual jurisdiction over the bishops.[37]

The central issue was not, however, episcopal character but episcopal jurisdiction. Defenders of the deprivals pointed to Solomon's removal of the high priest Abiathar (I Kings 2), and Elizabeth I's removal of Romanist bishops, as precedents for removing bishops from their jurisdictions in the church.[38] The Non-Jurors questioned the relevance of the analogies, asserting that the situations were different. In the case of Zadok and Abiathar, Zadok was already a high priest, and Solomon banished Abiathar for his part in Adonaijah's rebellion; Abiathar, however, had not been deprived of his priesthood. As for Elizabeth's deprivation of the Roman Catholic bishops, the latter were part of a heretical and schismatic communion. By their acts of heresy and schism, the "popish" bishops had deprived themselves; Elizabeth, therefore, was simply filling vacant sees and not depriving bishops. A further line of defense pointed to the dubious actions of Mary I, who had turned out the true catholic, orthodox, and reformed bishops, replacing them with "Romanists." It could be claimed, therefore, that Elizabeth had merely removed the usurpers and restored the rightful bishops to their sees.[39]

At the heart of the controversy over episcopal jurisdiction was the matter of the dioceses. While the Non-Juror clergy had allegedly not been deprived of their ordinations, the state had assumed the right to prevent them from publicly exercising their ministries, including diocesan oversight.[40] The Non-Jurors, on the other hand, maintained that episcopal consecration conferred the diocese to the bishop, and it could only be removed by bishops meeting in a provincial synod. Mark Goldie has called this defense of episcopal authority dubious. He questions how even a synod could deprive a bishop under the conditions set up by Henry Dodwell. Unfortunately, Goldie does not elaborate on why this argument restrained synods from depriving a bishop. The issue was not whether a bishop could be removed from office, rather the question concerned the proper procedure. Thus, the church, not the state, was charged with handling this matter.[41]

Non-Jurors grounded their defense of the spiritual nature of diocesan jurisdiction in the alleged apostolic origins of the diocesan system. According to this scenario, the Apostles and their successors, at the leading of the Holy Spirit, divided the supervision of the church's ministries among themselves. This occurred according to church law and totally independent of the magistrate. The correspondence between the diocesan boundaries and those of the imperial provinces was simply coincidental. At no point did the early leaders attempt to have the civil governor determine who received which assignment. If permission from the magistrate was necessary for determining jurisdiction, then the church would have been without a government until the fourth century or the attempts by the Apostles to set up such a system would have been a case of rebellion against the legitimate authorities. Logic ruled out the origination of diocesan boundaries in the state.[42]

In spiritual matters, the bishops stood above all other authorities. If the magistrate's rights conflicted with the church's in spiritual affairs, the magistrates were to forfeit their rights. Nothing was to stand in the way of spreading the gospel.[43] The relationship between bishop and flock was as inviolable as the relationship between the civil magistrates and their realm. Both ruled their spheres of government by divine right, and their subjects were not at liberty to rebel against them. Nathaniel Bisbie affirmed what he believed was the view of the ancient church that "one bishop, one church" was parallel to "one king, one state." He asserted that it was fatal to the unity of the church for there to be more than one bishop in a diocese.[44] Another analogy to the unbreakable relationship between bishop and people was that of husband and wife, with the bishop standing as Christ's proxy in the marriage of Christ and the church. To break off communion with the bishop severed one's relationship with Christ. Charles Leslie wrote:

> That this marriage to our Bishop, whereby we are, by proxy, married to Christ, cannot be dissolv'd, nor are we divorced from him, and marry'd to another Bishop, by any other means, than those which Christ has appointed; otherwise the marriage still remains: And a second Bishop is a second husband, that is an adulterer, while the first husband lives, and is not divorced for a just cause, and by an authority that is competent.[45]

The laity were to remain subject to their bishops as long as the bishops were not heretical in matters of Christian worship and doctrine. The fact that a bishop was prevented, by force, from fulfilling his episcopal duties did not dissolve the relationship between bishop and people, any more than the relationship between king and people or husband and wife would be dissolved because of forced absence. To do otherwise threatened the viability of the church as an independent spiritual society. One can see, in these descriptions, the strong attachment to divine-right theory and patriarchalism, but the theological foundations of these arguments are equally evident. Attachment to the bishop was on the same plane as allegiance to the king, in this case, the deposed James II. Non-Jurors considered episcopal character and diocesan jurisdiction to be synonymous and inseparable from one another; by intefering with the Non-Juror bishops' diocesan jurisdiction the government was in a state of schism.[46]

Non-Jurors did not see themselves as a schismatic party. The onus of the schism was placed on those who remained within the state church, for by remaining they affirmed the right of the state to interfere in the spiritual affairs of the church. Non-Jurors, however, did not all agree on the nature of the schism. This disagreement led some Non-Jurors to eventually return to the established church, while others continued to adhere to a parallel episcopacy long after the original Non-Juror bishops died.

Henry Dodwell interpreted the "schism" in terms of the injury done to the bishops; the schism existed until either the bishops were restored to office or they were dead. He believed that the see became vacant on the death of the lawful bishop, and since the unlawfully imposed successor held the strongest title to the see, he deserved the allegiance of the people of the diocese. Following the death of the deprived Bishop of Norwich, William Lloyd, in 1710, Dodwell sought the permission of Thomas Ken, the only living original Non-Juror bishop, to return to the established church, in accordance with the principles set out in a *Case in View, Considered* (1705). In the *Case in View, Now in Fact,* Dodwell declared that the schism had ended and those who remained outside the established church were in schism.[47]

George Hickes took a more rigid view of the situation. He believed the acts of deprivation had created an unrectifiable schism. He tried to dissuade Dodwell and Robert Nelson from returning to the established church, declaring that they returned at the peril of their souls, for the bishops and priests of the established church were unable to perform "valid acts of priesthood; their very prayers are sin; their Sacraments no Sacraments." While both Dodwell and Hickes believed that the church could not exist without bishops, Hickes had made certain that the Non-Juror episcopal succession could continue by joining with Archibald Campbell and James Gaddarer, two Scottish bishops, in consecrating Jeremy Collier, Samuel Hawes, and Nathaniel Spinckes as bishops in 1713. An earlier attempt to maintain the Non-Juror succession had led to the consecration of Hickes and Thomas Wagstaffe in 1693. These consecrations had been performed by William Lloyd, Bishop of Norwich; Francis Turner, Bishop of Ely; and Thomas White, Bishop of Peterborough, at the behest of William Sancroft.[48] Hickes believed the schism would end only when the offending parties acknowledged their schism and returned to the true, Non-Juror, church. The "schismatics" would need to have their ordinations authorized, the intruding bishops would have to repent, and the true church would have to reaffirm their episcopal character before they would be allowed to reclaim their diocesan jurisdiction. Hickes did not consider the deaths of the injured bishops to be sufficient to end the schism. In the meantime, the church functioned under the leadership of suffragan bishops, who served not as diocesan but as catholic bishops.[49]

The decline of the Non-Jurors as a viable ecclesiastical society had several causes. First, most of the deprived bishops, including Thomas Ken, did not attempt to continue their episcopal duties after their deprival. Second, Henry Dodwell, Robert Nelson, and other leading Non-Juror lay leaders returned to the established church following the death of William Lloyd. Finally, the Non-Jurors made no attempt to create a diocesan episcopate to replace the "schismatic" episcopate of the established church. They simply took over two suffragan titles created but not filled by Henry VIII. It is difficult to understand why so little progress was made by them. In some respects, the lack of a unified purpose plagued them. Although the Non-Jurors claimed a number of leading scholars in their ranks, they seemed to lack the organizing ability and foresight to create a lasting and growing system in the face of persecution. Paul Monod believes they had a considerable audience but could not take advantage of it. Their success was limited by their inability to proselytize openly.[50] Whatever the case, the Non-Jurors were not successful in creating a viable church without the protection of the state. The divisions within the Non-Juror communion possibly hindered their effectiveness as well. Thomas Ken and Robert Frampton, the deprived Bishop of Gloucester, never countenanced any of the separatist activities of the Non-Juror episcopate. Despite their failings, they were able to continue, sometimes tenuously as a communion until 1805.[51]

## The Independence of Provincial Synods

The Non-Juror schism paralleled the ongoing Convocation Controversy in the Church of England, which gave voice to high-church affirmations of ecclesiastical autonomy. The anonymous publication of the *Letter to a Convocation Man* (1697) was the first of several earnest calls for the summoning of the Convocation of Canterbury. The tract has been attributed to several authors, including Sir Bartholomew Shower, a Jacobite lawyer, and Francis Atterbury; most scholars, however, believe that Atterbury was the primary author. The *Letter* launched a protracted debate that involved many of Britain's most eminent theologians, including the future Archbishop of Canterbury, William Wake. The controversy centered on the question of who had the right to call and dismiss Convocation. An additional difficulty pertained to the frequency of its meeting. The current scholarly debate focuses on whether the foundation of Atterbury's case for a regularly sitting convocation was theological or political. The two major positions are epitomized by the works of Mark Goldie and G. V. Bennett. Goldie has sought to place Atterbury's roots in the writings of Non-Jurors such as Henry Dodwell, linking the Convocation controversy with the Non-Juror claims of ecclesiastical autonomy. Bennett has attempted to show that Atterbury appealed to the English constitution to prove that Convocation had the right to sit regularly.[52] There is merit in both positions, though most scholars follow Bennett; Atterbury, as Bennett has demonstrated, made considerable reference to the constitutional guarantees of Convocation.

Goldie has asserted that Atterbury transferred the Non-Juror's concern for ecclesiastical independence to the debate over Convocation in the established church.[53] There is, however, a lack of preciseness in Atterbury's view of church autonomy that raises questions concerning Goldie's thesis. In contrast to Goldie, Bennett denies that Atterbury ever advocated the complete separation of church and state, asserting that Atterbury desired to "achieve reconstruction in the Church in partnership with the State and the Politicians."[54]

In the *Letter to a Convocation Man,* Atterbury seems to espouse the existence of two separate and distinct powers, each having different spheres of influence. Yet, in the *Rights, Powers, and Privileges of an English Convocation* (1700, 1701), he denied that the earlier tract had claimed ecclesiastical independence from the state. He distinguished, in the later work, between the ability of the church to exist without the state, as it had during the first three centuries, and the complete separation of the state from church affairs. He did not perceive a contradiction between distinct powers in church and state and in royal supremacy.[55]

Atterbury was fully cognizant of the historical precedents for synods meeting without state approval. In the *Letter to a Convoca-*

*tion Man* he asserted that the church was a supernatural society with the inherent power of self government. Yet he proceeded to defend the right of Convocation to meet on the basis of the English constitution. This is stated even more explicitly in the second work. He contended that Convocation's right to assemble could be defended in two ways, either on its own basis, or as it related to Parliament. He emphasized the second of the two options, perceiving that a constitutional defense would be more effective.[56]

Atterbury believed that "the liberties" of the church were analogous to those of the state; therefore, according to the English constitution, church and state would stand or fall together. He concluded that whatever was true of Parliament should be true of Convocation. He saw Convocation as the church's highest deliberative body, equal to Parliament, whose rulings were subject only to the ratification of the king. The equality of Convocation to Parliament meant that the rulings of the former did not require the assent of the latter. He asserted that it was the constitutional right of the church to meet to conduct religious business. His basis was the *Praemunire* clause, summoning to Parliament the bishops, and with them, the deans, archdeacons, and representatives of the clergy. Although it seemed a major obstacle to his position, Atterbury contended that Henry VIII's "Act for the Submission of the Clergy" did not abrogate this right; for once a custom was followed for more than a century, it became law. Convocation, therefore, was to meet with every new Parliament. Attendance at Convocation, as outlined by the clause, was not only a duty, but it was a right. Custom and an act of Parliament, under Edward III, determined that Parliament and the Convocations of Canterbury and York were to meet annually. For William Wake, however, the historical record established that Convocation needed royal permission to meet. Although neither Atterbury nor Wake appealed to a theological basis for their views, they each interpreted the historical record differently.[57]

Church and state, at least in relation to Convocation, had comparable forms of organization. Atterbury believed it was expedient for the polities of church and state to be as similar as possible; though he thought that the structure of the church should remain as consistent with the original as possible. Convocation paralleled Parliament in having two houses—the upper house composed of the bishops, the lower house consisting of representatives of the clergy. He argued that it was the only synod in Christendom modeled on a parliamentary prototype; therefore, Convocation had all the rights and privileges that were necessary to be a house of

Parliament, including the right of each house to debate, vote, and adjourn.[58]

It did not go unnoticed that, while Convocation was prevented from gathering, the Church of Scotland met regularly in synods and assemblies. Atterbury plaintively asked that the episcopal church of England have the same rights as the Scottish kirk, which, he claimed, had set up its assemblies independently of the government, after attempts were made to adjourn them. Atterbury asked only that the Church of England have the same rights as all other churches in Christendom. Matthias Earbery, a Non-juror, declared that the restrictions set on the Church of England, while freedom was given to the Scottish kirk, placed the church under a yoke of slavery to which even the sects would refuse to submit.[59]

Atterbury emphasized that the Lower House of Convocation had an indisputable right to meet to do the business of the church. He pointed out that, whereas the bishops could vote on ecclesiastical issues in the House of Lords, the lower clergy's only forum for discussion was the Lower House of Convocation. As the controversy unfolded, Atterbury was elected Prolocutor of the Lower House of Convocation. As Prolocutor he attempted to forge an alliance with the Tory leaders in the House of Commons; he hoped that the alliance would further High Church programs in the face of opposition from the more liberal bishops who controlled the Upper House of Convocation.[60]

Although the Non-Jurors were not directly involved in the Convocation Controversy, since they remained outside the established church, they produced a significant literary defense of the church's right to meet in synods and assemblies. Henry Dodwell, as Mark Goldie has noted, affirmed the importance of synods in his defense of the deprived bishops. Whereas Atterbury's work was based primarily on political precedents, Dodwell developed a much more theological rationale, though he was not averse to making use of political and historical precedents. He presumed that synods were independent of state control; Convocation was, in his view, the preeminent assembly of the Church of England. Therefore, only Convocation had the right to deprive an English bishop, and consequently, Convocation alone could release the people from submission to their bishops. He maintained that a synod was the church's legislative assembly for deliberations and rulings on matters concerning the "reformation of manners" and heresy. On the basis of historical precedent, including the rulings of general councils, he affirmed the right of synods to meet twice a year, and he assumed that they would not meet if they were subject to the whim of the magistrate.[61]

There was a major difference between Atterbury and Dodwell, which calls into question Goldie's theory that Atterbury derived his position on Convocation from Dodwell. While Atterbury defended the right of the lower clergy to gather, Dodwell was concerned with an episcopal synod, which he believed was the only body that could canonically deprive bishops. The difference between Convocation and an ecclesiastical synod did not go unnoticed by Atterbury's opponents. Although the *Letter to a Convocation Man* had Dodwellian elements, upon close analysis there is little relationship between them. Atterbury, along with Henry Sacheverell, cast his lot with his Tory counterparts in Parliament, believing that this alliance was the best means of protecting the church.[62]

The Non-Jurors stressed synodical gatherings of the clergy, which were grounded in the first Jerusalem council (Acts 15:1–29). On the basis of the decisions of the Council of Nicea, they called for biennial synodical gatherings of the bishops to transact church business. These meetings were to proceed until all business was resolved, even though the magistrate might oppose the continuance of the assembly. Three types of synods were outlined: provincial, national, and ecumenical. Thomas Brett argued that provincial synods, such as the Convocations of Canterbury and York, were the proper place for the judging and deposing of bishops in cases of transgression, which had been true since Judas was defrocked for betraying Jesus. Although the deposed Non-Juror bishops were not brought before Convocation, attempts were made by the Lower House of Convocation to deprive Benjamin Hoadly, which resulted in the prorogation of Convocation in 1717. The fact that Christian emperors confirmed the right of the church to meet in synods was not the granting of a favor, but the recognition of their Christian obligation to protect the church. To impede the gathering of the church in synods was to reject Christ's authority over the church; since the church was an independent society, councils and synods were perceived to be the primary means of church government. The Non-Juror position must be differentiated from Atterbury's, for the Non-Jurors did not give the king or magistrate a role in either calling synods or in approving the results or their deliberations.[63]

The Convocation controversy served as a vehicle for the defense of ecclesiastical independence, but the High Church leadership, led by Atterbury, did not follow the Non-Jurors in making the independence of the church a necessary element of their ecclesiology. Atterbury, at certain points, seems closer to William Warburton's attempt to submerge the two societies' doctrine in a church-state alliance. The independence of Convocation rested in its right to meet and discuss any issue it considered necessary, and while Atterbury affirmed this, his method of defending this right differed markedly from the defenses made by Dodwell, Brett, and Earbery.

## Conclusion

The independence or autonomy of the church from the state played a central role in Non-Juror ecclesiology, and it played a more subdued role in High Church thought. It can be shown that the Non-Jurors were, in part, politically motivated, but their defense of the church, as an independent society free from government control, was also clearly theological. If the Non-Juror recourse to ecclesiastical independence was a politically motivated defense of their allegiance to the deposed monarchy, many other Anglicans rejected divine-right theory for equally political reasons. Divine-right monarchy, though it was transformed by those who conformed to the new political situation, continued to have considerable support after the Revolution, even among supporters of William and Mary and their successors. Jacobitism was as prevalent in the established church as it was in the Non-Juror communion; Atterbury was a good example of a High Church leader who was implicated in Jacobite activities after taking the oaths.[64]

In spite of any political motivations, Non-Jurors and High Churchmen may have had in affirming the autonomy of the church from the state, in the final analysis their position was deeply rooted in theological principles. The foundation of the church's existence came from Christ's commission of the apostles, and in turn, the bishops, to propagate the Gospel. Apostolic succession, not a royal decree, formed the basis of the Church of England. State involvement was limited to supporting church rulings with state rewards and penalties.

# 5

# The Doctrine of the Ministry

The heart of High Church and Non-Juror ecclesiology was the emphasis on the visibility of the church. The visible church was the sole repository of the means of salvation, and therefore one could only hope to receive salvation in the visible church. Two elements characterized the visible church: the clerical ministry and the sacraments. Both were essential to the existence of the church, since God had ordained the clergy to administer the sacraments to the faithful. Thus, without the ordained ministry, which High Churchmen and Non-Jurors linked to the doctrine of apostolic succession, the church could not exist. Yet by the end of the seventeenth century the necessity of the historic episcopate and clergy to either the existence of the church or to salvation was being challenged from both inside and outside the established church. While the Dissenters rejected the episcopate, many within the established church, including Benjamin Hoadly and Samuel Clarke, saw church government to be an indifferent matter. The heart of the Bangorian Controversy, which engulfed Hoadly in 1717, was Hoadly's rejection of authoritative vicegerents in the church. Gilbert Burnet, a leading Latitudinarian Bishop, believed that the ministry was necessary to keep order in the church, but the actual form ministry took was considered to be adiaphora. Deists such as John Toland chose to remain within the established church in spite of their rejection of orthodox Christianity, and they challenged the traditional church polity. They questioned the need for clergy, or laity for that matter, to subscribe to a particular form of the church polity, doctrine, or priesthood. To this vocal minority, the church's purpose did not include setting theological, ecclesiological, or liturgical boundaries. It was challenges such as this one by Deists that aroused the ire of high-church enthusiasts.[1]

High Churchmen and Non-Jurors, in contrast with their more liberal challengers, continued to stress the importance of an episcopally ordained ministry. They sought to provide a credible alternative to the reductionism of Benjamin Hoadly and other liberal Anglicans. The coupling of salvation with the reception of the sacraments meant that ministry constituted an essential element of High church and Non-Juror ecclesiology.

Unfortunately, with the exception of George Every, little attention has been given to the high-church doctrine of the ministry. Every, however, does not examine in any depth the underlying theological foundations of the High Church and Non-Juror doctrine of the ministry.[2]

This chapter will briefly examine the socioeconomic conditions experienced by the clergy in the late seventeenth and early eighteenth century, and then, mindful of this socioeconomic context, the focus will turn to the underlying theological basis of ministry. Issues taken up will include the divine authorization for ministry, the dignity of Christian ministry, the qualifications for ministry, and finally, the hierarchical nature of Anglican ministry.

## Clergy Lifestyles

Whether curate or bishop, the typical eighteenth-century Anglican clergyman faced a life of hardship. Few steps were taken by the Church of England in the years that followed the Reformation to restructure the diocesan and parish systems. The sporadic attempts at reforming the church in the intervening years included the creation of five new dioceses, enactment of a restriction on pluralism in the sixteenth century, the updating of canon law, and in the early decades of the eighteenth century, the creation of the Queen Anne's Bounty to provide financial assistance to the clergy. Peter Virgin notes that the central problems of pluralism, lay patronage, diocesan geography, and clerical discipline, were left largely unaddressed.[3]

Most eighteenth-century Anglican clergymen lived in poverty. Social structures forced impoverished clergy to work under great disadvantages, including the lack of books and the company of educated colleagues. Poverty also compelled many priests to find additional sources of income, leading to the exploitation of the clergy and their congregations. Yet, in spite of the low state of the clergy in the late seventeenth and early eighteenth centuries, the situation did not reach the nadir of the late eighteenth and early nineteenth centuries. Poverty was not limited to the lower levels of the priesthood, though rectors were rarely destitute. While the situation of vicars was mixed, depending on the amount of their tithe, curates were the most impoverished, receiving, at best, small stipends for their service.[4]

The problems inherent in the support of the Anglican clergy did not go unnoticed by eighteenth-century observers. Thomas Stackhouse, a High Churchman, complained that the poverty of the clergy led to idleness, sloth, unwarranted income, depression, clandestine marriages, intrusions into other parishes, and dereliction of one's duties. He protested that serious consideration had not been given to the clergy's situation, so that while wealthy congregations enriched their pastors, the stipends of the less-privileged clergy were diminished. He questioned the ability of a pastor to support a family on a stipend of thirty pounds a year. He lamented the sight of a "man of God" with his toes sticking out of his shoes, his heels worn out of his socks, and wearing a ruffled coat or tattered gown, so that even apprentices and "wags" made light of him. Worse, many clergymen were forced to sell their books to buy a petticoat or a wedding ring for their wives. The economic conditions not only brought misery to the clergy but devalued them in the eyes of society as well.[5]

The enduring practice of clerical pluralism, though it may not have been as wide-spread as previously believed, came under sharp criticism by both high-church and low-church observers. Stackhouse charged incumbents who only visited their parishes once a quarter with being more concerned with profits than souls. These unworthy clerics thought that an occasional sermon was worth hundreds of pounds, while they left the poor, the widowed, and the fatherless to fend for themselves. On the other hand, the poorly reimbursed curate, who continually resided in his parish, remaining faithful to his duties, suffered under a "small, precarious stipend." It was the latter who deserved, in the words of Paul, double honor (I Timothy 5:17–18).[6]

Besides these economic difficulties, the poorer clergy suffered further indignities at the hands of their wealthier colleagues. Stackhouse called on the more-affluent clergy to treat their impoverished colleagues with civility and respect, perhaps inviting them to their tables, instead of inviting the squire or rich merchant. He noted that there were rectors who related to their curates with an air of superiority, better suited for a "Persian Monarch than a Christian Priest; breaking jests upon their poverty, and making themselves merry with their misfortunes."[7]

Politics also infected the religious climate of the period. The Church of England was profoundly political, and few thought this to be abnormal. Perhaps the most blatant example of the political character of the church was the career of Benjamin Hoadly. Hoadly denied the relevance of visible churches, and yet, he was only too happy to accept the most prestigious ecclesiastical posts. G. F. A. Best writes that the importance of the church to the social and political structures was to great for anyone who did not have religious scruples to forsake. Affairs of state also interfered with episcopal oversight in the dioceses. Even the most committed bishops suffered under the requirement of residing in London for most of the year. In addition, failure to vote the party line in the House of Lords could lead to unfortunate consequences. Both William Wake and Thomas Secker fell into disfavor because of the their political independence.[8]

Despite the inconveniences and low state of affairs that confronted the clergy of the late seventeenth and early eighteenth centuries, the importance of the ordained ministry was eagerly defended, especially by High Churchmen and Non-Jurors. The impetus for the defense of the ministry, and especially episcopacy, came from several points. First, there were the attacks on the Anglican episopate from Roman Catholic and Presbyterian opponents; second, the deprivations of the Non-juror bishops and clergy led to defenses of the independence of the church and its leadership from state domination. The rediscovery of patristic studies in the seventeenth century may have also influenced high-church defenses of episcopacy and priesthood. The Church Fathers were, themselves, strong proponents of the rights of the clergy.[9]

## The Doctrine of the Ministry

"Ministry," "clergy," and "office" were synonymous terms for high churchmen. Ministry was hierarchical, ordained, and limited to a particular group of men.[10] In many ways this differed little from Anglican views held since the Reformation. Yet divergences did exist between the positions of Richard Hooker or Edward Stillingfleet and the High Churchmen and Non-Jurors. The writings of the ancient church convinced high churchmen that there was a normative form of church government; therefore, decisions concerning ecclesiastical polity could not be left to the state to determine.[11]

Anglican laity appear to have had few rights and little authority in the church. High churchmen dismissed the prerogative of the laity to preach, to baptize, or to consecrate the eucharist. They declared that clerical authority was not derived from the people but from God alone through the agency of apostolic succession. An episcopal commission was required to validate any ministerial act, and the commissions given to some men prohibited the activities of all others.[12]

Ministers were considered servants of God, not the people; as God's representatives they served as mediators between God and his people. Though the term "minister" implied service, or a servile state, high churchmen stressed that the clergy were Christ's servants, not humanity's. The majesty and power of Christ helped elevate the office; for the servants of one who had such great stature also must be honored. The manner in which one treated the stewards of God's mysteries was seen as a reflection of one's view of God. Strangely, the humility of Christ, including his washing the disciples' feet, did not seem to impact their understanding of the priesthood. In contrast, Gilbert Burnet stated that the dignity of the ministry was in the work being done, as exemplified by Christ taking the form of a servant and washing his disciple's feet, an action the disciple's feet, an action the disciples were called to imitate.[13]

High Churchmen and Non-Jurors conceived of ministry in terms of its purpose and duties. The clergy were God's chosen means of celebrating the sacraments, governing the church, as well as teaching, preaching, blessing, and saving God's people. They were the intermediaries between God and the people, declaring God's will and sealing his covenants.[14] The Non-Juror lay leader, Robert Nelson, pointed out the implications of being a minister of Christ.

> That they act by commission from Him, that they are his officers and immediate attendants, his domestics and in a peculiar manner his servants. That they are employed in his particular business, empowered and authorized to negotiate and transact for God; and that not only in some particular thing, but at large in all the outward administrations of the covenant of grace, or of reconciliation between God and man.[15]

The emphasis was on the sacerdotal work of the ministry, while the pastoral aspects of ministry were considered to be secondary.

## Divine Authorization for Ministry

Ministry, for High Churchmen and Non-Jurors, was entered into only with divine authorization. This view had developed toward the end of the Elizabethan era, and it culminated during the period of William Laud's dominance over the Church of England in the 1630s. It had evolved in contrast to the view of those, such as Richard Hooker, who wished to give a far greater place to the state in authorizing religious service. Although Hooker believed that episcopal authority descended from the Apostles, he also taught that church and state were unified, with the clergy as an estate of society. Because the New Testament had not imposed a rigid form of ministry, the state had the right to decide what form would best suit its needs. Latitudinarian divines, such as Edward Stillingfleet, followed Hooker in perceiving the episcopacy as a convenient, though expendable, form of church government. A more catholic trend began to appear in the 1590s, culminating in the Laudian emphasis on the continuity between the reformed Church of England and the pre-Reformation church. At the center of the Laudian position was the doctrine of the apostolic succession. It was this Laudian emphasis on episcopacy and apostolic succesion that would predominate in late seventeenth-and early eighteenth-century High Church and Non-Juror ecclesiology.[16]

In contrast to the Erastian impulses of the day, exemplified by Benjamin Hoadly, high churchmen rejected any suggestion that the commission for ministry derived from the state or the people. They claimed that there was no evidence, either biblical or historical, that placed the power of ordination in anyone but the Apostles and their successors. The church had the same rights and responsibilities as the civil state too authorize subordinate officers for their society. While the laity, including the monarch, might be invited to give their consent or offer nominations, the final decision concerning consecrations and ordinations belonged to the bishops.[17]

The origin of Christian ministry, according to high churchmen, was lodged in the person and work of Christ. Christ, in turn, passed the responsibility for Christian ministry to the Apostles, who conveyed the commission, by laying on of hands, to all bishops and priests. The ordained ministry had a divine commission to continue Christ's task of restoring humanity to God's favor. The biblical foundation for ministry was found in the Great Commission (Matthew 28:18–20; John 20:21). Only a select few received this special authorization from Christ. The clergy alone had the right to fulfill the two essential elements of the commission—teaching and baptizing in Christ's name. Christ gave the apostles and their successors sufficient power and authority to fulfill their commission. Christ's promise to be present until the end of the world transcended the apostolic era; thus, it served as the scriptural foundation for the doctrine of apostolic succession.[18] William Beveridge affirmed that Christ was to be present, by the Holy Spirit, to assist in the fulfillment of the apostolic commission.

> In the discharge, I say, of their Apostolical office; for we have still to remember that I observed before, even that these words were spoken to the Apostles and them by the Holy Spirit, here promised, cannot be understood only of His illuminating, of sanctifying, or comforting presence, which he vouchsafeth to all believers, as well as unto them; but it must be understood in such a sense as is proper to the Apostles, Pastors, governors of the Church in all ages: which in brief amounts to no more nor less than this, even that Christ, having constituted such an office in His Church for the government and edification of it to the end of the world; He here promiseth that he himself, by his Holy Spirit, will be always present at the execution of it, so as to make it effectual to the great ends and purposes for which it was designed.[19]

Apostolic succession, therefore, was based in Christ's promise to be present with the Apostles and their successors through the ages.

Although the bishops received all the essentials of the apostolic office, some items, including the immediate call of Christ, infallibility, and extraordinary gifts, such as tongues and miracles, belonged only to the Apostles. The essential element of the apostolic commission was the presence of the Spirit, who authorized their ministry. The rites of laying on of hands conveyed the Holy Spirit to bishops and priests. This "apostolic rite" was to be continued until the end of the world, guaranteeing that the Spirit poured out on the Apostles on the day of Pentecost would be conferred to every Christian minister.[20]

The episcopate was the sole repository of apostolic succession; for High Churchmen and Non-Jurors believed that the only insurance that the church would continue to exist was the permanence of its chief officers. The Church of England's retention of the historic episcopate at the time of the Reformation gave high churchmen confidence in the apostolic authority of their church. Charges that the derivation of the Anglican episcopate from Rome invalidated the English succession were answered forcefully. Matthias Symson admitted that Rome was in error on many counts. Yet, because of Roman orthodoxy in the essential doctrines of the Christian faith, its orders and succession were likewise valid. He noted that no Protestant church required a Catholic, who had renounced his errors, to be reordained.[21] Thus, Anglicans could claim a commission from God passed on through successive generations of episcopal consecrations and priestly ordinations, for without a proper commission all that a priest might do would be invalid.[22]

An effective episcopal consecration, traditionally, required the presence of three bishops, while one bishop was needed to ordain a presbyter or deacon. Although this had been the general practice of the English Church, the Usages party of the Non-Jurors, who generally took a rigid view of historical precedent, felt compelled to continue their succession through the offices of only one bishop. Roger Laurence, irregularly consecrated, with Thomas Deacon, by the Scottish bishop Archibald Campbell, defended his consecration on the basis of the extraordinary circumstances facing his movement. Episcopal ordination was, nonetheless, required, and presbyterial ordinations were considered void. Although presbyters might participate in an ordination, only bishops could confer the apostolic mantle.[23] In this they differed from the Anglicanism of Richard Hooker and Gilbert Burnet; although Hooker emphasized episcopal authority in ordination, he allowed for exceptions that would permit presbyterial ordinations in cases of necessity. Burnet wrote, similarly, that when people could no longer in good conscience attend the national church, they should seek out someone, even if holding lower orders, to form a church. He even affirmed the right of the people to choose a minister from their own midst if an ordained minister could not be found. He believed that this was in accord with the Thirty-nine Articles in cases of necessity. Higher churchmen rejected the excuse of necessity as a justification for presbyterian ordinations, for only episcopal ordination was valid.[24]

The universal validity of episcopal ordination transcended all national or denominational manifestations of the church. Thus, someone ordained in the Church of England had a valid commission throughout the "Holy Catholic Church," while a presbyterian ordination was void. Presbyterian ordination became a sticking point in the conversations of the 1680s concerning the comprehension of Presbyterians in the Church of England. High Churchmen claimed that neither scripture nor history supported the validity of presbyterian ordinations. Thus, from the High Church perspective, Presbyterian clergy would have to be reordained by Anglican bishops. This was, however, unacceptable to most Presbyterians.[25] High churchmen, for their part, refuted the Presbyterian appeal to the precedent of the fifth century Catholic father, Jerome. Though the Presbyterians held that Jerome affirmed the validity of nonepiscopal ordinations, their high-church respondents claimed that Jerome had only described the nomination of bishops by presbyters, not presbyterial ordinations. Thomas Brett dismissed Jerome's assertions that bishops and presbyters were originally the same office, stating that Jerome had gone against tradition at that point.[26]

Though apostolic succession formed the foundation of the High Church and Non-Juror doctrine of the ministry, these men also affirmed the continuity of the Christian Church with the Jewish dispensation. They believed that "church" offices that existed prior to the incarnation remained valid in the new church. Since the Jewish Law only allowed priests to offer sacrifices and perform other religious services, the same must also be true of the Christian Church. This meant that only the ordained clergy could administer the sacraments and perform other ministerial duties. An inward call to ministry did not eliminate the need for an external commission, such as that given by Moses to Aaron and the Levites.[27]

Ministry was accorded great dignity by High Churchmen and Non-Jurors, and that dignity derived, in part, from the doctrine of apostolic succession. This meant that the state could not remove the clergy's divine authorization and that obedience to them was required, for out of the clergy flowed the means of grace, which they alone could dispense. For Non-Jurors, the divine authorization of ministry demonstrated that their reaction was based on theological principles, not on political expedience. George Hickes asserted that the cause of the separation was the state's actions in putting new bishops on the thrones of those who had been unjustly and invalidly deposed.[28]

## The Dignity of Christian Ministry

The doctrine of the ministry, for High Churchmen and Non-Jurors, was theologically objective, with the dignity of the episcopally ordained ministry derived from the office itself, not from either the social position or the character of the person who filled the office. The dignity of the ministry came from the clergy's role as Christ's representatives or ambassadors, empowered to govern the church, pardon sins, and dispense God's words and sacraments. Thomas Stackhouse declared that neither riches nor poverty made a difference in the dignity of the ministry, so that "the curate that tramps it on foot, and the Rector that rides in his easychair chariot, and *no despict illinic,* are men of the same power and authority" with regard to their duties and calling within the church. Thus it did not matter what class or station of society that one came from, but the office that one filled.[29] Stackhouse maintained that his purpose in dwelling on the subject of ministerial dignity was not to magnify the office, but to remove the prejudices toward the poorer and less-learned clergy. He noted that "the glare and figure of an ecclesiastic is no way essential to his character; that a flaming gown and cassock have no more virtue in 'em, and perhaps less learning under them than the meanest threadbare jacket."[30] In short, it was the office itself, not the circumstances of a person's life, that gave dignity to the office.

The value of word and sacraments did not depend on the one who administered them, but on Christ's promise to be present with the celebrant of the holy office through the agency of the Holy Spirit. Without Christ's presence with the officiant, according to William Beveridge, "all the fine words and phrases in the world can never mortify one lust, nor convert one soul to God and goodness."[31] Non-Jurors, such as George Hickes, however, tended to waver on this issue, for they held that to submit to bishops who were in schism was sin.[32] Still, following the tone set by Bishop Beveridge, one comes back to Christ, the source of the commission to ministry, for the root of the dignity of the office of ministry.

## Qualifications for Christian Ministry

Christian ministry was not open to everyone. A prospective clergyman had to meet specific qualifications, some of which were spiritual and some pragmatic. Together with a call to ministry, one needed to acquire training in both theological and pastoral disciplines, and to demonstrate the personal traits necessary for effective ministry.[33]

A minister needed a call from the church and episcopal ordination before he could enter his office; gifts for ministry alone were not sufficient. Even Christ needed the anointing of the Holy Spirit before he entered his ministry. Christ in turn gave an outward commission to the Apostles, and this commission had been passed on through the centuries to their successors. With regard to the need for an outward call, William Roberts wrote that though the inward call was necessary, a commission for ministry entailed "being externally appointed and constituted to any Holy Office, either *immediately* by God himself, or *mediately* by those who are *divinely* authoriz'd to invest men therewith."[34]

Beyond the visible call, however, one needed suitable training. The clergy needed some rudiments of education in order to teach doctrine and refute error. George Bull advised candidates for ordination to develop a competent knowledge of four areas of theology, as well as a proficiency in biblical studies, which was the foundation of all theological disciplines. The four theological disciplines were speculative theology, apologetics, devotional or moral theology, and ethics. Practical theology, whether devotional or ethical, formed an important foundation for the practice of ministry. The study of ethics was extremely important, for ethics enabled clergy to help resolve parishioner's personal problems. Proper scriptural interpretation required the knowledge of antiquity, history, and philology. High churchmen recognized the danger in attempting to interpret the Bible without recourse to the understandings of previvious generations of scholars and preachers. Charles Leslie complained that many of his contemporaries had bypassed ecclesiastical history and the primitive Fathers, taking their knowledge of the faith secondhand from modern systems of divinity. He stated that the best method for studying theology was to start with the beginnings of Christian history and end with contemporary theology.[35]

The preponderance of seventeenth- and eighteenth-century Anglican clergy who either graduated from or attended Oxford or Cambridge demonstrated the importance given to a university education in the preparation for ministry. Gilbert Burnet and William Wake, however, criticized the universities for the quality of education they provided in theology and biblical studies. Burnet created a cathedral school to prepare candidates for ministry, but pressure from the universities closed it. A university education was, nonetheless, typical. Although Oxford had a reputation for being highchurch in orientation, former Cambridge students and graduates outnumbered Oxford alumnae among the Non-Jurors.[36]

Ministerial education, by itself, was not sufficient preparation for ministry. One also needed personal qualifications, such as prudence. Bull wrote "wisdom is the soul that animates and enlivens knowledge, without which a large knowledge is but like a huge carcass, a lifeless inactive thing."[37] With proper training and wisdom, the candidate for ministry needed to have lived a holy life. Teaching required the ability to model one's faith. Although the efficacy of the sacraments did not depend on the priest's personal holiness, preaching without holiness of life was lifeless.[38]

Although the lifestyles of many clergy did not approach dignified standards, each was called to an office of high solemnity and honor, at least in theory. The person called to the ministry, however, needed both a calling from the church and proper qualifications. The candidate for ministry required not only an inner call, perhaps more importantly, there was the need of an external call from the visible church, which was confirmed through episcopal ordination.[39]

## The Three Orders of the Clergy

The English church, like English society in general, was hierarchical. The Reformation had left intact the three-fold order of ministry, consisting of bishops, priests, and deacons. Two positions developed with regard to the hierarchy. Some divines, including Richard Hooker and James Ussher, either were ambiguous about the relationship between priest and bishop, or they equated them. Hooker occasionally conflated the two orders, with bishops being little more than a higher grade of presbyter, while Ussher argued, in his attempts to seek reconciliation with the Presbyterians, that the two orders were synonymous. High Churchmen, on the other hand, following Henry Hammond and John Pearson, stressed the distinctness of the three orders. Ministry was not only an earthly system, it was also a reflection of the heavenly order. Charles Leslie wrote that the hierarchical government of the church had its feet on the earth and extended up to Christ, the head of the church, who reigns in heaven. This reflected Leslie's belief that the church militant and the church triumphant were one.[40]

High Churchmen believed that the distinction of orders was an ancient paradigm. They attempted to trace the three-fold order back through the Apostles to Jewish practice. Bishops, priests, and deacons were compared to the Jewish hierarchy of high priest, priests, and Levites. The distinction of orders among Christians had begun with Jesus himself, with Christ, the twelve, and the seventy as models of the three-fold order of ministry. Following the resurrection, apostles, elders, and deacons governed the church. The final form saw the distinction between bishops and presbyters, so that the three orders were bishop, presbyter, and deacon. High churchmen seemed unaware that the development of the church's polity was gradual and at times ambiguous. They tended to see the history of ministry as a straight line from the apostles to the present. All other forms of ministry that existed historically were either ignored or seen as divergences from the apostolic norm.[41]

This emphasis on the distinction of orders would appear to undermine Francis Atterbury's attempt to use the high-church-dominated Lower House of Convocation to challenge the authority of the Whig bishops. Atterbury's actions were a striking contrast to the hierarchical system his theology taught. Yet Atterbury found this necessary in order to counter the unwillingness of the bishops to confront heresy, and the relaxed nature of contemporary English society and religion. Although theology undergirded the High Church response to their times, at points they felt constrained to push the borders of their theology so as to accomplish their goals.[42]

## EPISCOPACY

High Churchmen and Non-Jurors, despite Atterbury's challenge to the authority of the bishops in the Convocation Controversy, saw the episcopate as the fountainhead of the church. From the bishops flowed all valid ministry. There was a Cyprianic, episcopal exclusivity in the high-church program, one that had been defended throughout the seventeenth century by leading divines, including Joseph Hall, Henry Hammond, William Laud, Lancelot Andrewes, and Jeremy Taylor. In the eighteenth century, more moderate and liberal churchmen challenged the Cyprianic view of ministry. John Findon notes that the chief proponents of the Cyprianic view in the established church, Nathaniel Marshall, William Higdon, and John Johnson of Cranbrook, were limited to minor posts after 1715, and George Smalridge languished in the unimportant see of Bristol. John Potter, a strong proponent of episcopal supremacy in his *Discourse on Church Government* (1707), appears to have changed his views by 1714, denying that only one legitimate form of church government existed. Though as late as 1725, Potter, as Bishop of the diocese of Oxford, defended the belief that episcopally ordained clergy were required to administer properly the sacraments. Others who had defended a Cyprianic view of the church, such as Thomas Brett, left the established church, believing that their principles could no longer be espoused within it.[43]

Apologetics for the historic episcopate were an important element of the primitive scholarship of high churchmen such as Joseph Bingham, Francis Brokesby, John Potter, and William Sclater. They attempted to trace the authoritative position of the bishops in the church to the earliest stages of the church. Theological defenses of the episcopate were penned by several divines, including Thomas Brett and George Hickes.[44] At issue was the apostolicity of the office. Christ had promised to be present with the people of God through his Apostles, and by extension, through the bishops who succeeded the Apostles. This concept, that Christ was present in the ministries of the bishops, formed the basis of the doctrine of apostolic succession, and therefore, of divine-right episcopacy.[45] The episcopate was not only permissible, it was necessary. Thomas Ken based his refusal to abdicate the see of Bath and Wells on his apostolic commission.

> Shall I lay aside primitive and right Episcopacy, which hath such grounds from Scripture, both as to the divine wisdom so ordering his church among the Jews, so also by the example, precept, and direction evident from our Lord Jesus Christ, and the Holy Apostles in the New Testament, who preferred worthy persons for their piety, zeal, and holy gravity, to exercise a Christian authority over ministers and people for their soul's good, which might conflict with charity and humility, for the preservation of the Churches' peace and purity in the best and primitive times; such grave persons as for their age, were fathers; for their innocency, saints; for their industry, labourers; for constancy, confessors; for zeal, martyrs; for charity, brethren; for their light, angels; and venerable for all excellencies?[46]

Few in England were as respected and beloved as Thomas Ken, and yet he stood up strongly for the dignity and the divine institution of the episcopate, at a time when such a defense was considered questionable.

Divine-right episcopacy, based upon Christ's commission to the Apostles, was for some an indisputable fact. The divine standing of the episcopate was related to the perception that the existence and well being of the church depended on the presence of bishops who served as the guarantors of efficacious sacraments, which were the means of grace and ultimately of salvation. The divinely instituted episcopate was not a temporary enterprise, it was a permanent and universal institution. Searches of Scripture and antiquity failed to provide high churchmen with a sufficient rationale for altering the government of the church.[47] Charles Leslie, affirming both the universality and the permanency of the episcopate, noted that non-episcopal government was both recent and insignificant.

> The whole Christian World, as it always has been, so at this present is episcopal, except a few dissenters, who in less than two hundred years last past have arisen like a wart upon the face of the Western Church: For little more proportion do our Dissenters here, the Hugonots in France, the Presbyterians in Holland and Geneva, and thereabouts, bear to the whole body of the Latin Church, which is all episcopal, they will not appear so big as a mole.[48]

High churchmen rested comfortably in the knowledge that the

Church of England had retained the divinely ordained episcopate. Foreign Protestants, though they lacked an episcopate, might take comfort in the grace and mercy of God, but English Dissenters, who had access to a reformed episcopate, were without excuse, and their ministries and sacraments were invalid. Roger Laurence stirred up controversy when he published a rationale for being rebaptized following his conversion from Nonconformity to the Church of England. Laurence asserted boldly that lay baptism, that is, baptism performed by a non-episcopally ordained priest, was invalid.[49] High churchmen, because of their stress on the necessity of episcopal government, wrestled with the question of the orders of the foreign Protestant churches. Although most high churchmen believed that God would confer salvation on the foreign Protestants, they did question the refusal of the continental Protestants to seek episcopal ordination from either the English bishops or the Scandinavian Lutheran bishops. Joseph Betty caustically asserted that the Geneva church had "rebelliously and impiously rejected" the episcopate. Although they were not willing to unchurch the foreign Protestants for not having bishops, high churchmen did call for the restoration of episcopal government in their churches. They believed that such a step would enable the Protestant churches on the continent to fulfill their mission, and it would further the unity of the one holy catholic and apostolic church.[50]

The Church of England, for its part, retained the divinely ordained and ancient episcopate. High churchmen insisted that this episcopate had remained unimpaired and unbroken throughout the history of Christianity. Anglicans believed that Christianity, and with it the episcopate, had originally been planted in Britain in the first century, perhaps even by Paul. Charles Leslie noted that Clement of Rome had reported that Paul had preached to the "farthest bounds of the west," which, he said, implied Britain. Other evidence came from fourth century authors such as Theodoret and Eusebius, who professed that the Apostles had converted Britain. Brett made use of the work of Edward Stillingfleet, *The Antiquities of the British Churches,* as evidence for the apostolic establishment of the Anglican episcopate. Stillingfleet was a Latitudinarian bishop, yet he was able to give support to an important element of the High Church ecclesiology. The historical evidence, however, is largely silent until the fourth century. J. R. H. Moorman has stated, however, that the first mention of Christians, in Britain was by Tertullian in the year 200. Still, the presence of three bishops at the Council of Arles does demonstrate that episcopal organization had been in place for some time prior to the fourth century. Consequently, high churchmen believed that Britain's episcopal pedigree was as ancient as any other national church.[51]

The bishops, as the preeminent officers of the church, provided oversight to the church as a whole. Although episcopal sees might differ in terms of the size of their jurisdiction, their wealth, and their outward trappings, each bishop had an equal share of episcopal authority. In spite of their equality, however, there were different degrees of responsibility. In theory, High Church and Non-Juror divines recognized four levels of bishops: patriarchs, metropolitans, diocesan bishops, and suffragan bishops.

In the theory accepted by both High Churchmen and Non-Jurors, the patriarchs had jurisdiction over several provinces, a form of government modeled on the structure of the Roman Empire. Historically, the five patriarchies of Rome, Alexandria, Antioch, Constantinople, and Jerusalem had been entrusted with mediating disputes between metropolitan sees. While they were correct in recognizing that a few sees gained primacy in the first six centuries, the jurisdiction of the patriarchal sees may have been less official than they would have us believe. W. H. C. Frend notes that Antioch's suzerainty, unlike that of Alexandria, was not closely related to ethnic or geographical unity. Jerusalem's patriarchal claims were based largely on the presence of the Holy Places within its domains. Though eighteenth-century Anglicans did not recognize any form of patriarchal authority over the Church of England, the Non-Jurors, in their dialogues with the Greek and Russian Orthodox Churches, advocated a plan of union that would have placed the churches under the patriarchal authority of Jerusalem, which the Non-Jurors considered the "mother see." Metropolitans, or archbishops, oversaw an ecclesiastical province. Frend states that the importance of a particular see did not always match its secular importance. Still, important cities, such as Carthage, took precedence over their less-important neighbors in episcopal councils. The responsibilities of the metropolitans included the ratification of episcopal elections, the consecration of bishops, and the calling of provincial synods. In England, Canterbury and York held the status of metropolitan sees. The Archbishop of Canterbury held the additional title of Primate of all England, a title that he retains to the present day. Despite the appearance of a distinction in authority, high churchmen denied that patriarchs, primates, or metropolitans were of a higher order than the diocesan bishops. They appear to have recognized that the distinction in episcopal offices was gradual, corresponding to the growth of the church. They have grasped the early distinction of offices in the early church, but they placed it earlier than modern scholarship would allow. As for the primacy of Canterbury, this was not settled until 1353, three centuries after the papacy of Gregory VII. Prior to that settlement there was considerable controversy concerning the relationship of the two provincial sees.[52]

Diocesan bishops, of whom there were twenty-six in eighteenth-century England, were charged with ordaining presbyters and deacons, administering the office of confirmation, and providing ecclesiastical discipline. Finally, there was the allowance for suffragan bishops. Although Henry VIII enacted legislation that provided for suffragans to assist the bishops, none were consecrated in the seventeenth or eighteenth centuries. There were calls for a more equitable division of the dioceses and the appointment of suffragans, so that more effective oversight might be maintained, but these calls went unheeded. Thomas Brett believed that a bishop could oversee, at most, three hundred parishes, since a bishop could visit approximately one hundred parishes in a single year. Brett's figures stand in stark contrast to the massive size of the diocese of Lincoln, which had more than twelve hundred parishes.[53]

The eighteenth-century English church, while recognizing the possible existence of four degrees of bishops, retained only the two metropolitans and the diocesan bishops, with the Archbishop of Canterbury serving as Primate of all England. Although they affirmed the historical primacy of the patriarchs, the heretical nature of the Roman Church prevented the English Protestants, even the high-church clergy, from submitting their church to Rome's patriarchal jurisdiction. The Non-Jurors circumvented Rome's supremacy and proposed the primacy of Jerusalem. Among the Non-Jurors, George Hickes, and following his death, Jeremy Collier, took the title of primus, which made them first among equals among the Non-Juror bishops.[54]

Although one might theorize about different degrees of episcopal jurisdiction, for High Churchmen and Non-Jurors the essence of the issue of church and ministry was the episcopate itself, the only repository of apostolic succession. From the bishops the lower orders of ministry, presbyters, and deacons derived their commission and authority. Ministerial authority descended from Christ through each order of ministry, each dependent upon the apostolic commission passed on through the bishops.

## THE PRIESTHOOD

The second order of ministry in the Anglican Church was the priesthood (presbyter). The priesthood received its sacerdotal authority from the bishops, who were the sole bearers of apostolic succession. Matthias Symson wrote that a valid ordination required that the one who ordained priests "have a power to ordain, transmitted to him or them, by a continued succession from Jesus Christ, the founder and legislator of this society or religion."[55] Although the priesthood derived its power and authority from the episcopate, the presbyters were the true core of the church. The bishops conferred to presbyters the jurisdiction over the heart of the church's corporate life, the preaching of the word of God, and the celebration of the sacraments. William Beveridge's insistence that the existence of the church depended on the priesthood serves as evidence of the importance attached to the ministry of the presbyters, since without them the word of God would not be preached nor would the sacraments be administered. Although Beveridge may have stretched the truth, since the bishops could have filled any of the priestly roles, his statement underlined the key role presbyters played in the life of the English church.[56]

The Anglican priesthood, according to its defenders, was rooted in the scriptural office of presbyter, a term often used interchangeably in the New Testament with the Greek word for bishop (*episkopos*). Joseph Bingham noted that the Septuagint used the term *presbuteroi* for rulers or governors; thus, it had been employed not only as an indication of age but also of an office prior to the Christian era. In the church's usage, the term *presbyter* referred to one ordained to "discharge the several duties of that office and station, wherein he is placed."[57] While recognizing the interchangeable use of *episkopos* and *presbuteros* in Scripture, High Churchmen and Non-Jurors attributed this usage to the structure of the apostolic church. They contended that the Apostles served as the first bishops while the presbyter/bishops were a lower order of the ministry. This order, like the modern presbyter, lacked the authority to ordain or exercise episcopal jurisdiction. The division between presbyters and bishops occurred when the Apostles, by themselves, could no longer provide oversight to the growing church. The Apostles then passed their mantle to the bishops, who placed the care of the parishes in the hands of presbyters. For Thomas Brett, it was a question of responsibility, not nomenclature. Although presbyterial and episcopal responsibility existed as separate entities in the New Testament, the titles attached to them evolved over time. Following the apostolic age, the apostolic office became the sole domain of the bishops. Yet as William Sclater, a Non-Juror, pointed out, there was not only a change of title, but also of order that occurred in the consecration of the bishops; thus, the bishop was not simply a higher order of the priesthood, but a distinct order. Sclater defined presbyters as the bishop's curates, who had been authorized to "execute some extraordinary parts of the episcopal power."[58]

In the face of objections that Protestantism taught a priesthood of believers and not the priesthood of the clergy, high churchmen attempted to prove that a Christian priesthood was a New Testament concept. They conceded that the New Testament authors did not use the term *hiereis* (priest) to designate either presbyters or bishops, but this did not mean that the idea was absent from the New Testament. The Christian priesthood, according to its proponents, was rooted in the continuity between Judaism and Christianity. Although Christ had come to abolish the law of Moses and the Jewish priesthood, he instituted a new covenant, and with it a new priesthood (Hebrews 10:9). Further, the testimony of the earliest Christian Fathers, Clement of Rome and Ignatius, confirmed the existence of the priesthood in the New Testament church.[59]

The priest was God's vicar, or representative. His office was sacerdotal in nature, and it involved advocacy and mediation. Like the Jewish priest, the Christian priest also stood between God and humanity, interceding with God on behalf of his parishioners. Still, there was a qualitative difference between the two priesthoods; the Christian priesthood was rooted in the actions of Jesus Christ, the supreme high priest, who offered himself on the cross as a perfect and eternal sacrifice. Whereas the Jewish priesthood descended from Aaron, the Christian priesthood issued from Christ and his Apostles in an unbroken succession of episcopal consecrations. Thus, the foundations of the Christian priesthood were two-fold: continuity with the Jewish priesthood, and continuance of Christ's work of mediation and intercession (Hebrews 2:17; 5:1, 5–12).[60]

As a mediator, the Christian priest did not plead his own merits before God, but, as Joseph Bingham explained, a priest was "appointed to convey the people's devotions to God, and the will and blessings of God to the people."[61] As the mediator between God and humanity, the priest served as the steward of God's mysteries, making him a sacrificing priest, for he had the privilege of administering the sacraments, which were the means of grace. The link between the sacraments and salvation increased the importance and dignity of the priesthood, since only a divinely commissioned minister (a bishop was a priest as well) could minister baptism and eucharist.[62]

The priest/presbyter was commissioned to preach and to teach. This not only entailed the right to read scripture or give an oration, but it enabled the priest to provide "authoritative instruction."

While a lay person could teach from a natural capacity, the priest, as Christ's ambassador, uttered words that had the power to confer the benefits of the Gospel to all who listened. As stewards of God's word, the priests were entrusted with making sure that the doctrines and teachings of God were not distorted or corrupted.[63] Preaching was a great responsibility, requiring a knowledge of Scripture, ancient languages, judgment, and elocution. To accomplish this task, new preachers, and those without preaching skills were encouraged to read the homilies published by the Church of England to their congregations.[64] Presbyters were also pastors entrusted with the guidance of the laity, protecting them from danger and warning them away from evil and sin. They were called to visit the flock in times of sickness and affliction, providing pastoral discipline and giving absolution to the penitent.[65]

The priest's responsibilities for administering the sacraments, preaching, and pastoral oversight were shared with bishops who had the additional responsibilities of ordination and confirmation. Therefore, although every bishop was a priest, not every priest was a bishop.[66]

### THE DIACONATE

The deacon filled the third order of Anglican ministry, and like the presbyters, his authority was received with his ordination by the bishop. Even as the priests were to stay within the bounds of their order, deacons were warned not to exceed their commission by encroaching on the responsibilities of the priesthood. The origin of the office, according to Anglican views, lay in the seven ministers of the table of the Jerusalem church (Acts 6), in what Robert Nelson called the "murmuring of the Grecians . . . against the Hebrews." Seven men were selected from among the Hellenistic-Jewish Christians and ordained by the Apostles to care for the needs of the widows, the poor, and to serve the tables.[67] Yet, high churchmen pointed out, these spirit-filled men were qualified for more than serving tables. The seven had extraordinary gifts and they were competent students of scripture, as demonstrated in Stephen's apologetic for the Christian faith. The office may have included serving of tables, a role originally undertaken by the Apostles themselves, but it was much broader in scope.[68]

Deacons assisted the presbyters in looking after the poor and in leading worship. They also served as messengers for the bishops. While their duties were often "servile," they were also sacerdotal. The servile responsibilities included: service as a crier; giving directions in the service; preparing the altar; reading the Gospel; receiving the offerings and carrying them to the celebrant at the altar; carrying the cup, and sometimes the bread, to the faithful; and dismissing the people. Besides these "servile" ministries, the sacerdotal ministry of the deacon, undertaken in the absence of the priest or bishop, included the administration of baptism, preaching, and the offering of prayers. Philip the Evangelist exemplified the sacerdotal nature of the diaconate in preaching to the Samaritans and baptizing those who believed (Acts 8). Though they could administer the consecrated eucharist, they could not consecrate the sacrament itself. In this, Deacons were dependent on the priests.[69]

An office similar to, but different from that of the deacons, was that of the deaconess. Joseph Bingham pointed out the order's importance in the ancient church, noting New Testament references to the office (Romans 16:1). The duties of this ancient office included: the baptism of women, which at the time involved the immersion of adults and needed to be done with decency; private catechisms for women; ministries to sick or distressed women; ministry to the martyrs and confessors in prison, since women could gain access to prisoners more easily during persecutions; and finally, presiding over the widows. In spite of its importance to the early church, the order of deaconness had been discontinued. Therefore, the Christian ministry remained a male domain. No one, not even Bingham, advocated the restoration of the order of deaconess.[70]

Even as the priest served as the assistant to the bishop, the deacon assisted the priest in carrying out the sacred tasks of ministry. Each order was dependent on the order above it for its power and authority. Yet high churchmen attached great dignity to all three orders. Deacons, no less than priests or bishops, remained distinct from the laity, for like the two higher orders, they received ordination through the laying on of hands. Yet Thomas Brett lamented the fact that the contemporary Anglican church saw the deacon as little more than a probationary office, rather than as the distributors of church revenues and as the servants of the poor.[71]

## Conclusion

The three-tiered structure of Anglican ministry was the foundation of the church's existence, the salvation of God's people, and the orderly gathering of the church. The bishops were the bearers of apostolic succession, the source of all ecclesiastical authority. While the episcopate was the fountain of Christian ministry, each ministerial order had responsibilities peculiar to itself. Anglicans from every party affirmed the value of a three-fold order of ministry, at least on social or cultural grounds, but it was the High Church and Non-Juror divines who provided the theological and historical defense of these distinctions in ministerial office. From their examination of the biblical, theological, and historical record, they concluded that each office was indispensable to the church's well-being. Therefore their greatest argument was with the Dissenters, who argued for a different form of polity on theological, not cultural grounds. Though they may have emphasized episcopal authority and have recognized that bishops, by virtue of their commission to disciple the nations, could have fulfilled the sacerdotal responsibilities of the other two orders, they clearly understood that the effectiveness of this ministry would have been diminished without the assistance of the priests and deacons.

The responsibility for administering the sacraments linked the ministry to the question of the church and salvation. Salvation was found only in the visible church, where visible sacraments were administered by a visible priesthood. High Churchmen and Non-Jurors were ardent guardians of clerical prerogative, even if that meant, as was the case with the Non-Jurors, separating themselves from the national church. The perceived threat to the episcopate that came from the ejections of the Non-Juror bishops served to undergird the high-church belief in the independent integrity of the church. Even those High Churchmen who remained within the established church after 1691 insisted that they were ordained and commissioned to Christian ministry by God, not the state.

# 6

# Sacramental Theology

The sacramental theology of the High Church and Non-Juror divines was intrinsically related to their perceptions of the nature of the church and the ministry. Baptism and eucharist served as the bridges between church, ministry, and salvation. The sacraments were understood to be the means of grace offered by the church through the offices of an episcopally ordained clergy. These two sacred ordinances reminded recipients of the visible nature of the church, for communion with God was entered into through the tangible components of the sacraments. Yet, eighteenth-century English sacramental piety has been largely discounted or ignored, in spite of the close relationship among church, sacraments, ministry, and salvation in High Church and Non-Juror theology. Interpreters such as Gerald Cragg have followed nineteenth-century Victorian historians, including John Overton, Frederick Relton, and Charles Abbey, in depicting the eighteenth century as a period of religious laxity and distrust of mystery.[1]

This picture of indifference, corruption, and incompetence was first seriously challenged by the stunning accomplishment of Norman Sykes, and more recent scholarship has further challenged this perspective. Thus, as F. C. Mather asserts, the alleged laxity of English religious life was more apparent than real. He states that this supposition results from the lack of attention shown by historians to the catholic and sacramental piety that marked the high-church tradition. He attributes the "default in sacramental practice" to practical difficulties, not to a "distrust of mystery." Though Mather criticizes Norman Sykes for focusing on the latitudinarian elements of the church, Sykes deserves credit for initiating the process of reevaluating eighteenth-century English religious life. Sykes demonstrated that, despite the obstacles, a large percentage of adult parishioners did take part in the eucharist on Easter.[2] Still, eighteenth-century churchmen were concerned about the state of the church and the piety of its members, yet neglect of

116

the sacraments had predated the Reformation and was not unique to the eighteenth century. But the issues that attracted the attention of high-church apologists and theologians often focused on sacramental questions. Their opposition to occasional conformity, support for the Test Act, the schism within the Non-Juror movement, and the lay baptism controversy provide evidence of the importance that high churchmen affixed to the sacraments.[3]

The sacraments were not only catalysts for debate, they were a part of the Anglican identity. High-church understandings of the ministry, sacraments, and liturgy undergirded their belief that the Church of England was the only visible representation of the one holy catholic and apostolic church in England. The only qualification the Non-Jurors made was that they, and not the established church, were the remnant of the Church of England. In examining the High Church and Non-Juror conception of the sacraments, attention will be given to the somewhat scholastic questions of cause, necessity, and effect. Though baptism and confirmation find a key place in this discussion, special attention will be given throughout to the eucharist, and especially to divisive issues such as the doctrines of eucharistic presence and eucharistic sacrifice.[4]

## High Church Sacramental Theology

Article XXV of the Thirty-nine Articles defines the sacraments as outward signs of an invisible work of grace. This Augustinian definition of the sacraments required both an "invisible spiritual grace" and an "outward visible sign." Therefore, the conveyance of God's grace, which depended on a visible sign, further supported the high-church emphasis on the visible church. The sacraments were not, according to William Beveridge, "bare signs, but sure seals of righteousness by faith, whereby God doth not only signify his grace to us, but confirms our faith in it; and our faith being confirmed in the sacraments do thereby prove so advantageous to our souls."[5] The ambiguity of the definition of the sacramental elements as "outward signs of an invisible grace," may be, as D. E. W. Harrison and Michael Sansom point out, the cause of the confusion that exists with regard to the number of sacraments. Resolving the confusion, they believe, requires a firm definition of the meaning of grace and its signs. High Churchmen and Non-Jurors did in fact seek to provide a specific formula that would undergird their understanding of the nature of God's grace and the signs of that grace. The exception to the general high-church position on the sacraments came from Non-Juror liturgist Thomas Deacon, who defined sacraments more broadly as sacred acts and oaths and as divine mysteries. On the basis of his broadly defined theology of the sacraments, Deacon was able to include all spiritually significant ceremonies, including confirmation, under the sacramental rubric. Deacon appears to validate the comments of Harrison and Sansom concerning the confusion concerning the number of sacraments that develops from an ambiguous definition of the sacraments. Deacon divided the sacraments into two categories, the first relating to baptism and eucharist, which Christ had instituted as the means of grace. The second category consisted of ten lesser sacraments, including: "Five belonging to Baptism, namely Exorcism, Anointing with oil, the white garment, a taste of milk and honey, and Anointing with Chrism or ointment." The second five were "the sign of the cross, imposition of hands, unction of the sick, Holy Orders, and Matrimony." By 1747, when *A Full, True, and Comprehensive View of Christianity,* Deacon's largest work, was published, he had moved well beyond even the vast majority of Non-Jurors in his thinking.[6]

Like most Protestants, High Church and the majority of Non-Juror divines limited the definition of a sacrament only to baptism and the Lord's supper. Only two ordinances fulfilled the requirements of a true sacrament. The sacramental tests included institution by Jesus Christ, external symbols to represent inward graces, and the presence of divine promises annexed to the rites. Anglicans found a qualitative difference between the seven Roman Catholic sacraments and the two received by Protestants. Although the five additional Roman sacraments could be seen as sacred signs, they did not have the same intrinsic value as baptism and the eucharist. Therefore while High Churchmen and Non-Jurors affirmed that confirmation was an ancient custom and the proper means of conferring the Holy Spirit to a believer, they recognized that it lacked explicit institution by Christ. Instead of being a sacrament, they maintained that confirmation served to perfect the sacrament of baptism. True sacraments, therefore, were seals of the covenant between God and his people, through which pardon of sin could be conveyed. Thomas Wilson noted that the most compelling evidence for the transmittal of divine grace through the sacraments could be found in the visible effect in the recipient's life. This ethical or moral consequence of sacramental piety allowed the church to distinguish between the children of God and the children of the devil.[7]

High Churchmen and Non-Jurors carefully differentiated between the source of grace and the sign itself. The elements of bread, wine, and water depended solely on the power of God for their efficacy. The guarantee of sacramental effectiveness rested in God's promise to fulfill the terms of the covenant symbolized by the elements. This relationship between sign and grace has similarities to the position espoused by Bonaventure, the thirteenth-century Franciscan theologian. Bonaventure based the value of the sign on God's covenant with his people, wherein God promised to work in the soul of the person who made use of the sacrament.[8]

The sacraments were not *adiaphora,* but necessary elements of church life carrying essential spiritual benefits. The sacraments served as marks of the true church, as they did for the Reformers. Thomas Brett explained that the unity of the catholic church rested on the reception by all church members, no matter where they were in time and space, of the "same signs and badges of the people of God." Every member of the catholic church was initiated into the church through baptism, and each testified to his or her communion with Christ and with one another by "receiving of his Body and blood under the elements of bread and wine."[9] The physical act of receiving the sacraments separated those inside the church from those on the outside. There was no place for a spiritualist understanding of the sacraments, such as the one espoused by Quakers, for without a visible means of admitting members, the church would cease to exist as a society. The sacraments, according to high-church theology, clearly placed an indelible mark on the person of the believer and served as a key foundation to church life.[10]

## The Causes of the Sacraments

Though high-church tradition stressed the importance of the clergy's role in sacramental theology, it also affirmed, with the historic church, that God alone ensured the efficacy of the sacraments. While they emphasized the means of administering the sacraments, they also recognized the need for personal faith in the reception of the benefits of the sacraments. To understand the efficacy of the sacraments for salvation and spiritual growth one must examine the roles that God, the clergy, and personal faith played in high-church sacramental theology.

## THE ROLE OF GOD

The eucharistic bread and wine, by themselves, only sustained the physical body, and the baptismal waters only washed off external dirt, not the internal dirt of sin. Yet the power of God made bread, wine, and water effective means of conveying the grace of God. Unlike the English Reformers and contemporary broad churchmen who emphasized the reception of the "word" that accompanied the signs,[11] High Churchmen and Non-jurors stressed that God attached the promise of salvation to the sacramental action itself. The facility of the sacraments to bring remission of sins and eternal life rested on God's choice in ordaining them for this purpose. God, in turn, grounded the sacraments in Christ's sacrificial death on the cross. Therefore, anyone who received the sacramental elements also received pardon for sin, and unity with Christ.[12]

The salvific activity of God in the eucharist was coupled with God's presence in the eucharist. Though the doctrine of real presence was controversial even among High Churchmen and Non-Jurors, a significant portion of the high-church community endorsed the doctrine. The doctrine of eucharistic presence centered on the participation of the Holy Spirit in the eucharistic event. The Spirit's presence was seen in two different ways. The more moderate position stated that God poured out the Spirit on the believers as they received the sacramental elements. The second view, exemplified by Thomas Brett, held that the Spirit directly infused the elements themselves. Consequently, even though the substance of the elements did not change, the bread and wine became the body and blood of Christ. Despite the stress placed on Christ's presence in the sacraments, High Churchmen denied teaching the doctrine of transubstantiation.[13] They attempted to prove that transubstantiation was a deviation from the primitive doctrine of real presence. Ironically, John Johnson, the leading high-church sacramental scholar, turned the charges of transubstantiation against the Calvinists and Lutherans. He insisted that Lutherans and Calvinists believed that Christ's natural body was present in the sacramental elements, but he taught Christ's spiritual presence in the elements. He wrote, "it is certain the primitive doctrine, which I defend, is not only inconsistent with Transubstantiation, but with that Real Presence of the Body of Christ in the Eucharist, which is common opinion of Protestants abroad." Johnson appears to have misunderstood Calvin's position, as his view is very close to the Reformer's.[14]

With real presence defined in spiritual, not corporeal terms, high churchmen affirmed Christ's presence in virtue and in power but not in his natural body. Like Calvin, however, High Churchmen and Non-Jurors maintained that the elements remained bread and wine following consecration. Though the substance of the consecrated elements remained the same, by eating the bread and wine in faith, one spiritually received the body and blood of Christ. Yet they claimed that they were not receptionists, for they presupposed that Christ was objectively present with the sacrament prior to and independent of one's reception of the sacraments. Although this appears to be contradictory, high churchmen were trying to keep the proper tension between their espousal of eucharistic presence with their rejection of transubstantiation and consubstantiation. The mystery of the Spirit's activity enabled the communicant to receive spiritually Christ's body and blood while eating and drinking consecrated bread and wine. Without a change of substance, the Spirit was able to convey the fruit of Christ's sacrifice on the cross to the recipient. Though they remained close to Calvin's position, high churchmen moved beyond him by separating the Spirit's mediation of Christ's presence from the recipient's faith by placing it in the words of institution and the prayer of invocation. Faith simply made one worthy to receive the elements.[15]

John Chrysostom, the fourth-century bishop of Constantinople, defined the mystery of Christ's presence in the eucharist in terms of believing that what appears to be one thing is in reality something else. This somewhat ambiguous definition formed the basis of John Johnson's doctrine of eucharistic presence.

> And the case is very clear, that since the Sacramental Body and Blood are what they are by virtue of the presence of the Spirit; and that the secret operations of the Spirit are not to be perceived by our senses; and that therefore the Body and Blood of the Eucharist are such only in an invisible mysterious manner: therefore they are to be considered and received by us, not only outwardly as consecrated Bread and Wine, but inwardly with the eye and reach of our understanding and judgement; not as bare types and figures but as being in effect, though not in substance, what they represent.[16]

Although Christ was objectively present in the elements by the power of the Holy Spirit, this reality could be perceived only through the eye of faith.[17]

Even though High Churchmen and Non-Jurors rejected transubstantiation and spoke of Christ's body and blood being present representatively, spiritually, or sacramentally, they affirmed the real and permanent presence of Christ in the sacrament. Belief in Christ's permanent presence in the eucharist not only led them to handle the elements with reverence, but it also induced them to reserve a portion of the sacramental meal for later use. The purported ancient practices of reservation of the host and the priest's consumption of the leftover bread and wine provided further evidence of a permanent consecration.[18] Johnson concluded, based on this testimony, that the faith of the recipient was not responsible for transforming bread and wine into the body and blood of Christ.

> Now certainly the primitive Fathers never thought of sending mere bread and wine to their brethren or to the faithful who could not attend the public congregation; and consequently, they thought the benediction which they had received on the Lord's Table was not transient, so as to cease as soon as the celebration was concluded; and therefore they did not imagine that their being the Body and Blood of Christ depended on the faith of those who did eat or drink it.[19]

Although Brett and Johnson believed that the eucharist was more than mere bread and wine, the specter of transubstantiation caused them to skirt the issue of how the elements were changed into the body and blood of Christ.

There were many similarities between High Church and Calvinist doctrines of real presence, though they were never acknowledged. Yet, there were also parallels to Roman Catholic doctrine, especially the idea that Christ was present in the eucharist, independent of the faith of the recipient. W. Jardine Grisbrooke notes that even John Johnson did not find his theory completely satisfactory. Johnson rejected the idea of substantival change, but did not seem content with embracing virtualism. Grisbrooke points out that a number of the passages from the Fathers that Johnson examined seemed to "countenance substantialism, and to advocate 'excessive' reverence to the sacrament." Grisbrooke states that "the most determined opponent of transubstantiation could hardly say that Johnson is very successful in his attempt to explain them away."[20] In fact, high-church proponents of eucharistic presence appeared to tread a very thin line between traditional Anglican and Roman Catholic beliefs.

The sacraments, infused with the power of the Holy Spirit, were more than simple memorials. Although God could have chosen other means of imparting grace, he elected to work primarily through the sacraments to confer remission of sins and salvation. For High Churchmen and Non-Jurors, the presence of the Holy Spirit in and with the sacramental elements guaranteed eternal life, confirmed Christian faith, and increased the grace of God in the recipients.[21]

## THE ROLE OF THE CLERGY

The episcopally ordained priesthood was central to high-church sacramental thought. In contrast to the positions of the sixteenth-century Reformers, High Churchmen and Non-Jurors emphasized the sacerdotal nature of the priesthood. The priesthood mediated the grace and favor of God through the sacraments; thus, sacramental action took precedence over the proclamation of the word. Although they recognized the relationship between the proclamation of the word and the sacraments, they saw the word as preparatory to the sacraments, and not the cause of their validity. Apostolic succession undergirded their sacramental theology, for Christ authorized only the Apostles to administer the sacraments. The Apostles, in turn, empowered their successors, the bishops, and then the bishops, through ordination, authorized the priests/presbyters to administer the sacraments.[22]

The commission to baptize, like the institution of apostolic ministry, was found in Matthew 28:19, "Go ye therefore and disciple the nations." Thomas Brett declared that the "ye" in the commission pertained only to those who would be allowed to baptize. Christ commissioned the eleven Apostles who had gathered with him prior to the ascension, to be his vicegerents, and not the larger group of disciples who had followed him. Brett insisted that if Christ had intended to empower the entire church to fulfill the office, he would not have limited his commission to the eleven. The Apostles, in turn, were authorized to ordain elders (priests or presbyters) to carry out this commission on their behalf until the end of the age.[23] Though inferior ministers, such as Philip the Deacon and Ananaias the prophet, did baptize during the apostolic age, high-church divines affirmed that only the bishops, and those commissioned by them, had the right to baptize and exercise the cure of souls. Consequently, they intimated that the Apostles had previously authorized Philip and Ananaias to baptize.[24]

The Anglican articles of faith also limited the sacramental ministry to specific individuals. Roger Laurence asserted that Article Twenty-three made it illegal for the laity and the Dissenters to administer the sacraments. Laurence claimed that the articles of faith, as doctrinal statements, could not be changed at one's pleasure. Nonconformist clergy, since they lacked episcopal ordination, were seen as lay people. As lay people, they could not validly consecrate the eucharist or baptize an infant or new believer.[25]

Perhaps because he was aware of the danger of being charged with Donatism, Laurence distinguished between the authorization and the sanctity of the administrator, the latter having nothing to do with the efficacy of baptism. Although God alone conferred the gift of the Holy Spirit, Laurence questioned whether it was reasonable to expect God to "concur with the usurpations of those who act herein without his commission, nay in opposition thereto, [as is the case with us]."[26] Laurence and Brett agreed that Christ was obligated to ratify sacraments administered only by those he had commissioned; therefore, anyone baptized by a heretic or schismatic was to be rebaptized. Laurence rooted his call for the rebaptism of Dissenters in Cyprian's requirement that the schismatic Novationists were to be rebaptized. Laurence declared that because the Novationist priests and bishops were excommunicated as heretics and schismatics, their sacramental actions were invalid. Joseph Bingham, a High Churchman himself, responded to Laurence, stating that since the church supplied what was lacking in a schismatic baptism, rebaptism was unnecessary. George Every notes that while Bingham's position was more consistent with the patristic evidence, Laurence's work received a better response from the clergy.[27]

The more doctrinaire High Churchmen attempted to skirt the question of the validity of foreign, non-episcopal ordinations and sacraments. Though they denied unchurching foreign Protestants who lacked episcopal ordination, they insisted that the Dissenters were different. The latter had usurped the right to baptize when England had an episcopate that was both Protestant and apostolic. For High Churchmen, the Church of England was the only church in England that offered valid sacraments. Though they did question whether the foreign Protestants acted in opposition to episcopacy, they denied that it was their duty to judge the situation of other national churches. They did not question the sacraments of the continental Protestant churches, but they encouraged foreign Protestants to restore the episcopate to their churches. George Every and G. V. Bennett are correct, however, in stating that the rejection of lay baptism did question the validity of the sacraments celebrated by foreign Protestant clergy. This included the Lutheran Hanoverians, who ruled England after 1714. Bennett states that

Laurence's *Lay Baptism, Invalid,* had Jacobite tendencies; thus in one swing Laurence "delivered an attack on the dissenters and on the baptism of the Lutheran House of Hanover."[28] This put the Stuart pretender, James III, who had been baptized in the Catholic Church, in a better position religiously to be king—better than the Hanoverians, who as German Lutherans did not possess episcopally authorized baptisms. It also meant that the Non-Juror ordinations given by Hickes and his successors and those of the Roman Catholics were valid, but the Lutheran ministers of Hanover would have to be reordained if they sought to join the Church of England. Thomas Brett's decision to not take the oaths to George I most assuredly was determined, at least in part, by the religious situation of the Hanoverians. In 1714 Brett published *A Review of the Lutheran Principles: showing how they differ from the Church of England's.* Roger Laurence interpreted Brett's tract as a challenge to the validity of the Lutheran orders:

> You have proved that the pretended orders of the foreign reformed bodies are not originally derived from Presbyters but mere Laics who pretended to Divine Inspiration and so were no other than enthusiastic cheats.[29]

Though debate raged as to the validity of the foreign Protestant ordinations, high churchmen affirmed that the efficacy of the sacraments depended on proper administration, which required a properly ordained ministry. High Churchmen, such as Charles Wheatly, believed it was better for a child to remain unbaptized than to be baptized by a lay person.

> Our Church therefore, by prohibiting all from intermeddling in baptism but a *lawful* minister, plainly hints, that when baptism is administered by any others it conveys no benefit or advantage to the child, but only brings upon those who pretend to administer it the guilt of usurping a sacred office: and consequently that persons so pretendedly baptized (if they live to be sensible of their state and condition) are to apply to their lawful minister or bishop for that Holy Sacrament, of which they only received a profanation before.[30]

Unauthorized baptism was considered a sin, and it would be presumptuous of the Dissenters to think that God would validate unlawful sacraments. Though he may have stated his position more provocatively then most high churchmen would have liked, they probably would have agreed with Thomas Brett when he called the

Dissenter's celebration of the Lord's Supper a "profane mockery of the Divine ordinance."[31]

## THE ROLE OF THE RECIPIENT

High-church sacramental theology affirmed that God was the effective cause and the episcopally ordained minister the necessary mediator of the sacraments; still, it provided a place for the recipient's faith. Baptized infants required sponsors to speak on their behalf, promising that the child would be raised in the Christian faith. Church members communed with Christ in the Lord's supper, and they recognized the bread and wine to be the sacramental body and blood of Christ through faith. Faithful participation in the sacraments made the recipient a partaker of Christ and the benefits of his death.[32] While all high churchmen affirmed the necessity of faith, they differed in how they understood its place in sacramental theology. High church options ran from Daniel Waterland, who affirmed that the recipient's faith determined the sacrament's efficacy, to John Johnson, who gave a limited place to personal faith.

Waterland stressed that the sacraments allowed for the concurrence of the Holy Spirit and the human will as a moral agent. Without faith, reverence, and repentance, the external actions of the sacraments were worthless to the recipient. Reception of the sacraments also could be considered a moral virtue if performed in obedience to Christ. It expressed love for God, faith, hope, and humility. But as the appointed means of receiving salvation, the sacraments depended on faith to bring the act to completion.[33]

Johnson emphasized the power of the Holy Spirit, imparted through the prayer of invocation, to make the bread and wine the body and blood of Jesus. The transformation of the elements occurred prior to their distribution; thus, personal faith did not impact this transformation. Nonetheless, faith was required to distinguish the spiritual or sacramental body and blood of Christ from the natural body and blood of Christ.

> And the case is very clear, that since the Sacramental body and blood are what they are by virtue of the presence of the Spirit; and that the secret operations of the Spirit are not to be perceived by our senses; and that therefore the body and blood of the Eucharist are such only in an invisible mysterious manner: therefore they are to be considered and received by us, not only outwardly as consecrated bread and wine, but inwardly with the eye and relish of our understanding and judge-

ment; not as bare types and figures, but as being in effect, though not in substance, what they represent.[34]

Faith was necessary to apprehend the mystery and the value of the sacraments. The phrase "take, eat, this is my body" meant that they ate not only with their mouths, but also with their minds, for it was in their minds that they perceived that the bread was the "perfect representation of his natural body."[35]

The relationship of faith to the question of real presence was addressed by Johnson and Thomas Brett. Following the dictums of John 6:53–54, Johnson noted that Christ instructed his disciples to receive the sacramental body and blood both as an act of faith and through eating and drinking the elements. Johnson rejected both the Calvinist idea of receiving the spiritual body through the mind, and the Roman Catholic and Lutheran belief in eating the substantial body of Christ. But, like Luther, Johnson saw the text referring to more than receiving the word of Christ by faith. He asserted that the text commanded the necessity of the oral manducation of the sacramental elements; thus eating orally *(manducatio oralis)* and eating spiritually, or from the heart *(manducatio cordalis),* were brought together. While recipients of the eucharist ate bread with their mouths, they apprehended the perfect representation of Christ's natural body in the bread with their minds. Though their outward senses perceived only bread, by faith they received the bread as the body of Christ and ate it rationally. Despite the parallels with Luther, Brett and Johnson rejected any hint of eating and drinking the substantial body and blood of Christ.[36]

Following John 6, high churchmen such as Johnson, Thomas Wilson, and even Daniel Waterland, believed that one could only encounter Christ's body and blood in and through the eucharist. These words that Jesus spoke prior to the institution of the eucharist clarified the meaning of the Last Supper. Wilson wrote:

> Then they understood, that when before He had spoken of eating his flesh and drinking his blood, as necessary to eternal life, He did not mean it in such a manner as they then understood it, but in a spiritual manner, as he now explain'd it; namely, that Christ is our life—the food of our souls—in the sacrament. As common bread is the food of our bodies, so this is the support of our spiritual life.[37]

Participation in the sacramental meal brought the recipient the blessings of Christ's sacrifice. According to John 6, when one worthily received bread and wine, one ate and drank the body and blood of Christ.[38]

High Churchmen and Non-Jurors advocated frequent communion, though weekly communion was rarely attained in the eighteenth century. Waterland believed that one could not commemorate Christ's passion too often, yet the emphasis was to be upon worthy communicating.

> Here lies the main stress of all, not to urge frequency of communion so far as to render this Holy Sacrament hurtful or fruitless to the parties concerned; neither yet to abate so far as frequency as to make a kind of dearth or famine of this so salutary and necessary food.[39]

The importance attached to the worthy reception of the eucharist, however, was tempered by the realization that the universality of sin made every communicant theoretically unworthy to receive the eucharist. This meant that the accent needed to be placed on the manner of reception, not on the sanctified state of the communicant. Even as Paul instructed the fractious Corinthians to discern the difference between a meal and the body and blood of Christ (I Corinthians 11:27), the worthy recipient was to recognize the sacred significance of the sacrament, and, therefore, partake of the sacrament with reverence. Unworthy reception, according to William Beveridge, referred to people coming to the Lord's table to "receive the outward signs of bread and wine, without discerning by faith the Lord's body signified by them, and therefore without shewing any more regard and reverence to what they eat and drink there, than they do to any other meat and drink."[40]

Although High Churchmen and Non-Jurors emphasized the meaning of the sacrament, they did outline the prerequisites for worthy reception of the eucharist. The profile of a worthy communicant included: valid baptism, repentance of sin and a resolve to refrain from future sin, a sound Christian faith, competent knowledge of the sacrament's meaning, and a reverent approach to the sacrament. The major impediment to worthy reception was willful, or "gross," sin. John Johnson believed that the problem of unworthy recipients would be overcome if the church returned to its primitive constitution, and restore a proper discipline, so that those who were penitents could be prodded to repent and return to the altar. He complained that his contemporaries were either willing to die in their sins, or they were afraid that taking part in the eucharist unworthily would lead to damnation. England's pluralistic religious community proved to be an additional hindrance to frequent communion, since effective discipline was rendered impossible by the lack of a unified national church. Johnson's proposal that the primitive discipline should be restored was simply not realistic, given the state of English society.[41]

With the church as a whole, High Churchmen and Non-Jurors acknowledged that God was the source and power behind the sacraments, yet the emphasis fell upon the proper administration of the sacraments, and that required properly ordained clergy. The disagreement between the high churchmen and the Dissenters centered over the latter's lack of an episcopally ordained clergy. Both High Church and Non-Juror divines claimed that the Dissenting clergy operated in opposition to the lawful English episcopate. While high churchmen tended not to stress the role of personal faith, frequent and worthy reception of the sacrament was clearly their ideal.

## The Necessity of the Sacraments

Though baptism and the eucharist were considered the divinely ordained means of conveying salvation to the people of God, high-church divines held back from asserting their absolute necessity *(necessitas absoluta)*. Instead they stressed their hypothetical or consequent necessity *(necessitas ex suppositione or necessitas consequentiae)*. Christ's institution of the sacraments formed the basis of their necessity. There was no intrinsic obligation to be baptized or to receive the eucharist, except that the two ordinances had been divinely ordained to bring salvation to those who chose to make use of them. Although God could have adopted some other means of granting salvation, God chose these two symbolic rites to accomplish his purpose. In the sacraments, the communicant pledged to serve God faithfully, while God promised to provide the grace necessary for salvation. Christ's institution of the sacraments obligated him to fulfill the promises attached to those signs. Though high-church divines would not admit to the absolute necessity of sacramental reception, Christ's institution of the sacraments meant that intentional neglect of sacramental observance hindered one's salvation. By not making use of the ordained elements, they failed to keep their part of the covenant.[42]

The contingent nature of the sacraments allowed room for those who could not obtain valid sacraments because of ignorance or impossible circumstances. With regard to baptism, Roger Laurence stated that God could "dispense with his own institutes and give the spiritual graces annex'd to them, to whom he pleases." Still, the English Dissenters were in a dangerous situation, for they lived upon an episcopal government, but refused to submit to it. While God was "infinitely good" and would not punish people for circumstances beyond their control, those who were "slothful and negligent, the obstinate and perverse, we have no authority from Divine revelation to hope anything for their advantage."[43] The Quaker practice of inward baptism, with its rejection of visible symbols, was considered the most blatant and obstinate spurning of properly consecrated sacraments. Charles Leslie responded to them, declaring that by despising Christ's ordinance of water baptism, the Quakers had made themselves appear to be wiser than Christ, "as if he had appointed means either unnecessary or ineffectual to the ends for which they were intended!"[44]

The sacraments were necessary for salvation, yet no one presumed to question God's right to choose a different method. They appear to have reflected the late medieval Nominalists in the distinction between absolute powers *(de potentia absoluta)* and ordained powers *(de potentia ordinata)*, although they did not acknowledge their dependence. The Nominalists had rejected the Thomist view of the sacrament, which attributed an intrinsic and instrumental causality to the sacraments, enabling the elements to effect grace in the recipient. The Nominalist position stated that the efficacy of the sacraments was based on God's covenant promises, though God could do as he pleased with the sacraments *(de potentia absoluta)*.[45] Christ's institution of the sacraments made them obligatory. To refrain from participating in the sacramental worship of the Church of England, or the Non-Juror community, was a rejection of God's ordinances. With the opportunity the "true church" provided for properly administered sacraments, there was no reason for their neglect.

## The Effects of the Sacraments

Baptism and eucharist were marks of God's covenant with his people, and as a result, they were the means of entering and maintaining the relationship with God and his church. Reception of the sacraments, therefore, served to enable believers to live a full Christian life. Though high churchmen did not consider confirmation to be a sacrament, the exception to this view being Thomas Deacon, the relationship between baptism and confirmation warrants its consideration in this discussion. Confirmation was seen as a necessary completion of baptism and prerequisite to receiving the Lord's supper. The effects of each sacrament will be considered separately in the following discussion.

## THE EFFECTS OF BAPTISM

Baptism affected the lives of its recipients in two ways; first it initiated one into the covenant with God, and second it provided remission of sins. High-church understandings of baptism differed little from the historic Christian traditions. Yet, for at least some high churchmen, especially Roger Laurence, true Christian baptism was linked to episcopal government, thus separating them from Reformed and Lutheran Protestantism, as well as most Anglicans. Like most Protestants and Roman Catholics, they baptized infants born to church members as well as unbaptized adults. Because baptism preceded the reception of both confirmation and the eucharist, it served as the foundation for the rest of Anglican sacramental and liturgical doctrine and practice.

The apostolic commission to disciple the world and to baptize believers meant that the sacrament served to initiate the disciple into the earthly form of the Kingdom of God, the church, and into the covenant relationship with God (Matthew 28:19–20). Thus, baptism replaced the Jewish ordinance of circumcision as the sign of the covenant. William Beveridge asserted that Christ's ordination of baptism as the means of entering the covenant (perhaps reflecting the Nominalist understanding of *de potentia ordinata*), meant that it was "not only necessary, but generally necessary, to salvation, seeing it is the only way or means ordained by Him, whereby to be admitted into church, out of which there is no salvation."[46] Baptism was the seal, guaranteeing that each party in the covenant relationship would fulfill the terms of the covenant. Still, God was obligated only to ratify a covenant made by an authorized representative. Baptism, therefore, was void if not administered by a properly ordained bishop or priest.[47]

Although baptism replaced circumcision as the "sacrament" of initiation into God's covenant, it also stood in continuity with circumcision. The change of covenant signs was based on God's right to choose the form of initiation. George Hickes wrote:

Baptism doth nothing under the Gospel, which Circumcision did not as properly, and effectually under the Law. This was then as absolute and real a sacrament, as that now is. This did then as really initiate true believers, as that now doth.[48]

The parallel of baptism to circumcision helped provide a defense of the practice of infant baptism. The continuity between circumcision and baptism meant that infants should be baptized, even as the Jews circumcised their infant males. Although high-church divines admitted that the New Testament never explicitly commanded infants to be baptised, the parallel with circumcision, the implicit evidence from the New Testament, such as the household baptisms (Acts 16:15, 33; I Corinthians 1:16) and Jesus' practice of blessing the children (Mark 10:13), and the testimony of the early church sufficiently sanctioned the practice for the contemporary church.[49]

While baptism initiated a person into a covenant relationship with God, it also made that person a disciple or an apprentice of the Christian faith. This raised the question of whether an infant could be a true disciple. Thomas Brett responded that it was the act of baptism, not the decision of the person baptized, that made someone a disciple. He distinguished between the terms *disciple* and *teach* (Matthew 28:19–20). Since a disciple was a learner, baptism admitted a person to the "school of Christ." Teaching followed discipleship, with baptism as the point of entry. Like the Jewish child circumcised because of the decision of the child's parent, the Christian infant became a disciple based on his or her parents' faith. This view was grounded in the belief that children, whether Christian or pagan, belonged to their parents, and therefore, they inherited their parent's religion. If this were not true, William Beveridge declared, then Christian children were worse off than Jewish children, who had received the sign of the covenant.[50]

This position differed markedly from that taken by the Latitudinarian divine Samuel Clarke, who made a strong linkage between belief and baptism. For Clarke baptism signified a person's solemn decision to obey the Gospel. He went on to define "believing" as repenting and believing the Gospel (Mark 1:5). Whereas Brett and Beveridge discounted the faith and belief of the recipient as necessary prerequisites for baptism, Clarke stressed them. For Clarke baptism was simply a sign of faith, not an effective cause of salvation. He believed that without obedience to the Gospel baptism had no spiritual purpose, "but [was] a mere natural washing of the body, without fruit or efficacy." High churchmen emphasized that God used the sacrament to administer grace, bringing faith and salvation to the recipient.[51]

Although infants could not profess faith for themselves, high-church divines thought that they did have within them the "seeds of repentance and faith." These seeds had the potential to grow into perfection, since the vows contained the promise of fulfillment. While adult initiates made the same promise to fulfill their vows as the parents and sponsors of baptized children, there was the possibility, in each case, that the terms of the covenant would not be fulfilled. Though adults were required to demonstrate their faith and repentance, infants were baptized on the basis of sureties given by parents and guardians. When children reached the age of discretion, they would have to fulfill the terms of the covenant, as if they had made the vows themselves. In this way, High Churchmen and Non-Jurors maintained the Anglican traditions.[52]

The second benefit accrued through baptism was pardon, or remission of sins, which led to new birth in righteousness. The waters of baptism symbolized the washing away of sins, freeing the recipient from the power of sin. The visible sign of washing powerfully embodied the process of regeneration. Charles Wheatly explained the relationship between washing and forgiveness of sins.

> For as that is the first office done unto us after our natural births, in order to cleanse us from the pollution of the womb (Ezekiel 16:4); so when we are admitted into the church, we are first baptized, (whereby the Holy Ghost cleanses from all the pollution of our sins, and renews us unto God, [Titus 3:5], and so become, as it were spiritual infants, and enter into a new life and being; which before we had not).[53]

The importance of the metaphor of washing the recipient of his or her sin was linked to the belief that humanity was infected by original sin. Therefore, the church baptized infants to free them from the consequences of the fall of Adam, whose guilt was passed on to each succeeding generation.[54]

THE EFFECTS OF CONFIRMATION

Although Anglicans did not give confirmation sacramental status, the fact that only bishops could perform the rite made it a significant element of church life. Yet the actual practice of the rite was hindered by numerous obstacles. Though bishops were canonically required to make a triennial visit to each parish in their diocese, parliamentary duties and the size of many dioceses hindered fulfillment of this requirement. Even the most diligent bishops found this duty difficult to fulfill.[55]

High Churchmen and most Non-Jurors followed Protestant practice and excluded confirmation from the list of sacraments, but some of them, notably Thomas Deacon and Henry Dodwell, pushed this definition. Deacon explicitly taught that confirmation was a sacrament, which he believed could be administered to infants following their baptisms. Henry Dodwell gave confirmation a role on a par with baptism. He saw baptism as a preliminary rite, one that was beneath the dignity of an Apostle to perform. This necessitated a second rite, a higher baptism, that would seal with oil instead of water to secure eternal life for the recipient.[56] The views of Deacon and Dodwell were not, however, representative of the high-church doctrine of confirmation. The limitation of the rite of confirmation to bishops resulted from following the practice of the catholic church and primitive tradition. The sacred office of confirmation, while it was not a sacrament, fulfilled the need of those baptized in infancy to renew the vows made on their behalf by their godparents. The failure to fulfill the promises made at one's baptism would bring the forfeiture of the blessings promised to the recipients of baptism. Confirmation enabled people to affirm that they were Christians of their own choice. This rite, therefore, gave the church greater security, since the leadership would then know that all church members were willing to live according to the Gospel. The laying on of hands by the bishop confirmed the baptismal vows and conferred the Holy Spirit.[57]

The biblical basis of the confirmation was found in the conferral of the Holy Spirit on the Samaritan believers through the laying on of the apostles' hands. Though Philip, a deacon, baptized the new believers, the Jerusalem church sent Peter and John to lay hands on the Samaritans and pray for them. This resulted in the conferral of the Holy Spirit (Acts 8:14–17). The Church Fathers verified that although the biblical evidence for confirmation was limited, it was, nonetheless, there. The Fathers also affirmed that bishops were charged with the responsibility for the rite.[58] John Potter claimed that the rite of confirmation was a permanent and fundamental part of Christianity. In defense of this proposition, he appealed to Hebrews 6:1–2, which placed the laying on of hands immediately following baptism. He believed that this could only refer to confirmation. Confirmation might take place immediately after a baptism if an apostle or bishop were present, or when it could be conveniently administered (Acts 8). If an apostle or bishop was not available, the rite would be postponed until the candidate could be brought to the bishop.[59]

Although confirmation lacked sacramental status, without it[59] baptism appeared to lose its efficacy once a child reached the age of discretion. Charles Wheatly stated that while baptism was sufficient for salvation, it pertained only to children who had died before committing actual sin. Notwithstanding the fact that baptism washed the former Adamic guilt away and made one an heir of God's promise of eternal life, without confirmation one remained an infant in the faith, unable to resist temptation. Wheatly explained, "baptism conveys the Holy Ghost only as the spirit or principle of life; it is by Confirmation that he becomes to us the Spirit of strength, and enables us to stir and move ourselves." Thus, confirmation provided the equipment and empowerment to battle temptation.[60]

The rite of confirmation preserved church unity by calling on the recipients to obey the hierarchy. It called for a renewal of Christian life and brought an admonition to not dishonor the Christian faith. It advanced the believer to a higher level of church life, giving him or her the right to partake of the Lord's supper. Candidates for confirmation faced strict requirements, since the rite conferred great benefits. Requirements included a thorough instruction in Christian doctrine, the meaning of confirmation, the purpose of the episcopate, and the duties toward God, neighbor, and self. Proper preparation also included a time of prayer and fasting.[61]

Parents, godparents, and clergy were charged to prepare catechumens better for confirmation. Henry Stebbing declared that the lack of care shown by parents and godparents in raising children in the faith was scandalous. He called on priests to pay greater attention to the catechizing of the children, so that they would not be embarrassed by the children's lack of knowledge when presented to the bishop.[62]

The question of sacramental status appears to be a moot point, for without this rite a church member was not filled with the Holy Spirit nor could he or she partake of the Lord's supper. The only real hindrances to sacramental status were the lack of an explicit institution of the ordinance by Christ, and a visible symbol such as water, or bread and wine. Non-Jurors rectified the latter problem by restoring the practice of anointing with oil. Yet the importance of the action seems to contradict the belief expressed by Philip Stubbs that confirmation was not a sign of an inward work of grace, for this does not equate well with the belief that confirmation conveyed the Holy Spirit to the recipient.[63]

The stress placed on the rite of Confirmation gives further credibility to the centrality of episcopal government to high-church ecclesiology. Despite their unwillingness to grant confirmation sacramental status, the fact that only bishops could confirm, theoretically gave the act greater importance than either baptism or the

Lord's supper, which could be administered by lower orders of clergy.

## THE EFFECTS OF THE LORD'S SUPPER

The eucharist was the apex of High Church and Non-Juror worship. Many high churchmen described the Lord's supper in sacrificial language. For some it was a sacrifice of praise and thanksgiving, acknowledging Christ as Lord and as savior, and for others it was a material sacrifice of bread and wine. Sacrificial language employed by High Churchmen and Non-Jurors, such as John Johnson, George Hickes, and Thomas Brett, forms the basis of mature high-church eucharistic doctrine, differentiating it from traditional Anglican positions. Thomas Brett and Thomas Deacon, freed from the shackles of the state church, took Johnson's doctrines and created liturgies that would give expression to the distinctive elements of his theology.[64] The root of the problem with the traditional doctrines and liturgies, as identified by Brett and Johnson, was the loss of the doctrine of eucharistic sacrifice. While they believed that sacrificial language was present in the 1549 Liturgy, they insisted that it was removed in the 1552 edition. This development was traced to the meddling of Calvinistic foreigners Martin Bucer and Peter Vermigli.[65]

Although most high churchmen affirmed the definition of the eucharist as a commemorative sacrifice—that is, a memorial of Christ's sacrifice on the cross[66]—more advanced proponents of eucharistic sacrifice professed to its propitious nature. A propitious sacrifice required a material offering that could be offered to God to plead the merits of the cross. This did not mean, however, that they presumed that the eucharist supplemented the merits of the cross, for the cross was the foundation of the sacrifice. John Johnson wrote that while the oblation of bread and wine did not intrinsically expiate or atone for sin, because the eucharist was a "full and perfect representation of the Sacrifice of Christ's body and blood" the eucharist imparted the effects of Christ's atoning sacrifice to communicants. In the oblation of the eucharist, the bread and wine became for the recipient all that Christ had done on the cross, as if "we had him actually lying on our altars." The Non-juror liturgies of Thomas Brett and Thomas Deacon sought to restore the prayer of oblation, so as to give expression to this view. Brett believed that the omission of the prayer of oblation following the institution narrative in the 1552 liturgy was deliberate, and that it needed to be restored if there was to be a valid consecration of the eucharist.

The oblation became one of the four "usages" that eventually would divide the Non-juror movement.[67]

Precedent for the doctrine of eucharistic sacrifice was found in the Old Testament. Brett and Johnson emphasized the need for offering God a gift to procure his blessings. Johnson gave a five-fold definition of a sacrifice, on which he could base his doctrine of eucharistic sacrifice.

> 1. Some material thing, either animate, or inanimate, offered to God, 2. for the acknowledging of the dominion, and other attributes of God, or for the procuring Divine blessings, especially remission of sin, 3. upon a proper altar, (which yet is rather necessary for the external decorum than the internal perfection of the Sacrifice,) 4. by a proper officer, with agreeable rites, 5. and consumed or otherwise disposed of in such a manner as the author has appointed.[68]

Though the eucharist might have all the properties of a true sacrifice, the doctrine's proponents distinguished between the eucharistic sacrifice and the sacrifice of the cross. The efficacy of the eucharist, like the Jewish sacrifices, was derived from the cross.[69]

The eucharistic sacrifice, though it did not add to the merits of Christ's death and sufferings, enabled those who had sinned since the event of the cross to receive pardon for their sins. Forgiveness of sins was given on the condition that the believer comply with two provisos: first, a sacrificial offering had to be made to God for one's sins; second, this sacrifice, furnished by Christ, had to be applied to the believer in the Lord's supper.[70]

Although they walked a thin line, high churchmen rejected the realism of the Tridentine language. The elements had no propitiatory value in themselves; they simply communicated the benefits of Christ's sacrifice on the cross to the recipients. There would have been no need for the commemorative sacrifice of the eucharist if Christ could have personally applied the benefits of the cross to all believers at the time of his sacrifice, but the eucharist was needed to apply the benefits to future generations, born after that "great sacrifice."[71]

The terms *sacrifice* and *oblation* were used interchangeably to define the eucharist. The eucharist reenacted Christ's high-priestly offering of himself as a living sacrifice. This oblation occurred not on the cross, but in the eucharist. In the Last Supper, Christ offered himself up as a sacrifice. It was at that point, and not on the cross, that the oblation was made. The shedding of blood was undertaken by those who nailed Christ to the cross, but the sacri-

fice preceded that event; thus the cross was the necessary consequence of the oblation made at the Last Supper. Thomas Brett
asserted that Christ suffered and died according to his will in the
eucharist, culminating in his death "in deed" on the cross. The
beneficial nature of the cross, therefore, resulted from Christ's voluntary offering of himself for the sins of the world. Johnson put
this view in different terms; whereas Christ offered himself spiritually in the eucharist, he offered himself corporally on the cross.
Although it comprised two actions, it was one oblation.[72] Edwin
Echlin states that there is a marked contrast between the views
of Johnson and the sixteenth-century Reformers. The Reformers
denied that Christ had offered himself as a sacrifice in the Last
Supper as proof against the doctrine of the sacrifice of the Mass.
Power points out that there were some in attendance at Trent who
related the eucharistic sacrifice to Christ's offering of himself in the
Last Supper. He writes: "it was this offering that was sacramentally
represented in the mass, but because of the real presence it could
be said that it was the victim of the sacrifice of the cross that
was offered." While the language is similar, high-church Anglicans
rejected the idea that Christ was offered as the victim in the eucharist.[73]

Although there was disagreement over the nature of the sacrifice,
sacrificial language was predominant among high-church exposi-
tions of eucharistic doctrine. Johnson believed that the Anglican
eucharist fulfilled his definition of sacrifice. The bread and wine
provided a material offering, the eucharist acknowledged God's
dominion, Christ's institution of the eucharist brought divine blessing, the table of the Lord was a proper altar, the Anglican priests
were proper officers to preside at the event, and the sacrifice was
consumed by eating, which was the manner Christ had appointed.[74]
Whereas Daniel Waterland might have been reluctant to agree with
this definition, this would not have been true of most high
churchmen. Waterland, representing the more centrist elements of
the Anglican church, was not willing to go as far as Johnson, Brett,
and Hickes on the question of eucharistic sacrifice. Richard Buxton, however, does note that Waterland found it more dangerous
to ascribe too little rather than too much to the sacrament.[75]

Whether or not they affirmed the sacrificial language espoused
by Johnson, Hickes, and Brett, High Churchmen and Non-Jurors
believed that the Lord's supper communicated the benefits of the
cross to the people of God. The elements were not simply types or
representative images, they were the instruments of Christ's work
in the lives of his people. The rite not only caused the participant

to remember the blessings Christ purchased by his death, but it imparted those blessings to the participants. They did not receive common bread and wine in the Lord's supper, but inwardly they received the body and blood of Christ.[76] The eucharist was not simply a sign but an effective means of imparting salvation.[77]

While baptism cleansed one from pre-baptismal sins, it neither prevented one from sinning, nor did it bring forgiveness for post-baptismal sin. The eucharist, on the other hand, brought forgiveness of post-baptismal sins. For High Churchmen and Non-Jurors, salvation was conditional. Sin constituted a breach in the covenant with God that could be filled only through the eucharist. This, in turn, required frequent opportunities to partake of the eucharist.[78]

A more subtle benefit than pardon for sin was spiritual nourishment of the soul. The body and blood of Christ, received spiritually, nourished the inward soul, even as bread and wine nourished the body. The eucharist was a medicine that supplied to the soul needed grace, in particular, sanctifying grace.[79] Waterland explained that the fruit of sanctifying grace was the enrichment of the soul (Galatians 5:22; Ephesians 5:9), immortality of the body (Romans 8:9–10), and the sealing of the whole person for future glory (Ephesians 1:13–14; 4:30; II Corinthians 1:22). The effective cause of the sanctifying grace was the conferral of the Holy Spirit in the eucharist.[80]

The eucharist served to give inner strength to meet temptation, hardship, and difficulty. When taken frequently, the eucharist gave strength to face one's spiritual enemies. It gave assurance of the resurrection to eternal life, calming fears concerning one's eternal state. Confidence in the resurrection, based on a sealed pardon and renewed grace, helped preserve Christians from weariness in the face of their pilgrimage and holy war.[81]

The eucharist also had an ethical dimension expressed in the call for communicants to receive the sacrament worthily. The requirements of self-examination, repentance, faith, and charity served as an instrument for encouraging Christians to grow in virtue. John Johnson affirmed that covenanting with God required a "sincere love and charity for all men,"humility, rejection of unjust means, patience, chastity and temperance, and true penitence. Yet high churchmen recognized that the eucharist provided the grace and strength of the Holy Spirit that was needed for moral virtue.[82]

Although the eucharist had many spiritual benefits, it also had temporal benefits; for instance, the corporate nature of the supper helped establish the covenant between believers. The single loaf symbolized that the church, in communication with Christ, was one body (I Corinthians 10:17). As Christians from around the world gathered for the eucharist, they became mysteriously, the one body of Christ. Johnson stated that through the offering of the one loaf to God, "we offer not only the sacramental body of Christ, but His mystical body, the Church; and are thereby understood to profess, that we look on all good Christians as united to Christ and each other, as the several grains are kneaded into one loaf."[83]

Though it might seem incongruous with the respect given to the eucharist, most high churchmen gave affirmation to the use of the sacrament as a political test. The Test Act, passed in 1673, required holders of a civil office to receive the eucharist in an Anglican church prior to taking office. The purpose of the test was to exclude Roman Catholics and Dissenters from serving in public office. While Whig politicians desired to either eliminate the act or to modify it so that Dissenters could be included, high churchmen strongly supported its continuation. Although one might see this as a profane usage of a sacred act—Daniel Defoe called the use of the sacrament as a civil test "a vile prostitution of it, and contrary to the very nature and design of the Gospel institution"—high churchmen supported the Test Act as a means of protecting the church from being dominated by a government composed of non-Anglicans.[84] Thomas Sherlock stated that the Test Act provided the best evidence that the government would ensure the "security of the ecclesiastical constitution." He believed that since the Lord's supper was the best means of demonstrating a person's sincerity toward the church and religion, only a sacramental test of government officials could guarantee the safety of the church. Yet the test was not the reception of the sacrament itself; the test was taking communion in the Church of England. Support of the Test Act accompanied high churchmen's opposition to the practice of occasional conformity. The latter practice allowed Dissenters to hold office without converting to the Church of England. High churchmen believed that, although it allowed Dissenters to bypass the Test Act, occasional conformity—not the sacramental test— dishonored the sacrament. Henry Sacheverell warned of those "crafty, faithless, and insidious persons, who can creep to our altars, and partake of our sacraments that they may be qualify'd more secretly and powerfully to undermine us." He called the practice a "*religious* piece of *political hypocrisy,* as even no heathen government would have endur'd." Though it might seem strange to use the sacrament as a political test, High Churchmen believed that its holy nature made the sacrament the strongest safeguard for the continued existence of both church and state.[85]

## Conclusion

Sacramental theology formed a central position in the framework of High Church and Non-Juror ecclesiology. It provided incentives for protecting the independent integrity of the church as the reservoir for the means of grace. It gave purpose to their political battles to maintain the central place of the established church in English society. It was clearly linked to the resistance of High Churchmen and Non-Jurors to any effort that would undermine the episcopal foundation of the Church of England. While High Churchmen were not the largest religious party in England, they had a major influence on eighteenth-century Anglican sacramental thought. John Johnson provided the basis for Non-Juror and Anglo-Catholic liturgical formulations, and as Darwell Stone points out, Daniel Waterland's more centrist eucharistic theology continued to prevail at the beginning of the nineteenth century. Though they differed at points on the effects of the sacraments, the tangibleness of the sacraments—the water, bread, and cup—exemplified the high-church affirmation of the visible church. While they upheld Protestant sacramental doctrine by affirming only two sacraments, the relationship of those sacraments to the church, the ministry, and to salvation served to reinforce the essential place of the church in the life of the Christian believer.[86]

# Epilogue

Although, as S. C. Carpenter has declared, the "church in 1688 turned over a leaf and began again," many eighteenth-century English churchmen would have rejected the implications of that thesis.[1] Change may have been in the wind, but for a considerable portion of the population adherence to traditional patterns of social, religious, and political discourse remained strong. Latitudinarians may have dominated an Erastian state church and many among the common people may have been indifferent toward religious things, but a "righteous remnant" persisted in holding to the ecclesiological principles of William Laud and the Caroline divines. The High Churchmen and Non-Jurors of the late seventeenth and early eighteenth centuries faced a myriad of challenges, from the accession to the throne of a Dutch Presbyterian in 1689 and then of a German Lutheran in 1714, to the onslaught of the contractarian voluntarism of John Locke. Deism and Nonconformity challenged the church from the outside, and the liberalism of Benjamin Hoadly and Samuel Clarke confronted high churchmen from within the Church of England. Throughout this season of conflict, High Churchmen and Non-Jurors continued to define the church in traditional terms, emphasizing the visibility and apostolicity of the church, the necessity of an episcopally ordained ministry, and the centrality of the sacraments as the appointed means of receiving grace and salvation.

Political issues dominated the late seventeenth and early eighteenth centuries, but High Churchmen and Non-Jurors used a theological rationale to defend the church and its ministry and to define the church's relationship to the state. The integrity and continued existence of the visible, catholic, and apostolic church in England in the face of perceived political threats and theological heterodoxy was their utmost concern.

Controversy and dispute rocked the English religious scene in the early years of the eighteenth century, and high churchmen played a very important role in the developments. High-church agitation sparked the Convocation Controversy, as Francis Atterbury and his supporters attempted to provide the church with a semblance of self-government. Although Atterbury pursued political means to fulfill his quest, the underlying issue was theological. The Test and Corporation Acts, even though they appeared to prostitute the sacrament before political expediency, received continued support from High Churchmen. Supporters of the acts believed that only coercion could shore up the vital interests of the state church. The fact that salvation could only be found within the one, holy, catholic, and apostolic church meant that the established church was the sole repository of the means of grace and salvation in England.

The Dissenters' rejection of the divinely ordained episcopate placed them outside the realm of salvation. This view caused major problems in both church and state, as is evidenced by the lay baptism controversy, which emerged from the publication of Roger Laurence's tract *Lay Baptism, Invalid.* Laurence not only challenged the validity of the Dissenters' ministerial orders, but perhaps more importantly, from a political standpoint, if upheld it would have undermined the claims of George I, a German Lutheran, to be head of the Church of England and a Christian monarch.

Many Anglicans believed that the deprivation of bishops and clergy who refused to take the oath of allegiance to William and Mary was an attack on the church. Those high churchmen who faced the loss of their church offices because of their political beliefs found cause to defend the church's complete autonomy from the state. Many Non-Jurors sought solace in the study of what they believed was the pristine and free church of the earliest Christian centuries.

Though they may have seemed out of step with the changing times, High Churchmen and Non-Jurors continued to define the true church in terms of the primitive ideal located in the early centuries of Christendom.[2] They described this church as episcopal, catholic, and holy. The catholicity and unity of the church were guaranteed by the doctrine of apostolic succession that found embodiment in the person of a bishop who traced his consecration back through a historic succession of bishops to Christ's commission of the Apostles. Salvation was to be found only within the sacred corridors of this church, so that heavenly verities were encountered in the earthly and visible expression of the church. Charles Leslie expressed this belief very clearly, stating that the divinely appointed hierarchy that governed the church had its foot on the earth and extended up to its head, Jesus Christ, who reigned in heaven.[3]

High Church and Non-Juror divines did not present a monolithic theological face to the world. Their thought was characterized by different emphases and nuances. William Beveridge remained rooted in the Restoration Church, combining a Calvinist theology with an emphasis on the visible and apostolic church. Francis Atterbury and Henry Sacheverell continued to espouse the beneficial alliance that existed between church and state, whereas Henry Dodwell, George Hickes, and Thomas Brett defended the church's subsistence as an autonomous society completely separate from the state. Still, neither Beveridge nor Atterbury, neither Sacheverell nor Dodwell, neither Hickes nor Brett believed that there was any road to God except the one that led through the episcopal and apostolic church that had existed in that nation from before the Reformation. The claim of the Dissenters to be a viable ecclesiological option to the episcopal church in England was coldly rejected.

The emphasis on the visible nature of the church, its apostolicity, and the stress on episcopacy and sacraments also emerged later in the eighteenth century in the writings of High Church divines such as William Jones of Nayland; George Horne, Bishop of Norwich; and Charles Daubney, Archdeacon of Salisbury, culminating in the thought of the Tractarians. Jones, like William Beveridge and Thomas Brett before him, saw the church as an ark outside of which there was no hope of salvation. For him, as with his high-church predecessors, "the Church then, must, in its nature, be a society manifest to all men. Some may slight it, and despise it, and refuse to hear it; but they cannot do even this, unless they know where it is found."[4] J. H. L. Rowlands believes that "true High Church principles were limited to a few pious individuals" in the eighteenth century, but Jonathan Clark sees these same descendents of the early eighteenth-century High Churchmen and Non-Jurors as evidence of the continuance of the *ancien regime* in England throughout the eighteenth century and into the early decades of the nineteenth century. Despite the controversial nature of Clark's defense of an *ancien regime* in eighteenth-century England, he has correctly stated that high-church Anglicanism remained strong if not dominant throughout the eighteenth century and into the nineteenth century.[5]

The doctrine of apostolic succession, which Louis Weil calls the "key to the ecclesiastical system" of the Tractarian movement, is found fully developed in early eighteenth-century high-church thought. Weil acknowledges that the Tractarians appropriated this doctrinal construct from the older High Church party. Like their predecessors, Tractarians rooted in their theory of apostolic succession the Church of England's catholicity, the sacraments' efficacy, and the integrity of their doctrine. The centrality of episcopacy to the catholic doctrine of the church was a common thread running from Caroline theologians, including Henry Hammond, through late seventeenth and early eighteenth-century high churchmen such as William Beveridge, John Potter, Henry Dodwell, and Thomas Brett, to the nineteenth-century Oxford divines, including John Henry Newman, Richard Hurrell Froude, and John Keble.[6] W. J. Copeland, a Tractarian, wrote glowingly of the Non-Juror defense of apostolic succession in an article in the *British Critic.*

> They became witnesses to that peculiar position which the Church of England occupies as modelled on the primitive church, the church of the first three centuries, carefully preserving the Apostolical succession of its ministry, and thus securing the validity of its ministrations, maintaining the sublime and mysterious nature of the Christian sacraments, and distinguished, alike from the innovations of popery on the one hand, and of ultra-Protestantism on the other.[7]

Thus, the High Churchmen and the Non-Jurors of the early eighteenth century served as a span in the bridge between two great movements: the Caroline divines of the mid-seventeenth century and the Oxford Movement of the nineteenth century.

Although High Churchmen and Non-Jurors did not dominate either church or state, their influence on key political and theological issues of the period, as well as on future developments, demonstrates clearly that they were not simply eccentric fringe groups. High Churchmen took leading roles in the controversies surrounding Convocation, occasional conformity, attempts at repealing the Test Act, and the Bangorian Controversy. While Norman Sykes' works, especially his *Church and State in England in the XVIIIth Century,* were masterful defenses of the English church in the eighteenth century, they do not give sufficient place to high-church piety and thought. F. C. Mather challenged Sykes' treatment of the church, and we have attempted to follow Mather in uncovering the important nuances of the High Church and Non-Juror ecclesiologies.[8]

This study has underlined the theological aspects of the high-church program, demonstrating that Jonathan Clark is correct in asserting that the works of the Non-Jurors, in particular, but also of the juring High Church party, were not simply "ephemera" to be ignored. The theological and political perspectives espoused by these divines would influence later generations of Anglicans in England, Scotland, and America. Many of the emphases of the Oxford Movement were presaged by the efforts of the High Churchmen and Non-Jurors, who defended the church's apostolic integrity in the last decade of the seventeenth century and through the early decades of the eighteenth century. Owen Chadwick states that the major differences separating the old high-church parties and the Oxford Movement were the element of feeling, the use of poetry, the sense of awe and mystery, and the profundity of reverence that pervaded Tractarian thought. In the end, the difference between the two efforts was a matter of atmosphere, not doctrine.[9]

Many questions raised by the earlier movement were realized in the 1830s. Emancipation of Roman Catholics and Dissenters freed members of these two groups to hold civil office, including Parliamentary office. The battle cry "the Church in Danger" raised by Tory High Churchmen such as Atterbury and Sacheverell in the early part of the eighteenth century was hoisted again in the early 1830s. Geoffrey Rowell maintains that the repeal of the Test and Corporation Acts (1828), the Catholic Emancipation Bill (1829), and the passage of the Reform Bill (1832) significantly weakened the constitutional position of the established church. Facing the prospects of a parliament that was no longer exclusively Anglican, High Churchmen had to acclimate themselves to the new idea that their church would no longer be the church of the nation. Now a parliament that included non-Anglicans would be the legislative body over the Church of England. It was this reality confronted by the church in the 1830s that churchmen of the early eighteenth century feared.[10]

The predicted consequences of a state church dominated by non-Anglicans had led to use of the sacrament as a political test and as opposition to occasional authority. Even as early as the late eighteenth century, High Churchmen such as Charles Daubney contemplated the question of disestablishment. Like the Non-Jurors who proceeded him, he sought to ground the authority of the church in its divine origins, not in its civil establishment. For Daubney and his High Church colleagues, disestablishment was still a threat and not a part of their program, but they laid the groundwork for the Tractarian embrace of the concept. High Churchmen in the nineteenth century, like those who went before them, remained apprehensive about the viability of the episcopacy if Parliament came to be dominated by liberals of the order of Benjamin Hoadly, Roman Catholics, and Dissenters. The controversies that plagued the Church of England in the eighteenth and nineteenth centuries were, at bottom, questions of authority. Whether it was the Non-Juror assertion of their independence as a religious society or Atterbury's call for the resurrection of Convocation, concerns about church authority experienced by eighteenth-century high churchmen were similar to those of John Keble, Richard Hurrell Froude, and John Henry Newman.[11]

High churchmen not only influenced later defenders of episcopacy and the church's spiritual independence, but they strongly impacted the sacramental and liturgical thought of later churchmen. The doctrines of eucharistic presence and sacrifice, brought to maturity by George Hickes and John Johnson, found liturgical expression in the works of Thomas Brett and Thomas Deacon. Brett and Deacon, taking advantage of their freedom from state interference, created a liturgy that restored the prayer of invocation and the oblation, and that gave fuller expression to the doctrine of eucharistic presence.[12] The writers of the *Tracts for the Times* recognized the importance of this work, stating that the doctrine of eucharistic sacrifice, which they themselves were defending, had "found refuge among the Non-Jurors and our brethren of the Scottish Church."[13] G. J. Cuming has assessed the impact of these liturgies, whose publication led to the division of the Non-Juror communion, as being disproportionate to the size of that movement.

> For the first time a deliberate attempt had been made by an organized body of Anglicans (for so they regarded themselves) to create a liturgy on truly primitive lines. They used the best patristic scholarship of their day to correct what they regarded as the errors of the Book of Common Prayer. In so doing they brought to maturity the work of the pioneers, from Taylor to Whiston, and opened the way for many liturgies of later years. Above all, they regained from the Fathers the conception of the eucharist as a sacrifice.[14]

The effects of the Non-Juror liturgies were felt most keenly by the nonjuring Scottish Episcopalians, and through them, by the emergent American Episcopal Church in the 1780s and 1790s. Many Scottish Episcopalians continued to use the 1637 liturgy of William Laud, but the Scottish bishops Archibald Campbell and James Gadderar worked closely with their English colleagues, bringing many English developments into the Scottish church. After the rapprochement of Thomas Brett with the Non-Usages party in 1734, Campbell became the primary leader of the Usages party in England. Gadderar and Thomas Rattray both produced liturgies that reflected the sacramentalist views of Johnson, Brett, and Deacon. Rattray's *An Office for the Sacrifice of the Holy Eucharist* (1744) was based on both the Scottish Liturgy of 1637 and the primitive Liturgy of St. James which Thomas Brett had translated into English.[15] The most important Scottish liturgy, however, was the one edited by Thomas Falconer and Robert Forbes in 1764, which became the official liturgy of the Scottish Episcopal Church. W. Jardine Grisbrooke, in his study of the English liturgies of the seventeenth and eighteenth centuries, states that the 1718 liturgy of Brett and Deacon was the primary source of all Anglican rites that descended from the 1764 liturgy. Edward Echlin notes that although there are differences between the two liturgies, the Scottish liturgy follows the Usagers in their focus on the oblation and the invocation of the Spirit.[16]

The Non-Juror liturgical influences extended through the Scottish church to the American Episcopal Church, as Samuel Seabury was sent by the Episcopal Church of Connecticut in 1784 to seek consecration by the Scottish bishops. Seabury, having been rebuffed by the English bishops who required an oath of allegiance to the king as a prerequisite for consecration, promised to recommend the Scottish liturgy to the American church. In 1785 Seabury produced a liturgy modeled on the one he received from the Scottish Episcopalians. At the first convention of the American church, Seabury and William White were commissioned to revise the 1662 prayer book, but the convention did adopt a modified form of the Scottish prayer of consecration that included the oblation and prayer of invocation that were important elements of the Non-Juror liturgy.[17]

The High Churchmen and Non-Jurors, whose theological and political thought was developed in the context of both political and religious challenges, deserve to be recognized as important contributors to the religious life of eighteenth-century England. Although they may not have had the same immediate impact as Edmund Gibson and Benjamin Hoadly in the eighteenth century or the Tractarians in the nineteenth century, they stand as proponents of an important tradition with a lasting legacy.

# Notes

## INTRODUCTION

1. S. C. Carpenter, *Eighteenth Century Church and People* (London: John Murray, 1959), 2. For an overview of the religious activity of the age see Gordon Rupp, *Religion in England 1688–1791* (Oxford: Clarendon Press, 1986).

2. The term churchman(men) is not intended to be taken in a gender-exclusive sense, but since the term has been used historically to describe the parties of the Anglican church, it seems appropriate to continue its use. The phrase High Church (capitalized) will be used to designate the High Church party in the Church of England, while high church/high-church (uncapitalized) will be used inclusive of both the High Church party and the Non-Jurors, who are theologically and ecclesiologically high church, but are outside the bounds of the established church.

3. Paul Kleber Monod, *Jacobitism and the English People 1688–1788* (Cambridge: Cambridge University Press, 1989), 17–19.

4. Carpenter, *Eighteenth Century Church,* 56–57. J. C. D. Clark, *English Society 1688–1832* (Cambridge: Cambridge University Press, 1985), 119–98. Howard Erskine-Hill, "Literature and the Jacobite Cause: Was there a Rhetoric of Jacobitism?" in *Ideology and Conspiracy: Aspects of Jacobitism, 1689–1759,* ed. Eveline Cruickshanks (Edinburgh: John Donald Publishers, Ltd., 1982), 59–60. John Findon, "The Non-Jurors and the Church of England 1689–1716" (D.Phil. Diss., Oxford University, 1978). L. M. Hawkins, *Allegiance in Church and State* (London: George Routledge and Sons, Ltd., 1928), 41–49. William H. Hutton, *The English Church from the Accession of Charles I to the Death of Anne (1625–1714)* (London: MacMillan and Co., Ltd., 1903; reprinted, New York: AMS Press, 1970), 236. Margaret Jacob, *The Newtonians and the English Revolution 1689–1720* (Ithaca: Cornell University Press, 1976), 72–99. J. P. Kenyon, *Revolution Principles: The Politics of Party 1689–1720* (Cambridge: Cambridge University Press, 1990), 5–34, 69–82. R. J. Smith, *The Gothic Bequest: Medieval Institutions in British Thought 1688–1863* (Cambridge: Cambridge University Press, 1987), 11–28. W. A. Speck, *Reluctant Revolutionaries: Englishmen and the Revolution of 1688* (Oxford: Oxford University Press, 1988), 18. Gerlad M. Straka, *The Anglican Reaction to the Revolution of 1688* (Madison: University of Wisconsin Press, 1962), 80–83. Gerald M. Straka, "The Final Phase of Divine Right Theory in England, 1688–1702," *English Historical Review* 77 (October 1962): 638–58.

5. Owen Chadwick, *The Spirit of the Oxford Movement* (Cambridge: Cambridge University Press, 1990), 5.

6. The attempts to root ecclesiology and theology in the writings and practices of the early church are discussed in my article, "The Search for the Primitive Church: The Use of Early Church Fathers in the High Church Anglican Tradition, 1680–1745," *Anglican and Episcopal History* 59 (September 1990): 303–29, as

well as in chapter 2 following. Cf. Smith, *Gothic Bequest,* 29–30. Smith notes that while the early Non-Jurors, such as Collier and Hickes, retained interest in medieval precedent, later Non-Jurors looked more to patristic sources. On the latitudinarian emphasis, see Isabel Rivers, *Reason, Grace, and Sentiment: A Study of the Language of Religion and Ethics in England, 1660–1780; Volume 1, Whichcote to Wesley* (Cambridge: Cambridge University Press, 1991), 25–26.

7. Roy Porter, "The English Enlightenment," in *The Enlightenment in National Context* (Cambridge: Cambridge University Press, 1981), 1–2, 4. Margaret Jacob, *The Radical Enlightenment: Pantheists, Freemasons and Republicans* (London: George Allen and Unwin, 1981), 22–23. J.G.A. Pocock, "Post-Puritan England and the Problem of the Enlightenment," in *Culture and Politics from Puritanism to the Enlightenment,* Perez Zagorin, ed. (Berkeley: University of California Press, 1980), 92–100.

8. Charles J. Abbey and John H. Overton, *The English Church in the Eighteenth Century,* 1st ed., 2 vols. (London: Longmans, Green and Co., 1878), 1:1. Gerald R. Cragg, *The Church and the Age of Reason 1648–1789,* rev. ed. (Baltimore: Penguin Books, Inc., 1970), 71–72, 75–76. W. A. Speck has pointed out that the threat to the church in the eighteenth century came more from Deism and atheism than from Roman Catholics and Nonconformists. The dreaded increase of dissent under the Whig toleration never materialized. W. A. Speck, *Stability and Strife in England 1714–1760* (Cambridge: Harvard University Press, 1977), 100–101. Concerning the High Church–Tory alliance, see H. T. Dickinson, *Liberty and Property* (New York: Holmes and Meier Publishers, 1977), 13–56. J. A. W. Gunn, *Beyond Liberty and Property* (Kingston and Montreal: McGill-Queen's University Press, 1983), chapter 4. Geoffrey Holmes, *The Trial of Doctor Sacheverell* (London: Eyre Methuen, Ltd., 1973), 41–43. On the question of ecclesiastical independence, see Mark Goldie, "The Non-Jurors, Episcopacy, and the Origins of the Convocation Controversy," in *Ideology and Conspiracy: Aspects of Jacobitism, 1689–1759,* Eveline Cruickshanks, ed. (Edinburgh: John Donald, 1982), 15–35. The question of ecclesiastical autonomy will be addressed in full in chapter 4. Kenyon, *Revolution Principles,* 83–101.

9. John Findon has asserted that the Non-Juror separation was a "direct result of a political Revolution." His dissertation, therefore, is focused on the influence of political ideas on the Church of England. Findon, "The Non-Jurors and the Church of England," 3. Cf. Norman Sykes, *Church and State in England in the XVIIIth Century* (Cambridge: Cambridge University Press, 1934, reprinted, Hamden, CT: Archon Books, 1962), 285–86. Guy Martin Yould, "The Origins and Transformation of the Non-Juror Schism, 1670–1715" (Ph.D. Diss., University of Hull, 1979), 306. Some work has been done on Latitudinarian ecclesiology, but the high-church doctrine has been largely neglected; see John Marshall, "The Ecclesiology of the Latitude-men 1660–1689," *Journal of Ecclesiastical History* 36 (July 1985): 407–27.

10. George Hickes (1642–1715) was the titular Non-Juror Bishop of Thetford (1694–1715), and the recognized leader of the Non-Juror community. Educated at Oxford (B.A., 1663; M.A., 1665; B.D., 1675; D.D., 1679), he was Dean of Worcester prior to being deprived in 1690 for his refusal to take the oath of allegiance.

11. George Every, *The High Church Party 1688–1718* (London: S.P.C.K, 1956), xiii, 1–2. J.G.A. Pocock has stated that the stress on divine-right monarchy and the Anglo-Catholic implications of an apostolic church only found expression among a "handful of extremists on the fringe of the nonjuring secession." The following study, however, will attempt to dispel the view that divine-right episco-

pacy was held only by those on the fringe. Pocock, "Problem of the English Enlightenment," 100–101.

12. Francis Atterbury (1662–1732), a graduate of Christ Church, Oxford, served, successively, as Archdeacon of Totnes, Dean of Carlisle, and Dean of Christ Church, before being consecrated Bishop of Rochester in 1713. He also received an appointment as Dean of Westminster with his episcopal nomination. In 1723 he was deprived of all offices and exiled for his Jacobite activities.

13. Thomas Brett (1667–1745), a graduate of Corpus Christi College, Oxford (LL.B., 1689; LL.D., 1697), was rector of Rucking, when he converted to the Non-Jurors in 1715. He was later consecrated as a Non-Juror bishop (1716), and became one of the movement's leading figures. Henry Dodwell (1641–1711) graduated from Trinity College, Dublin and was a key lay leader of the Non-Juror movement, defending their separation over the deprival of the Non-Juror bishops. Prior to his deprival in 1691, he was appointed as Camden Professor of History at Oxford University (1688). He returned to the established church in 1710 after the death of William Lloyd, Bishop of Norwich, who was the last remaining Non-Juror bishop, with the exception of Thomas Ken, Bishop of Bath and Wells, who also returned to the established church. Samuel Hill (1648–1716) was educated at Oxford and served as rector of Kilmington and as Archdeacon of Wells.

14. The theological rationale behind the Convocation Controversy is discussed more fully in chapter 4. Also see G. V. Bennett, *The Tory Crisis in Church and State 1688–1730* (Oxford: Clarendon Press, 1975), 48–56 and Goldie, "Origins of the Convocation Controversy," 15–35. On the attempts to prevent the repeal of the Test and Corporation Act and the Occasional Conformity Act see Bennett's *Tory Crisis in Church and State,* 214–21, and Every, *High Church Party,* 33–36, 105–24, 163–67.

15. William Law (1686–1761), a Cambridge graduate, is better known for his devotional writings, but he was also an able controversialist. He was deprived in 1714 of his fellowship for refusing to take the oath to George I, and he joined with the Non-Jurors. Andrew Snape (1675–1742) was a graduate of King's College, Cambridge, where he later served as provost before being named Vice-chancellor of Cambridge University (1723).

16. William Beveridge (1637–1708) received his education at St. John's College, Cambridge. He served, successively, as vicar of Ealing, St. Peter's, Cornhill, and as Archdeacon of Colchester, before being consecrated Bishop of St. Asaph in 1704. John Potter (1674–1747), educated at Oxford, served as Regius Professor of Divinity at Oxford prior to being appointed Bishop of Oxford (1715) and then Archbishop of Canterbury (1737). Henry Sacheverell (1674–1724), an Oxford graduate, served as Senior Dean of Arts, Magdalen College, Oxford, and Bursar of the college, prior to being named rector of St. Andrews, Holborn (1713).

17. Joseph Betty (1693–1731) was a fellow of Exeter College, Oxford. William Roberts (1673–1741) was rector of Jacobstown, Devon and prebendary of Exon. Matthias Symson (b. 1675) was Canon of Lincoln.

18. Abbey and Overton, *English Church in the Eighteenth Century,* 1:1–6. Hutton, *English Church,* 241. John H. Overton and Frederick Relton, *The English Church From the Accession of George I to the End of the Eighteenth Century (1714–1800)* (New York: The Macmillan Company, 1906), 1.

19. Sykes, *Church and State,* 1–5, 34–40, 283. Also see his other treatments of the English church: Norman Sykes, *From Sheldon to Secker: Aspects of English Church History 1660–1768* (Cambridge: Cambridge University Press, 1959); Norman Sykes, *Old Priest and New Presbyter* (Cambridge: Cambridge University

Press, 1956); Norman Sykes, *Edmund Gibson* (Oxford: Oxford University Press, 1926); and Norman Sykes, *William Wake Archbishop of Canterbury,* 2 vols. (Cambridge: Cambridge University Press, 1957). The Whig interpretation of history is discussed and critiqued in Herbert Butterfield, *The Whig Interpretation of History* (New York: W. W. Norton and Company, 1965).

20. J. H. Overton, *The Nonjurors: Their Lives, Principles and Writings* (New York: Thomas Whittaker, 1903), 14. Monod, *Jacobitism and the English People,* 139.

21. J. C. D. Clark, "On Moving the Middle Ground: The Significance of Jacobitism in Historical Studies," in *The Jacobite Challenge,* Eveline Cruickshanks and Jeremy Black, eds. (Edinburgh: John Donald Publishers, Ltd., 1988), 177. Clark, *English Society,* 146–47. J. C. D. Clark, *Revolution and Rebellion* (Cambridge: Cambridge University Press, 1986), 16, 176. The renewed interest in Tory and Jacobite political thought can be seen in the recent works of Linda Colley, J. A. W. Gunn, Paul Monod, and Daniel Szechi, as well as Clark's works. Linda Colley, *In Defiance of Oligarchy* (Cambridge: Cambridge University Press, 1982). Gunn, *Beyond Liberty and Property.* Daniel Szechi, *Jacobitism and Tory Politics 1710–1714* (Edinburgh: John Donald Publishers, Ltd., 1984). John Morrill, "Sensible Revolution," in *The Anglo-Dutch Moment,* Jonathan I. Israel, ed. (Cambridge: Cambridge University Press, 1991), 95–96.

22. Studies of the high-church movements include: Bennett, *Tory Crisis in Church and State.* G. V. Bennett, "Conflict in the Church," in *Britain after the Glorious Revolution, 1689–1714,* Geoffrey Holmes, ed. (New York: St. Martins Press, 1969), 155–75. G. V. Bennett, "The Convocation of 1710: An Anglican Attempt at Counter-Revolution," in *Studies in Church History: Councils and Assemblies,* G. J. Cuming and Derek Baker, eds. (Cambridge: University of Cambridge Press, 1971), 12:311–19. Every, *High Church Party.* Goldie, "Origins of the Convocation Controversy," 15–35. F. C. Mather, "Georgian Churchmanship Reconsidered: Some Variations in Anglican Public Worship 1714–1830," *Journal of Ecclesiastical History* 36 (April 1985): 255–83. Findon, "Non-Jurors and the Church of England," 3. Yould, "Origins of the Non-Juror Schism." Both Findon's and Yould's studies end with the death of George Hickes in 1715. Findon has attempted to focus on the political rather than theological issues of the Non-Juror movement.

## CHAPTER I. HIGH CHURCH ECCLESIOLOGY IN THE CONTEXT OF RELIGIOUS LIBERALISM AND NONCONFORMITY

1. S. C. Carpenter, *Eighteenth Century Church and People* (London: John Murray, 1959), 2. Peter Harrison, *"Religion" and the Religions in the English Enlightenment* (Cambridge: Cambridge University Press, 1990). Paul Langford, *A Polite and Commercial People: England 1727–1783* (Oxford: Clarendon Press, 1989), 259. W. A. Speck, *Stability and Strife: England, 1714–1760* (Cambridge: Harvard University Press, 1977), 91–94, 100–101. Roland Stromberg, *Religious Liberalism in Eighteenth-Century England* (London: Oxford University Press, 1954), ix–x.

2. J. C. D. Clark, *English Society 1688–1832* (Cambridge: Cambridge University Press, 1985), 284–85. Margaret Jacob, *The Newtonians and the English Revolution 1689–1720* (Ithaca: Cornell University Press, 1976), 34–35. C. John Sommerville, *Popular Religion in Restoration England* (Gainesville: University

Presses of Florida, 1977), 21–30, 139–42. Isabel Rivers, *Reason, Grace, and Sentiment: A Study of the Language of Religion and Ethics in England, 1660–1780, Volume 1: Whichcote to Wesley* (Cambridge: Cambridge University Press, 1991), 7.

3. Charles J. Abbey and John H. Overton, *The English Church in the Eighteenth Century,* 2 vols. (London: Longmans, Green and Co., 1878), 1:1, 4–6. Gerald R. Cragg, *Reason and Authority in the Eighteenth Century* (Cambridge: Cambridge University Press, 1964), 2–3. Harrison, *"Religion" and Religions,* 99. John Redwood, *Reason, Ridicule and Religion: The Age of Enlightenment in England, 1660–1750* (Cambridge: Harvard University Press, 1976), 12–13. Gerard Reedy, "Barrow, Stillingfleet on the Truth of Scripture," in *Greene and Centennial Studies* (Charlottesville: University Press of Virginia, 1984), 37–38. Stromberg, *Religious Liberalism,* 1. Some recent scholars, however, have challenged the extent to which Locke influenced political and ecclesiastical thought during this period, especially in terms of the influence of contract theory on Whig politicians and theologians. J. A. W. Gunn, *Beyond Liberty and Property* (Montreal: McGill-Queen's University Press, 1983), 173. Clark, *English Society,* 45–50.

4. Roger L. Emerson, "Latitudinarians and the English Deists," in *Deism, Masonry, and the Enlightenment,* J. A. Leo Lemay, ed. (Newark: University of Delaware Press, 1987), 30. Emerson points out that there was a major difference between Latitudinarians and Deists, for while the former gave a place to revelation the latter rejected it. Donald Greene, "Latitudinarianism and Sensibility: The Genealogy of the 'Man of Feeling' Reconsidered," *Modern Philology* 75 (1977): 176–77. Rivers, *Reason, Grace, and Sentiment,* 66–68. Gordon Rupp, *Religion in England, 1688–1791* (Oxford: Clarendon Press, 1986), 29–31. John Spurr, "'Latitudinarianism' and the Restoration Church," *The Historical Journal* 31 (January 1988): 61–82. Robert Sullivan, *John Toland and the Deist Controversy* (Cambridge: Harvard University Press, 1982), 55.

5. Cragg, *Reason and Authority,* 181–182. Eldon J. Eisenach, *Two Worlds of Liberalism: Religion and Politics in Hobbes, Locke, and Mill* (Chicago: University of Chicago Press, 1981), 61–64. J. G. A. Pocock, "Post-Puritan England and the Problem of the Enlightenment," in *Culture and Politics from Puritanism to the Enlightenment,* Perez Zagorin, ed. (Berkeley: University of California Press, 1980), 92–100. Redwood, *Reason, Ridicule and Religion,* 13. Rivers, *Reason, Grace, and Sentiment,* 34. George H. Sabine and Thomas Landon Thorson, *A History of Political Theory,* 4th ed. (Hinsdale, IL: Dryden Press, 1973), 433–34, 437–38.

6. John Dunn, *John Locke* (Oxford: Oxford University Press, 1984), 1–21.

7. Gerald R. Cragg, *From Puritanism to the Age of Reason* (Cambridge: Cambridge University Press, 1966), 114–17. Cragg, *Reason and Authority,* 5–6, 66–67. Stromberg, *Religious Liberalism,* 19. Sullivan, *John Toland,* 91, 113–14, 122–25, 208–10. Jonathan Clark, in his book *English Society,* 46–48, is the most recent observer to charge Locke with heterodoxy. Clark, in fact, believes that Locke's primary influence was among religiously heterodox groups and not on political theory.

8. John Locke, *The Reasonableness of Christianity,* George W. Ewing, ed. (Washington: Regnery Gateway, 1965), 16–20. Peter Byrne, *Natural Religion and the Nature of Religion* (London: Routledge, 1989), 45–51, 71–72. Gerard Reedy, *The Bible and Reason* (Philadelphia: University of Pennsylvania Press, 1985), 135–41. Cf. Cragg, *Reason and Authority,* 12. Eisenach, *Two Worlds of Liberalism,* 86–89. I. T. Ramsey, "Introduction," in John Locke, *The Reasonableness of Chris-*

*tianity with A Discourse of Miracles and part of A Third Letter Concerning Toleration,* I. T. Ramsey, ed. (Stanford: Stanford University Press, 1958), 9–12. Reedy, "On the Truth of Scripture," 22–25. Stromberg, *Religious Liberalism,* 52– 57. Sullivan, *John Toland,* 222–23.

9. Locke, *Reasonableness of Christianity,* 128, 149, 168–72. Cragg, *Puritanism to the Age of Reason,* 124–30. William Spellman, "Archbishop John Tillotson and the Meaning of Moralism," *Anglican and Episcopal History* 56 (December 1987): 421–22.

10. John Locke, "A Letter Concerning Toleration, being a Translation of the *Epistola de Tolerantia,*" in *The Works of John Locke,* new ed., 10 vols. (London: Thomas Tegg, W. Sharpe and Son, 1823, reprinted, Scientia Verlag Aalen, 1963), 6:13. Cf. Reedy, *Bible and Reason,* 138–39.

11. Locke, "Letter Concerning Toleration," 6:5–6, 11, 21, 30, 33. Cf. Cragg, *Reason and Authority,* 183. Eisenach, *Two Worlds of Liberalism,* 82–83.

12. Locke, "Letter Concerning Toleration," 6:14–15, 28–36. Locke, *Reasonableness of Christianity,* 122–23, 186–90. Clark, *English Society,* 46–48. John Spurr, "The Church of England, Comprehension and the Toleration Act of 1689" *English Historical Review* 104 (October 1989): 943–44. See Henry Rack, "'Christ's Kingdom Not of this World': The Case of Benjamin Hoadly Versus William Law Reconsidered," *Studies in Church History: Church, Society, and Politics,* Derek Baker, ed. (Oxford: Basil Blackwell, 1975), 278–79, and Speck, *Stability and Strife,* 95, on Locke's influence on Hoadly. On the influence of Peter King on John Wesley see Frank Baker, *John Wesley and the Church of England* (Nashville: Abingdon Press, 1967), 148–49, and Rupp, *Religion in England,* 438– 40. Cf. Maurice Cranston, *John Locke* (New York: The Macmillan Company, 1957), 438.

13. Locke, "Letter Concerning Toleration," 6:45–47.

14. Emerson, "Latitudinarianism and the English Deists," 30–43. Reedy, *Bible and Reason,* 10–13.

15. Harrison, *"Religion" and Religions,* 28.

16. Joseph Betty, *The Divine Institution of the Ministry, and the Absolute Necessity of Church Government: A Sermon Preached before the University of Oxford on Sunday the 21st of September, 1729,* 2nd corrected ed. (London, 1729), 17–19. John Potter, *A Discourse on Church Government: Wherein the Rights of the Church and the Supremacy of Christian Bishops are Vindicated and Adjusted,* 5th ed. (London: 1839), 2–11. William Roberts, *The Divine Institution of the Gospel Ministry and the Necessity of Episcopal Ordination,* 4th ed. (London, 1753, preached 1709), 7, 23–24. Matthias Symson, *The Necessity of a Lawful Ministry* (London, 1708), 9–10. These works exemplify the high-church assertion of the primacy of the church and episcopally ordained ministry in Christian life. This high-church ecclesiology will be treated in depth in the chapters that follow.

17. Harrison, *"Religion" and Religions,* 28–31. Jacob, *Newtonianism and the English Revolution,* 28–30. John Marshall, "The Ecclesiology of the Latitudemen 1660–1689: Stillingfleet, Tillotson, and 'Hobbism',", *Journal of Ecclesiastical History* 36 (July 1985): 407–27. Rivers, *Reason, Grace, and Sentiment,* 25–26, 33. Rupp, *Religion in England,* 31. G. V. Bennett, however, contends that William's appointments to the bench were Tories rather than Whigs. G. V. Bennett, "Conflict in the Church," in *Britain After the Glorious Revolution, 1689–1714* (New York: St. Martins Press, 1969), 160–61. G. V. Bennett, "King William III and the Episcopate," in *Essays in Modern English Church History,* G. V. Bennett and J. D. Walsh, eds. (London: A. & C. Black Ltd., 1966), 104–5. I. M. Green, *The Reestab-*

*lishment of the Church of England 1660–1663* (Oxford: Oxford University Press, 1978), 168–77.

18. Gilbert Burnet, *An Exposition of the Thirty-nine Articles of the Church of England* (London, 1699), 180. Like Burnet, Benjamin Hoadly defined the church as a voluntary society, thus applying Locke's theories of church and state. Cf. Speck, *Stability and Strife*, 95.

19. Benjamin Hoadly, *A Preservative Against the Principles and Practices of the Non-Jurors Both in Church and State*, 2nd ed. (London, 1716), 55–57. Marshall, "Ecclesiology of the Latitude-men," 411–13, 421–23. Speck, *Stability and Strife*, 94–95. Sullivan, *John Toland*, 267–69. Norman Sykes, "Benjamin Hoadly, Bishop of Bangor," in *The Social and Political Ideas of Some English Thinkers of the Augustan Age*, F. J. C. Hearnshaw, ed. (New York: Barnes and Noble, Inc., 1923), 139–40. [Edward Welchman], *A Defense of the Church of England From the Charge of Schism and Heresie* (London, 1693), 10–12.

20. Benjamin Hoadly, "The Happiness of the Present Establishment, and Unhappiness of Absolute Monarchy: A Sermon Preached at the Assizes at Hereford, March 22, 1708," in *The Works of Benjamin Hoadly, D.D.*, 3 vols. (London, 1773), 2:113. Benjamin Hoadly, "A Letter to a Clergyman in the Country Concerning the Votes of Bishops on Occasional Conformity," in *The Works of Benjamin Hoadly, D.D.*, 3 vols. (London, 1773), 1:27–28. Arthur Ashley Sykes, *The Authority of the Clergy and the Liberties of the Laity Stated and Vindicated* (London, 1720), viii. For the opposition to the Test and Corporation Acts see: Arthur Ashley Sykes, *The Corporation and Test Acts, Shown to be of No Importance to the Church of England,* (London, 1736). Sykes (1684–1756), a Cambridge graduate and rector of Rayleigh, Essex, was the leading clerical supporter of Hoadly's position. Cf. Stromberg, *Religious Liberalism*, 91. Sullivan, *John Toland,* 267–69. Sykes, "Benjamin Hoadly," 122–23.

21. Emerson, *Latitudinarianism and the English Deists*, 30–35. Jacob, *Newtonians and the English Revolution*, 34–35.

22. Harrison, *"Religion" and Religions*, 61–74. Harrison affirms the contention of Charles Leslie that Charles Blount, not Edward Herbert, founded Deism. Margaret C. Jacob, *The Radical Enlightenment: Pantheists, Free Masons and Republicans* (London: George Allen and Unwin, 1981), 22–23.

23. Matthew Tindal, *The Rights of the Christian Church, Asserted, Against the Romish, and all other Priests who claim an Independent Power over It* (London, 1707), 80. Roger Emerson notes that, unlike liberal Anglicanism, Deism was "principally associated with the denial of revealed religion." Emerson has sought to demonstrate that Deism was not the natural outcome of Latitudinarianism. Emerson, "Latitudinarians and the English Deists," 28–30.

24. Matthew Tindal, *Christianity as Old as Creation: of the Gospel, A Republication of the Religion of Nature* (London, 1730; reprinted, Stuttgard-Bad Cannstatt: Friedrich Frommann Verlag, 1967), 20–21. [Matthew Tindal], *Four Discourses on the Following Subjects: viz. I. Of Obedience to the Supreme Powers and the Duty of Subjects in all Revolutions. II. Of the Laws of Nations, and the Rights of Sovereigns. III. Of the Power of the Magistrate, and the Rights of Mankind in Matters of Religion. IV. Of the Liberty of the Press* (London, 1709), 251, 261. [Tindal], *Rights of the Christian Church*, 174, 314. John Toland, "The Primitive Constitution of the Christian Church," *A Collection of Several Pieces of Mr. John Toland* (London, 1726), 2: 138–39, 146–49, 170, 196–97. Cf. Sullivan, *John Toland*, 128–32.

25. [Tindal], *Rights of the Christian Church*, 20, 29, 33, 35, 37. [Tindal], *Four*

*Discourses,* 243, 255. Cf. Clark, *English Society,* 295–97. Cragg, *Reason and Authority,* 185–86. Gunn, *Beyond Liberty and Property,* 50–51, 138. Sullivan, *John Toland,* 226.

26. Cragg, *Church and the Age of Reason,* 50–52. Green, *Reestablishment of the Church of England,* 84–87, 150–54. Christopher Hill, *The Century of Revolution, 1603–1714,* 2nd ed. (New York: W. W. Norton & Company, 1980), 210–11. Irvonwy Morgan, *The Nonconformity of Richard Baxter* (London: Epworth Press, 1945), 13–20. John Spurr, "Schism and the Restoration Church," *Journal of Ecclesiastical History* 41 (July 1990): 409–10. Michael R. Watts, *The Dissenters, From the Reformation to the Revolution* (Oxford: Clarendon Press, 1978), 57–58, 90–91.

27. Richard Baxter, "The Christian Directory: Christian Ecclesiastics," in *The Practical Works of Richard Baxter,* 23 vols. (London, 1830), 5:162, 247–49, 251. N. H. Keeble, *Richard Baxter: Puritan Man of Letters* (Oxford: Clarendon Press, 1982), 24, 27. William M. Lamont, *Richard Baxter and the Millennium* (Totowa, NJ: Rowman and Littlefield, 1979), 240. Morgan, *Nonconformity of Richard Baxter,* 91–98, 102–4.

28. Baxter, "Christian Directory," 5:285. Peter King, *Enquiry into the Constitution, Discipline, Unity and Worship of the Primitive Church* (London, 1691), 3, 7–8. Watts, *Dissenters,* 315–16.

29. Baxter, "Christian Directory," 5:164–65. Rupp, *Religion in England,* 108. Watts, *Dissenters,* 59.

30. Watts, *Dissenters,* 95–99. Cf. Rupp, *Religion in England,* 116–19.

31. Philip Doddridge, *A Course of Lectures,* 2nd ed., S. Clark, ed. (London, 1776), 490–91. Doddridge (1702–51) was a Nonconformist divine, pastor, and educator.

32. John Owen, *The True Nature of a Gospel Church and Its Government (1689),* abridged and edited by John Huxtable (London: James Clarke & Co., Ltd., 1947), 35–38. James E. Bradley, "Toleration, Nonconformity, and the Unity of the Spirit: Popular Religion in Eighteenth-Century England," in *Church, Word, and Spirit,* James E. Bradley and Richard Muller, eds. (Grand Rapids: William B. Eerdmans Publishing Company, 1987), 183–87. Cf. Rupp, *Religion in England,* 119–20. Watts, *Dissenters,* 315–17.

33. Owen, *True Nature of a Gospel Church,* 25–30. Watts, *Dissenters,* 317–18.

34. Philip Doddridge, *Free Thoughts on the Most Probable Means of Reviving the Dissenting Interest* (London, 1730), 6. Cf. Bradley, "Toleration, Nonconformity, and the Unity of the Spirit," 184–85, 187–99. Alan C. Clifford, "The Christian Mind of Philip Doddridge (1702–1751): the Gospel according to an Evangelical Congregationalist," *Evangelical Quarterly* 56 (October 1984): 237–38. Rupp, *Religion in England,* 127.

35. Watts, *Dissenters,* 319. Bradley, "Toleration, Nonconformity, and the Unity of the Spirit," 188–89. Cf. Rupp. *Religion in England,* 132–33.

36. A. C. Underwood, *A History of the English Baptists* (London: Carey Kingsgate Press, Ltd., 1947), 119, 128. Rupp, *Religion in England,* 130–31.

37. Rupp, *Religion in England,* 129–32. Underwood, *History of the English Baptists,* 119–32.

38. Rupp, *Religion in England,* 138–43.

39. Robert Barclay, "The Anarchy of the Ranters and other Libertines, the Hierarchy of the Romanist and other Pretended Churches, equally Refused and Refuted in a Two-fold Apology for the Church and People of Called in Derision Quakers," in *Truth Triumphant Through the Spiritual Warfare, Christian Labours*

*and Writings of the Able Servant of Jesus Christ, Robert Barclay* (London, 1692), 202–3. Rupp, *Religion in England,* 143, 151. Watts, *Dissenters,* 300–301.

40. Green, *Re-establishment of the Church of England,* 143–51. Douglas Lacey, *Dissent and Parliamentary Politics in England, 1661–1689* (New Brunswick, NJ: Rutgers University Press, 1969), 19–22. Spurr, "Church of England, Comprehension, and the Toleration Act," 928–33. Norman Sykes, *Church and State in England in the XVIIIth Century* (Cambridge: Cambridge University Press, 1934; reprinted, Hamden, CT: Archon Books, 1962), 8–13. Roger Thomas, "Comprehension and Indulgence," in *From Uniformity to Unity 1662–1962,* Geoffrey Nuttall and Owen Chadwick, eds. (London: S.P.C.K., 1962), 191–92, 195. Watts, *Dissenters,* 223–27.

41. G. V. Bennett, *The Tory Crisis in Church and State, 1688–1730* (Oxford: Clarendon Press, 1975), 8–10. Bennett, "Conflict in the Church," 158–59. Lacey, *Dissent and Parliamentary Politics,* 64–72. Spurr, "Church of England, Comprehension, and the Toleration Act," 935–39. Norman Sykes, *From Sheldon to Secker: Aspects of English Church History 1660–1768* (Cambridge: Cambridge University Press, 1959), 70–72. Thomas, "Comprehension and Indulgence," 191.

42. George Every, *The High Church Party, 1688–1718* (London: S.P.C.K., 1956), 28. Lacey, *Dissent and Parliamentary Politics,* 64–70. Thomas, "Comprehension and Indulgence," 212–14. Watts, *Dissenters,* 251–52.

43. Every, *High Church Party,* 19–21, 28, 32. Lamont, *Richard Baxter and the Millennium,* 212–13. Sykes, *Sheldon to Secker,* 83–84, 86–87.

44. Richard Baxter, *Of National Churches* (London, 1691), 1–2, 6–9, 29. Lamont, *Richard Baxter and the Millennium,* 212–17, 242–49, 258–59, 267–69.

45. Every, *High Church Party,* 28. Rupp, *Religion in England,* 113–14. Spurr, "Church of England, Comprehension, and the Toleration Act," 944–45.

46. Bennett, *Tory Crisis in Church and State,* 10–12. Bennett, "Conflict in the Church," 161. Every, *High Church Party,* 34–35. Sykes, *Sheldon to Secker,* 84–91. Thomas, "Comprehension and Indulgence," 247–53. Watts, *Dissenters,* 259–61.

47. Bennett, "Conflict in the Church," 161–66. Bennett, *Tory Crisis in Church and State,* 11. Every, *High Church Party,* 33. Sykes, *Sheldon to Secker,* 89–96. The Dissenters would have to wait until the beginning of the nineteenth century before the Test and Corporation acts were repealed, allowing Dissenters the freedom to hold office in England; it was not until 1871 that religious tests were abolished at the Universities. Cf. E. A. Payne, "Toleration and Establishment: I," in *From Uniformity to Unity,* Geoffrey Nuttall and Owen Chadwick, eds. (London: S.P.C.K., 1962), 258.

48. Watts, *The Dissenters,* 264.

49. Bennett, "Conflict in the Church," 162–63. Bennett, *Tory Crisis in Church and State,* 11–13. Speck, *Stability and Strife,* 91–92, 102. Watts, *Dissenters,* 384–86.

50. James E. Bradley, "Nonconformity and the Electorate in Eighteenth Century England," *Parliamentary History* 6 (1987): 243. James E. Bradley, "Whigs and Nonconformists: 'Slumbering Radicalism' in English Politics, 1739–1789," *Eighteenth-Century Studies* 9 (Fall 1975): 6–7. K.R.M. Short, "The English Indemnity Acts 1726–1867," *Church History* 43 (1973): 366. Cf. Bennett, *Tory Crisis in Church and State,* 13–14. Cragg, *Church and the Age of Reason,* 55.

51. Bennett, *Tory Crisis in Church and State,* 14. Christopher Hill, "Occasional Conformity," in *Reformation, Conformity and Dissent,* R. Buick Knox, ed. (London: Epworth Press, 1977), 199, 216–17. Sykes, *Sheldon to Secker,* 96–97.

52. [Daniel Defoe], *Case of the Protestant Dissenters in England Fairly Stated* (London, 1716), 8. [Daniel Defoe], *An Enquiry into the Occasional Conformity of Dissenters, in Cases of Preferment* (London, 1701), 21–25. Henry Sacheverell, *Political Union* (London, 1710), 24. Cf. Langford, *Polite and Commercial People,* 294–95. Payne, "Toleration and Establishment," 261–62. Watts, *Dissenters,* 265–66.

53. Sacheverell, *Political Union,* 20, 24. Cf. Geoffrey Holmes, *The Trial of Doctor Sacheverell* (London: Eyre Methuen, Ltd., 1973), 40, 42–43.

54. Bennett, *Tory Crisis in Church and State,* 68–73, 78–82, 150. Every, *High Church Party,* 109–10. Holmes, *Trial of Doctor Sacheverell,* 16–17, 42–43. Sykes, *Church and State in England,* 34–35. Sykes, *Sheldon to Secker,* 97. Watts, *Dissenters,* 265–66.

55. Langford, *Polite and Commercial People,* 294–95. Short, "English Indemnity Acts," 366–70. Watts, *Dissenters,* 267.

56. Bennett, *Tory Crisis in Church and State,* 48–56. Bennett, "Conflict in the Church," 165–66. Gerald M. Straka, *The Anglican Reaction to the Revolution of 1688* (Madison: University of Wisconsin Press, 1962), 19–20. Sykes, *Church and State in England,* 300–309. Norman Sykes, *William Wake: Archbishop of Canterbury, 1657–1737,* 2 vols., (Cambridge: Cambridge University Press, 1957), 1:80–156. See chapter four for a fuller discussion of the theological underpinnings of the controversy.

57. Bennett, "Conflict in the Church," 161. Bennett contends in his article that the majority of William's appointments were moderate Tories rather than Whigs. They were, nonetheless, opposed to the views of high Tories like Atterbury.

58. Bennett, *Tory Crisis in Church and State,* 56–62. Bennett, "Conflict in the Church," 166. Gunn, *Beyond Liberty and Property,* 137–38. William Marshall, *George Hooper 1640–1727: Bishop of Bath and Wells* (Milborne Port, Dorset: Dorset Publishing Company, 1976), 70–80.

59. G. V. Bennett, "The Convocation of 1710: An Anglican Attempt at Counter-revolution," in *Studies in Church History: Councils and Assemblies,* G. J. Cuming and Derek Baker, eds. (Leiden: E. J. Brill, 1971), 7:312–19. Bennett, *Tory Crisis in Church and State,* 109–18, 125–34. Rupp, *Religion in England,* 62–69.

60. Rupp, *Religion in England,* 64.

61. Sykes, *Church and State in England,* 361–62. The controversy derives its name from the fact that Hoadly was Bishop of Bangor at the time the confrontation erupted.

62. Benjamin Hoadly, "The Nature of the Kingdom or Church of Christ," in *The Works of Benjamin Hoadly, D.D.,* 3 vols. (London, 1773), 2:406. A. A. Sykes, a key supporter of Hoadly, took a similar view of the church and salvation; Sykes, *Authority of the Clergy,* 42. Cf. George Hickes, *The Constitution of the Catholic Church, and the Nature and Consequences of Schism* (London, 1716), 94–101. Benjamin Hoadly, *A Preservative Against the Principles and Practices of the Non-Jurors both in Church and State,* 2nd ed. (London, 1716), 89–91. Bennett, *Tory Crisis in Church and State,* 214–15. Cragg, *Reason and Authority,* 194. Henry D. Rack, "'Christ's Kingdom Not of this World': The Case of Benjamin Hoadly Versus William Law Reconsidered," in *Studies in Church History: Church, Society and Politics,* Derek Baker, ed. (Oxford: Basil Blackwell, 1975), 12:276–78. Speck, *Stability and Strife,* 94–95. Norman Sykes, *Church and State in England,* 290–3.

63. Hoadly, "Nature of the Kingdom," 2:409.

64. William Law, "Three Letters to the Bishop of Bangor," *The Works of the*

*Reverend William Law, M.A.*, 9 vols. (London, 1762, reprinted, Setley: G. Moreton, 1892), 1:4. Cf. Henry Stebbing, *Remarks Upon a Position of the Right Reverend the Lord Bishop of Bangor Concerning Religious Sincerity* (London, 1718), 11–14. Stebbing (1687–1763), a High Churchman and a graduate of St. Catherine's Hall, Cambridge, held several livings, was Archdeacon of Wiltshire, Chancellor of Sarum, and from 1748, Rector of Redenhall.

65. Benjamin Hoadly, *An Answer to the Reverend Dr. Hare's Sermon Intitul'd, Church Authority Vindicated* (London, 1719), 166–70.

66. Hoadly, "Nature of the Kingdom," 2:404.

67. Andrew Snape, *A Letter to the Bishop of Bangor* (Dublin, 1717), 10–11.

68. Benjamin Hoadly, *An Answer to the Reverend Dr. Snape's Letter to the Bishop of Bangor*, 10th ed. (London, 1717), 20–23. Benjamin Hoadly, "An Answer to the Representation Drawn up by the Committee of the Lower House of Convocation," in *The Works of Benjamin Hoadly, D.D.*, 3 vols. (London, 1773), 2:459.

69. Hoadly, "Answer to the Lower House," 2:473.

70. Law, "Three Letters to the Bishop of Bangor," 1:13.

71. Hoadly, "Answer to the Lower House," 2:478. Francis Hare, *Church Authority Vindicated in a Sermon Preached at Putney, May 5, 1719*, 4th corrected edition (London, 1720), 28. Thomas Sherlock, "Preface: The Vindication of the Corporation and Test Acts," in *The Works of Bishop Sherlock*, 5 vols. (London, 1830), 4:427–28. Sherlock, (1678–1761), the son of William Sherlock, Dean of St. Paul's, was educated at Cambridge, and like his father he was appointed Master of the Temple in 1704. Sherlock became the most prominent High Churchman and Tory church leader during the reigns of the first two Georges, serving as Bishop of Bangor (1728), Salisbury (1734), and London (1748).

72. Sherlock, "Preface," 4:426. Cf. Sykes, *Church and State in England*, 341.

73. Hoadly, *Preservative Against the Non-Jurors*, 33. Sykes, *Church and State in England*, 332–33.

74. Frank Baker, *John Wesley and the Church of England* (Nashville: Abingdon Press, 1967), 42–43, 137–59. Sykes, *Church and State in England*, 390–92.

75. Every, *High Church Party*, 169–81. Gunn, *Beyond Liberty and Property*, 164–85. Richard Sharp, "New Perspectives on the High Church Tradition: Historical Background, 1730–1780," in *Tradition Renewed*, Geoffrey Rowell, ed. (Allison Park, PA: Pickwick Publications, 1986), 4–23. For the continuance of the Tory party in the face of Whig domination see Linda Colley, *In Defiance of Oligarchy* (Cambridge: Cambridge University Press, 1982).

76. John Morrill, "The Sensible Revolution," in *The Anglo-Dutch Moment*, Jonathan I. Israel, ed. (Cambridge: Cambridge University Press, 1991), 95–96.

## CHAPTER 2. SOURCES OF AUTHORITY: SCRIPTURE, TRADITION, AND REASON

1. William Sherlock (1641–1707), graduated from Cambridge and served as rector of St. George's, Botolph Lane, London, and Master of the Temple, prior to his appointment as Dean of St. Paul's in 1691.

2. William Beveridge, "*Ecclesias Anglicana Ecclesia Catholica;* or the Doctrine of the Church of England Consonant to Scripture, Reason, and Fathers in a Discourse upon the Thirty-nine Articles Agreed Upon in the Convocation Held at London MDLXII," in *The Theological Works of William Beveridge, D.D.*, 12 vols. (Oxford: John Henry Parker, 1845), 7:x, 365. William Sherlock, *An Apology for Writing Against the Socinians in Defence of the Doctrines of the Holy Trinity*

*and Incarnation* (London, 1693), 12–13. Cf. Paul Avis, *Anglicanism and the Christian Church* (Minneapolis: Fortress Press, 1989), 63–67. Frederick F. Bruce, "Scripture in Relation to Tradition and Reason," in *Scripture, Tradition and Reason,* Richard Bauckham and Benjamin Drewery, eds. (Edinburgh: T & T Clark, Ltd., 1988), 35–36. Gerald R. Cragg, *Freedom and Authority* (Philadelphia: Westminster Press, 1975), 99, 110. Pedro Thomas Meza, "The Question of Authority in the Church of England, 1689–1717," *Historical Magazine of the Protestant Episcopal Church* 42 (March 1973): 63–86. Paul Elmer More, "The Spirit of Anglicanism," in *Anglicanism,* Paul Elmer More and Frank Leslie Cross, eds. (New York: Macmillan Company, 1957), xxiv–xxv. Gerard Reedy, "Barrow, Stillingfleet on the Truth of Scripture," in *Greene and Centennial Studies* (Charlottesville: University Press of Virginia, 1984), 37–38.

3. Gerald R. Cragg, *Reason and Authority in the Eighteenth Century* (Cambridge: Cambridge Unviersity Press, 1964), 2–3. Gerald R. Cragg, *The Church and the Age of Reason 1648–1789* (Baltimore: Penguin Books, 1970), 71–72, 159–61. Peter Harrison, *"Religion": and the Religions in the English Enlightenment* (Cambridge: Cambridge University Press, 1990), 28, 99. John Redwood, *Reason, Ridicule and Religion, The Age of Enlightenment in England 1660–1750* (Cambridge: Harvard University Press, 1976), 13, 203–4. Gerard Reedy, *The Bible and Reason* (Philadelphia: University of Pennsylvania Press, 1985), 135–37. Isabel Rivers, *Reason, Grace, and Sentiment: A Study of the Language of Religion and Ethics in England, 1660–1780, Volume I: Whichcote to Wesley* (Cambridge: Cambridge University Press, 1991), 66–77. William Spellman "Archbishop John Tillotson and the Meaning of Moralism," *Anglican and Episcopal History* 56 (December 1987): 409.

4. See chapter 4 for a much fuller discussion of the high-church understanding of the relationship of church and state.

5. Gilbert Burnet, *An Exposition of the Thirty-nine Articles of the Church of England,* 3rd ed. (London, 1705), 72, 78. William Law, "Three Letters to the Bishop of Bangor," in *The Works of the Reverend William Law, M.A.,* 9 vols. (London, 1762; reprinted, Setley: G. Moreton, 1892), 1:73–74. Cf. Reedy, *Bible and Reason,* 4. Harrison, *"Religion" and Religions,* 99.

6. Beveridge, *"Ecclesia Anglicana",* 7:191–92.

7. Thomas Brett, *Farther Proof of Tradition, to Explain and Interpret the Holy Scriptures* (London, 1720), 3–8.

8. Benjamin Hoadly, *An Answer to the Reverend Dr. Hare's Sermon intitul'd Church Authority Vindicated* (London, 1717), 128–29. Thomas Stackhouse, *A Compleat Body of Speculative and Practical Divinity,* 3rd ed. (London, 1743), 46. Stackhouse (1677–1752), a High Churchman, attended Cambridge and served as the minister of the English Church at Amsterdam (1713–31) and Curate of Finchley (1731–52). Arthur Ashley Sykes, *Some Remarks on Mr. Marshall's Defense of our Constitution in Church and State* (London, 1717), 78. Cf. Avis, *Anglicanism,* 272–73. Cragg, *Reason and Authority,* 12. Cragg, *Church and the Age of Reason,* 159–60. Roger L. Emerson, "Latitudinarianism and the English Deists," in *Deism, Masonry, and the Enlightenment,* J. A. Leo Lemay, ed. (Newark: University of Delaware Press, 1987), 28, 30.

9. Henry Stebbing, *A Rational Enquiry into the Proper Methods of Supporting Christianity, So Far as it Concerns the Governors of the Church* (London, 1720), 17, 20. Cf. Stackhouse, *Compleat Body of Divinity,* 46. Thomas Brett, *A Collection of the Principle Liturgies, used by the Christian Church in the Celebration of the Holy Eucharist. With a Dissertation upon Them* (London, 1720), vi.

10. Stackhouse, *Compleat Body of Divinity,* 66; Bevereidge, *"Ecclesia Anglicana,"* 7:194–95. Law, "Three Letters," 1:74.

11. Matthias Earbery, *A Review of the Bishop of Bangor's Sermon, and his Answer to the Representation of the Committee of the Lower House of Convocation,* 2 parts (London, 1718, 1:32). William Law, "The Case of Reason, or Natural Religion Fairly and Fully Stated," *Works,* 2:107, 109–10. Charles Leslie, "A Short and Easy Method with the Deists, Wherein the Certainty of the Christian Religion is Demonstrated by Infallible Proof from Four Rules, which are Incompatible, to any Imposture that ever yet has been, or that can Possibly Be," *The Theological Works of the Reverend Mr. Charles Leslie,* 2 vols. (London: 1721), 1:15. Earbery (1657–1740), educated at St. John's College, Cambridge, was the incumbent of Neatishead, Kent, prior to his conversion to the Non-Jurors in 1715. Leslie (1650–1722), a Non-Juror and active Jacobite, graduated from Trinity College, Dublin, and served as Chancellor of Connor before being deprived for his refusal to take the oaths to William and Mary. He spent the remainder of his life abroad in exile, returning to Ireland in 1721. Cf. Cragg, *Church and the Age of Reason,* 160–63; Redwood, *Reason, Ridicule and Religion,* 148–50; Reedy, *Bible and Reason,* 46–47. The appeal to miracles was the standard defense of the truthfulness of Scripture, on the part of both Latitudinarians and High Churchmen.

12. Stackhouse, *Compleat Body of Divinity,* 45–46. [Nathaniel Spinckes], *No Sufficient Reason for Restoring the Prayers and Directions of King Edward the Sixth's First Liturgy* (London, 1718), 2–3. Spinckes (1653–1727), educated at Jesus College, Cambridge, was rector of St. Martin's, Salisbury, when he was deprived in 1690. He was consecrated as a Non-Juror bishop in 1713 and became the leader of the Non-Usages party.

13. Brett, *Collection of the Principle Liturgies,* vii–viii. Brett, *Farther Proof,* m .4–5. cf. Law, "Three Letters to the Bishop of Bangor," 1:73; Law, "Case of Ream.son," 2:201.

14. Stackhouse, *Compleat Body of Divinity,* 45–46, 53, 66. Beveridge, *"Ecclesia Anglicana,"* 7:205, 213. Thomas Brett, *Tradition Necessary to Explain and Interpret the Holy Scriptures* (London, 1718), 136. Samuel Hill, *The Catholic Balance: Or a Discourse Determining the Controversies Concerning, I. Tradition of Catholic Doctrine. II. The Primacy of S. Peter and the Bishop of Rome. III. The Subjection and Authority of the Church in a Christian State: According to the Suffrages of the Primest Antiquity* (London, 1687), 37. Law, "Three Letters," 1:79. William Wake, *The Principles of the Christian Religion Explained: In a Brief Commentary upon the Church Catechism,* 2nd ed. (London, 1700), 20. Cf. Reedy, *Bible and Reason,* 90–95.

15. G. V. Bennett, *Tory Crisis in Church and State 1688–1730* (Oxford: Clarendon Press, 1975), 17. Cragg, *Reason and Authority,* 12, 93. Redwood, *Reason, Ridicule and Religion,* 143–44. Reedy, *Bible and Reason,* 136–37. Norman Sykes, *From Sheldon to Secker: Aspects of English Church History, 1660–1768* (Cambridge: Cambridge University Press, 1959), 153, 157. Cf. chapter 1 for a fuller discussion of the thought of Locke and the Deists.

16. Law, "Case of Reason," 2:60–61. Robert Nelson, *A Companion for the Festivals and Fasts of the Church of England with Collects and Prayers for each Solemnity* (London, S.P.C.K., 1841), 244–45. Nelson (1656–1715), a leading Non-Juror layman and devotional writer, was active in a number of charitable and religious organizations, even though he had left the established church. He returned to the Church of England in 1711 at the death of William Lloyd, deprived

Bishop of Norwich. Stackhouse, *Compleat Body of Divinity,* 17. Cf. Avis, *Anglicanism,* 65, 110–11.

17. G. V. Bennett, "Patristic Tradition in Anglican Thought, 1660–1900" *Oecumenica* (1971–72): 63, 66–67.

18. Bennett, "Patristic Tradition," 73. Burnet, *Exposition of the Thirty-Nine Articles,* 75–77. Robert D. Cornwall, "The Search for the Primitive Church: The Use of Early Church Fathers in the High Church Anglican Tradition, 1680–1745," *Anglican and Episcopal History* 59 (September 1990): 305–6. Eamon Duffy, "Primitive Christianity Revived; Religious Renewal in Augustan England," in *Studies in Church History,* Derek Baker, ed. (Oxford: Basil Blackwell, 1977), 298–99. Benjamin Hoadly, "The Nature of the Kingdom, or Church of Christ," in *The Works of Benjamin Hoadly, D.D.,* 3 vols. (London, 1773), 2:405.

19. Duffy, "Primitive Christianity Revived," 287. Cf. Bennett, "Patristic Tradition," 74–75.

20. Earbery, *Review of the Bishop of Bangor's Sermon,* 1:48. William Lowth, *Directions for the Profitable Reading of the Holy Scriptures,* 2nd ed. (London, 1712), 27–30. Lowth (1660–1732), who demonstrates high-church propensities, was a graduate of St. John's College, Oxford, held the livings of Buriton and Petersfield, Hampshire, and was the father of Bishop Robert Lowth. Cf. Bennett, "Patristic Tradition," 75–76; Duffy, "Pritimive Christianity Revived," 296–98.

21. John Henry Newman, *Apologia Pro Vita Sua* (New York: Longmans, Green and Co., 1947), 23. Cf. Robert Dudley Middleton, *Newman at Oxford: His Religious Development* (London: Oxford University Press, 1950), 107.

22. Jeremy Collier, trans., *A Panegyrick Upon the Maccabees, by St. Gregory of Nazianzen: Of Unseasonable Diversions, by Salvian: A Description of the Pagan World; A Consolary Discourse to the Christians of Carthage Visited by a Mortality; Of the Advantage of Patience; these three by St. Cyprian: Done into English by Jeremy Collier* (London, 1716). Nathaniel Marshall, ed. and trans., *The Genuine Works of St. Cyprian,* 2 Vols. (London, 1717). William Wake, ed. and trans., *An English Version of the Genuine Epistles of the Apostolic Fathers, With a Preliminary Discourse Concerning the Use of those Fathers* (London, 1693), Brett, *Collection of Liturgies.* Henry Dodwell, *Dissertationes Cyprianici* (Oxford, 1684); Henry Dodwell, *Dissertationes in Irenaeum* (Oxford, 1689). Cf. Cornwall, "Search for the Primitive Church," 315–20, 324.

23. Richard Bauckham, "Tradition in Relation to Scripture and Reason," in *Scripture, Tradition and Reason,* Richard Bauckham and Benjamin Drewery, eds. (Edinburgh: T. & T. Clark, Ltd., 1988), 122.

24. Bennett, "Patristic Tradition," 67–68.

25. Brett, *Tradition,* 1–3, 41–42, 146. John Johnson, "The Unbloody Sacrifice and Altar Unvailed and Supported," *The Theological Works of Rev. John Johnson, M.A.,* 4 vols. (Oxford: John Henry Parker, 1847), 1:31–32. Johnson (1662–1725), a High Churchman, graduated from Cambridge and served as vicar of Cranbrook, Kent. Lowth, *Directions for the Proper Reading of Scripture,* 28. Cf. [Henry Dodwell], *The Doctrine of the Church of England Concerning the Independency of the Clergy on the Lay Powers, To those Rights of Theirs which are Purely Spiritual, Reconciled with our Oath of Supremacy and the Lay-Deprivations of the Popish Bishops at the Beginning of the Reformation* (London, 1697), IV–V. Earbery, *Review of the Bishop of Bangor's Sermon,* 1:3. This was in line with traditional Anglicanism, including Thomas Cranmer and John Jewel, cf. Avis, *Anglicanism,* 41–42. Despite their preference for patristic studies, many high churchmen, including Jeremy Collier and William Wake, were proficient medieval

scholars; R. J. Smith, *The Gothic Bequest: Medieval Institutions in British Thought, 1688–1863* (Cambridge: Cambridge University Press, 1987), 11–42.

26. John Calvin, *Institutes of the Christian Religion,* 2 vols., John T. McNeil, ed., Ford Lewis Battles, trans. (Philadelphia: Westminster Press, 1960), 1:18–23. Johnson, "Unbloody Sacrifice," 1:31. Charles Leslie, "A Dissertation Concerning the Use and Authority of Ecclesiastical History," in *The Theological Works of the Rev. Mr. Charles Leslie,* 2 vols. (London, 1721), 1:728. Cf. Bauckham, "Tradition in Relation to Scripture," 124–25.

27. Lowth, *Directions for Reading,* 27.

28. [Jeremy Collier], *Reasons for Restoring Some Prayers and Directions as they Stand in the Communion Service of the First English Reform'd Liturgy, Compiled by the Bishops in the 2d and 3d Years of the Reign of King Edward VI,* 4th ed. (London, 1718), 32–33. Collier (1650–1726), a graduate of Cambridge, was rector of Ampton, Suffolk, and then Lecturer at Gray's Inn. He became a Non-Juror bishop in 1713. He became the primus of the Non-Juror bishops at the death of George Hickes in 1715. John Potter, *The Bishop of Oxford's Charge to the Clergy of His Dioceses at his Triennial Visitation in July 1719* (London, 1720), 27–28. Daniel Waterland, "A Vindication of Christ's Divinity: Being a Defence of Some Queries, Relating to Dr. Clarke's Scheme of the Holy Trinity, in Answer to a Clergyman in the Country," in *The Works of the Reverend Daniel Waterland, D.D.* (Oxford: Clarendon Press, 1823), 1.2:324–25. Waterland (1683–1740), a graduate of Magdalene College, Cambridge, was a moderate with High Church leanings. He served as Archdeacon of Middlesex from 1730 to 1740.

29. Brett, *Tradition,* 45, 49–50, 143. Francis Brokesby, *An History of the Government of the Primitive Church For the First Three Centuries and the Beginnings of the Fourth* (London, 1712), xxxiii. Brokesby (1637–1714), a graduate of Cambridge and biographer of Henry Dodwell, served as rector of Rowley, East Riding, Yorkshire before being deprived in 1690. Archibald Campbell, *The Doctrines of a Middle State Between Death and the Resurrection* (London, 1721), xi. Campbell (d. 1744), was the Scottish Non-Juror Bishop of Aberdeen from 1721–1724, when he resigned over the Usages controversy. He resided in London during this period, and after 1732 was the leader of the Usages party. Thomas Deacon, *Compleat Collection of Devotions Both Public and Private, Taken from the Apostolic Constitutions, the Ancient Liturgies, and the Common Prayer Book of the Church of England* (London, 1734), iv–v. Deacon (1697–1753) was a Non-Juror liturgist, scholar, and from 1734 bishop of the British Orthodox Church in Manchester. Hill, *Catholic Balance,* 15–16. John Hughes, "Preliminary Dissertations to St. Chrysostom's *De Sacerdotio,*" in George Hickes, *Two Treatises on the Christian Priesthood, and on the Dignity of the Episcopal Order,* 4th ed. (Oxford: John Henry Parker, 1847), 3:310–311. Hughes (d. ca. 1710) was a Fellow of Jesus College, Oxford, and a Non-Juror at his early death. Charles Leslie, "The True Notion of the Catholick Church, in Answer to the bishop of Meaux's Letter to Mr. Nelson: To Which is Prefixed the Letter itself," in *The Theological Works of the Reverend Mr. Charles Leslie,* 2 vols. (London, 1721), 1:581. [William Scott], *No Necessity to Alter the Common-Prayer; Or the Unreasonableness of the New Separation* (London, 1718), 13–14. Scot was a member of the Non-Usages party. Waterland, "Vindication of Christ's Divinity," 1.2:324–25. Cf. Bauckham, "Tradition in Relation to Scripture," 119. Cornwall, "In Search of the Primitive Church." 312–15.

30. Brett, *Tradition,* 65–66, 72, 82–83. Charles Leslie, "The True Notion of the

Catholic Church," in *The Theological Works of the Rev. Mr. Charles Leslie,* 2 vols. (London, 1721), 1:581.

31. Brett, *Tradition,* 134–35. Cf. Paul Langford, *A Polite and Commercial People, England 1727–1783* (Oxford: Clarendon Press, 1989), 242.

32. Brett, *Tradition,* 1–2. Hughes. "Preliminary Dissertations," 3:304–5.

33. Lowth, *Directions for Reading Scripture,* 28. Cf. Deacon, *Compleat Collection of Devotions,* 103–11.

34. Bauckham, "Tradition in Relation to Scripture," 119. Cragg, *Freedom and Authority,* 99, 145, 183.

35. Beveridge, "*Ecclesia Anglicana,*" 7:464–65. Brett, *Farther Proof,* 71. Brett, *Tradition,* 23–24. George Hickes, *The Case of Infant Baptism* (London, 1685), 39–40. 45. Law, "Three Letters to the Bishop of Bangor," 1:72–74.

36. Brokesby, *History of Government,* viii–ix.

37. Bauckham, "Tradition in Relation to Scripture," 118–19. Cf. Thomas Wagstaffe, the younger, who speaks of Scripture and Tradition as being "inseparable conveyances." [Thomas Wagstaffe], *The Necessity of an Alteration* (London, 1718), 152–53. Wagstaffe (1692–1770), the son of the Non-Juror bishop Dr. Thomas Wagstaffe, was ordained a Non-Juror priest in 1719, and served from 1738–70 in Rome as the Anglican chaplain to James III and Prince Charles Edward.

38. Brett, *Farther Proof,* 122. Cf. Reinhold Seeberg, *The History of Doctrines,* Charles Hay, trans. (Grand Rapids: Baker Book House, 1977), 2:431–32.

39. Brett, *Farther Proof,* 4–5, 7–15, 22–23. Brett, *Tradition,* 143. [Spinckes], *No Sufficient Reason For Restoring the Prayers,* 2–3. On the Usages Controversy see Henry Broxap, *The Later Non-jurors* (Cambridge: Cambridge University, 1924), 35–65.

40. Brett, *Farther Proof,* 6.

41. Brett, *Farther Proof,* 28–29. Cf. Bauckham, "Tradition in Relation to Scripture," 118–19.

42. Brett, *Tradition,* 118–20. Brett, *Farther Proof,* 43–44; [Wagstaffe], *Necessity of an Alteration,* 3. Cf. Broxap, *Later Non-Jurors,* 35–65. Cornwall, "Search for the Primitive Church," 310–11. See chapter 7 for a discussion of the liturgy and the eucharist.

43. Brett, *Tradition,* 27. Collier, *Reasons for Prayers,* 18–19.

44. Cragg, *Reason and Authority,* 93. Cragg, *Freedom and Authority,* 99, 121. Cragg, *Church and the Age of Reason,* 70–72. Charles J. Abbey and John H. Overton, *The English Church in the Eighteenth Century,* 2 vols. (London: Longmans, Green and Co. 1878), 1:284–86. Bennett, *Tory Crisis in Church and State,* 17. Redwood, *Reason, Ridicule, and Religion,* 12–13. Reedy, *Bible and Reason,* 37–39. Although he denies that Locke was a major political influence in the Glorious Revolution, Jonathan Clark asserts that Locke's major contribution to the early eighteenth century was the advocacy of Arianism. Cf. J.C.D. Clark, *English Society 1688–1832* (Cambridge: Cambridge University Press, 1985), 45–50.

45. John Sharp, "Sermon I: Faith and Reason Reconciled," *The Theological Works of the Most Reverend John Sharp, D.D.,* 5 vols. (Oxford: Oxford University Press, 1829), 5:1–18. Cragg, *Reason and Authority,* 20–21. Sharp (1645–1714), a graduate of Cambridge, served as Dean of Canterbury, prior to being consecrated as Archbishop of York. In this position, he helped advise the high-church-leaning Queen Anne. John Hunt, *Religious Thought in England,* 3 vols. (London: Strahan and Co., 1871), 2:114.

46. Charles Leslie, "The Truth of Christianity Demonstrated: With a Disserta-

tion Concerning Private Judgement and Authority," in *The Theological Works of the Reverend Mr. Charles Leslie*, 2 vols. (London 1721), 1:189.

47. Daniel Waterland, "A Review of the Doctrine of the Eucharist As Laid Down in Scripture and Antiquity," in *The Works of the Reverend Daniel Waterland* (Oxford: Clarendon Press, 1823), 7:6, 438–39.

48. Nelson, *Companion to the Festivals*, 282–83. Cf. Charles Leslie, "The Socinian Controversy Discuss'd in Six Dialogues: Wherein the Chief Socinian Tracts publish'd of Late Years, are Considered," in *The Theological Works of the Reverend Mr. Charles Leslie*, 2 vols. (London, 1721), 1:223. Lowth, *Principles for Reading Scripture*, 107. Sharp, "Sermon I," 5:10–11.

49. Nelson, *Companion to the Festivals*, 283. Leslie, "Socinian Controversy," 1:223.

50. George Smalridge, "Sermon XXXIII: The Use of Reason in Religion," *Sixty Sermons Preached on Several Occasions*, 2nd ed. (London, 1727), 342. Smalridge (1663–1719), a High Churchman, graduated from Christ Church, Oxford. He served as deputy Regius Professor of Divinity before being consecrated as Bishop of Bristol.

51. Henry Stebbing, *A Rational Enquiry into the Proper Methods of Supporting Christianity, So Far As it Concerns the Governors of the Church* (London, 1720), 34–35. Smalridge, "Sermon 33," 343–45.

52. Smalridge, "Sermon 33," 344.

53. Leslie, "Socinian Controversy," 1:223. Lowth, *Directions for Reading Scripture*, 112–113. Stackhouse, *Compleat Body of Divinity*, 19.

54. Lowth, *Directions for Reading Scripture*, 109. Law, "Case of Reason," 2:67.

55. Law, "Case of Reason," 2:116. Cf. Cragg, *Reason and Authority*, 96–98.

56. Cragg, *Reason and Authority*, 93–98. Leslie, "Socinian Controversy," 1:247. Leslie, "Truth of Christianity," 1:136. Lowth, *Directions for Reading Scripture*, 109–12.

## CHAPTER 3. THE NATURE OF THE CHURCH

1. George Every, *The High Church Party, 1688–1718* (London: S.P.C.K., 1956), xiv. Geoffrey Holmes, *The Trial of Doctor Sacheverell* (London: Eyre Methuen, Ltd., 1973), 45, 64–67. J. P. Kenyon, *Revolution Principles: The Politics of Party 1689–1720* (Cambridge: Cambridge University Press, 1990), 83–101. W. A. Speck, *Stability and Strife: England 1714–60* (Cambridge: Harvard University Press, 1977), 91.

2. H. F. Woodhouse, *The Doctrine of the Church in Anglican Theology 1547–1603* (London: S.P.C.K., 1954), 1–2. John Rogers (1679–1720), a graduate of Corpus Christi College, Oxford, served as Subdeacon of Wells and Chaplain to George, Prince of Wales.

3. See chapter 1 for a discussion of competing ecclesiologies of the period. The relationship of church and state will be developed in full in chapter 4; on those issues see: G. V. Bennett, "Conflict in the Church," in *Britain After the Glorious Revolution*, Geoffrey Holmes, ed. (New York: St. Martin's Press, 1969), 155–75. G. V. Bennett, "The Convocation of 1710: An Anglican Attempt at Counter-revolution," in *Studies in Church History: Councils and Assemblies*, G. J. Cuming and Derek Baker, ed. (Leiden: E.J. Brill, 1971), 7:311–19. G. V. Bennett, *The Tory Crisis in Church and State 1689–1730* (Oxford: Clarendon Press, 1975). G. V. Bennett, "King William III and the Episcopate," in *Essays in Modern English Church History*, G. V. Bennett and J. D. Walsh, eds. (New York: Oxford University Press, 1966), 104–31. Mark Goldie, "The Nonjurors, Episco-

pacy and the Origins of the Convocation Controversy," in *Ideology and Conspiracy: Aspects of Jacobitism 1688–1759*, Eveline Cruickshanks, ed. (Edinburgh: John Donald, 1982), 15–35. Gerald M. Straka, *The Anglican Reaction to the Revolution of 1688* (Madison: University of Wisconsin Press, 1962). Gerald M. Straka, "The Final Phase of Divine Right Theory in England, 1688–1702," *English Historical Review* 77 (October 1962): 638–58. Norman Sykes, *Church and State in the XVIIIth Century* (Cambridge: Cambridge University Press; reprint, Hampdon, CT: Archon Books, 1962). Norman Sykes, *From Sheldon to Secker: Aspects of English Church History 1660–1769* (Cambridge: Cambridge University Press, 1959). Norman Sykes, *William Wake, Archbishop of Canterbury*, 2 vols. (Cambridge: Cambridge University Press, 1957).

4. The independence of the church is discussed in depth in chapter 4.

5. John Potter, *The Bishop of Oxford's Charge to the Clergy of His Diocese at His Triennial Visitation in July 1719* (London, 1720), 8–9.

6. Benjamin Hoadly, "The Nature of the Kingdom, or Church of Christ," in *The Works of Benjamin Hoadly, D.D.*, 3 vols. (London, 1773), 2:404. Benjamin Hoadly, "An Answer to the Representation Drawn up by the Committee of the Lower House of Convocation," in *The Works of Benjamin Hoadly, D.D.*, 2:459, 477. William Law, "The Letters to the Bishop of Bangor," in *The Works of the Reverend William Law, M.A.*, 9 vols. (London, 1762; reprinted, Setley: G. Moreton, 1892), 1:92–93. Joseph Trapp, *The Real Nature of the Church or the Kingdom of Christ*, 2nd ed. (London, 1717), 3–4. Trapp (1679–1747), a graduate of Wadham College, Oxford and president of Sion College, Oxford, was a High Church opponent of Hoadly. For a discussion of Hoadly's ecclesiology, see chapter 1 on the Bangorian Controversy.

7. William Beveridge, "*Ecclesia Anglicana, Ecclesia Catholica;* or the Doctrine of the Church of England Consonant to Scripture, Reason, and Fathers in a Discourse upon the Thirty-nine Articles Agreed upon in the Convocation held at London MDLXII," 2nd rev. ed., in *The Theological Works of William Beveridge, D.D.*, 12 vols. (Oxford: John Henry Parker), 7:357–58. Gilbert Burnet, *An Exposition of the Thirty-nine Articles of the Church of England*, (London, 1699), 180–83. Cf. Pedro Thomas Meza, "Gilbert Burnet's Concept of Religious Toleration," *Historical Magazine of the Protestant Episcopal Church* 50 (September 1981): 227–28.

8. Thomas Brett, *The Independency of the Church Upon the State as to its Pure Spiritual Powers* (London, 1717), 54. John Hughes, "Preliminary Dissertations to St. Chrysostom's *De Sacredotio*," in George Hickes, *Two Treatises on the Christian Priesthood, and on the Dignity of the Episcopal Order*, 4th ed., 3 vols. (Oxford: John Henry Parker, 1847), 3:293–94.

9. Paul D. Avis, *The Church in the Theology of the Reformers* (Atlanta: John Knox Press, 1981), 1–9. Richard Hooker, *Of The Laws of Ecclesiastical Polity*, Georges Edelen, ed., 3 vols. (Cambridge: Belknap Press of Harvard University Press, 1977), 1:194–98. Robert Faulkner, *Richard Hooker and the Politics of a Christian England* (Berkeley: University of California Press, 1981), 119. W. D. J. Cargill Thompson, "The Philosopher of the 'Politic Society': Richard Hooker as a Political Thinker," in *Studies in Richard Hooker*, W. Speed Hill, ed. (Cleveland: The Press of Case Western Reserve University, 1972), 53–54. Woodhouse, *Doctrine of the Church*, 43–46.

10. John Potter, *A Discourse on Church Government: wherein the Rights of the Church and the Supremacy of Christian Bishops are Vindicated and Adjusted*, 5th ed. (London: Samuel Bagster, 1839), 21.

11. Law, "Three Letters to the Bishop of Bangor," 1:90, 92, 101–2. Henry Stebbing, "A Defence of the First Head of the Report of the Committee of the Lower House of Convocation," in *Polemical Tracts; or a Collection of Papers Written in Defence of the Doctrines and Discipline of the Church of England* (Cambridge: Cambridge University Press, 1727), 58–59, 62. Trapp, *Real Nature of the Church*, 4, 8.

12. Charles Leslie, "The Case of the Regale and the Pontificate, Restated," in *The Theological Works of the Rev. Mr. Charles Leslie* (London, 1721), 1:671. Trapp, *Real Nature of the Church*, 3.

13. Samuel Hill, *The Catholic Balance: Or a Discourse Determining the Controversies Concerning I. Tradition of Catholic Doctrines. II. The Primacy of S. Peter and the Bishop of Rome. III. The Subjection and Authority of the Church in a Christian State: According to the Suffrages of the Primest Antiquity* (London, 1687), 134–35. John Kettlewell, "The Practical Believer: Or the Articles of the Apostles Creed, Drawn out from a True Christian's Heart and Practice, In Two Parts" (London, 1718). *A Compleat Collection of the Works of the Reverend and Learned John Kettlewell, B.D.*, 2 vols. (London, 1719), 1:680. Kettlewell (1653–95), a Non-Juror, was a graduate of St. Edmund Hall, Oxford and vicar of Coleshill, Warwickshire, prior to being deprived in 1690. Law, "Three Letters to the Bishop of Bangor," 1:106. Potter, *Discourse on Church Government*, 9, 21–22. Stebbing, "Defence of the Report to Convocation," 58–59.

14. Paul D. Avis, *The Church in the Theology of the Reformers* (Atlanta: John Knox Press, 1981), 29–30. H. F. Woodhouse, "Sixteenth-Century Anglican Theology," in *A History of Christian Doctrine*, Hubert Cunliffe-Jones and Benjamin Drewery, eds. (Philadelphia: Fortress Press, 1980), 418–19.

15. Beveridge, *"Ecclesia Anglicana,"* 1:362–63. William Beveridge, "Sermon IV: Salvation in the Church Only, Under such a Ministry," in *The Theological Works of William Beveridge, D.D.*, 12 vols. (Oxford: John Henry Parker, 1842), 1:65. Hughes, "Preliminary Dissertations," 3:295. Kettlewell, "Practical Believer," 1:664. John Potter, "A Charge Delivered to the Clergy of the Diocese of Oxford, in July 1725," in *The Theological Works of the Most Reverend Dr. John Potter, Late Archbishop of Canterbury*, 3 vols. (Oxford, 1753), 1:406–8, 413–14. John Sharp, "Sermon VI: A Sermon on I Corinthians XII.13," in *The Theological Works of the Most Reverend John Sharp, D.D.*, 5 vols. (Oxford: Oxford University Press, 1829), 5:100. See chapters 5 and 6 for further discussions of the relationship of preaching and the sacraments to the church.

16. Cyprian, "Letter 33: The Problem of the Lapsed," in *Early Latin Theology*, Library of Christian Classics: Ichthus Edition, S.L. Greenslade, ed. (Philadelphia: Westminster Press, 1956), 145. Cf. Burnet, *Exposition of the Thirty-nine Articles*, 180. John Findon has also taken note of the Cyprianic view of the church that pervaded High Church and Non-Juror ecclesiology; John Findon, "The Nonjurors and the Church of England, 1689–1716" (D.Phil. Diss., Oxford University, 1978), 174. Cf. Beveridge, *"Ecclesia Anglicana,"* 7:363. Beveridge, "Sermon IV," 1:67–68. Thomas Brett, *The Divine Right of Episcopacy, and the Necessity of an Episcopal Commission for Preaching God's Word, and For the Valid Ministration of the Christian Sacraments, Proved from the Scriptures, and the Doctrine and Practice of the Primitive Church* (London, 1718), 56–58, 83. Potter, "Charge to the Clergy in 1725," 1:406–8. Potter, *Discourse on Church Government*, 210.

17. William Beveridge, "Sermon XI: Ministers of the Gospel, Christ's Ambassadors," in *The Theological Works of William Beveridge, D.D.*, 12 vols. (Oxford: John Henry Parker, 1842), 1:200.

18. See chapter 5 for a discussion of ministry and the episcopate.

19. Joseph Betty, *The Divine Institution of the Ministry and the Absolute Necessity of Church Government: A Sermon Preached before the University of Oxford on Sunday the 21st of September, 1729*, 2nd ed. (London, 1729), 10–22, 34–35. George Hickes, *Two Treatises, of the Christian Priesthood, and on the Dignity of the Episcopal Order*, 4th ed., 3 vols. (Oxford: John Henry Parker, 1847), 1:67. Cf. Every, *High Church Party*, 4–7, 17, 115–116. Every notes that Anglicans such as Thomas Tenison, Archbishop of Canterbury, saw episcopacy as convenient but not necessary. This contrasts markedly with high-church doctrine. Findon, "Non-Jurors and the Church of England," 171–74, 182. Woodhouse, *Doctrine of the Church*, 71–73, 93.

20. William Beveridge, "Sermon CII: The Exemplary Holiness of the Primitive Christians," in *The Theological Works of William Beveridge*, 12 vols. (Oxford: John Henry Parker, 1844), 4:444. Thomas Brett, *Tradition Necessary to Explain and Interpret the Holy Scriptures* (London, 1718), 66. [Henry Dodwell], *The Doctrine of the Church of England Concerning the Independency of the Clergy on the Lay Powers, to those Rights of theirs which are Purely Spiritual, Reconciled with our Oath of Supremacy and the Lay Deprivations of the Popish Bishops at the Beginning of the Reformation* (London, 1697), IV–V. Hill, *Catholic Balance*, 15–16. Kettlewell, "Practical Believer," 1:679. John Sharp, "Sermon V: A Sermon on I Corinthians XII.13," in *The Theological Works of the Most Reverend John Sharp*, 5 vols. (Oxford: Oxford University Press 1829), 5:89. See chapter 2 for a full discussion of the authority of tradition.

21. [Dodwell], *Doctrine of the Church of England*, VI.

22. William Beveridge, "Sermon II: The Institution of Ministers," in *The Theological Works of William Beveridge, D.D.*, 12 vols. (Oxford: John Henry Parker, 1842), 1:42–43. William Beveridge, "Sermon IX: The Preparatory Duties for Holy Orders," in *The Theological Works of William Beveridge, D.D.*, 12 vols. (Oxford: John Henry Parker, 1847), 1:159. John Kettlewell, "Of Christian Communion, to be Kept on in the Unity of Christ's Church, and among the Professors of Truth and Holiness," in *A Compleat Collection of the Works of the Reverend and Learned John Kettlewell, B.D.*, 2 vols. (London, 1719), 2:570–71. Kettlewell, "Practical Believer," 1:679.

23. William Beveridge, "Sermon VII: Christ's Church Established on a Rock," in *The Theological Works of William Beveridge, D.D.*, 12 vols. (Oxford: John Henry Parker, 1842), 1:130–31, 174. Thomas Brett, *The Extent of Christ's Commission to Baptize: A Sermon Shewing the capacity of Infants to receive and the utter incapacity of our Dissenting Teachers to Administer Christian Baptism* (London, 1712), 22. Potter, "Charge Delivered to the Clergy in 1725," 1:441.

24. Law, "Three Letters to the Bishop of Bangor," 1:7–8, 73. Cf. Benjamin Hoadly, *An Answer to the Rev. Dr. Snape's Letter to the Bishop of Bangor*, 10th ed. (London, 1717), 22–23. Benjamin Hoadly, *A Preservative Against the Principles and Practices of the Non-Jurors Both in Church and State*, 2nd ed. (London, 1716), 78–88. Andrew Snape, *A Letter to the Bishop of Bangor* (Dublin, 1717), 10.

25. Beveridge, "*Ecclesia Anglicana*," 7:359. Thomas Brett, *An Account of Church Government and Governours*, 2nd ed. (London, 1710), 4–5. George Bull, *A Vindication of the Church of England From the Errors and Corruptions of the Church of England* (London, 1719, reprint, Oxford: John Henry Parker, 1840), 155–56. Bull (1634–1710), educated at Exeter College, Oxford, was rector of Suddington and Archdeacon of Llandaff before his consecration as Bishop of St.

David's in 1705. Hill, *Catholic Balance* 44–45. Ken, *Church Catechism,* 26–27. Kettlewell, "Practical Believer," 1:665. Potter, *Discourse on Church Government,* 23–24. Stebbing, "Defence of the Report," 62. Wake, *Principles of the Christian Religion,* 63. Cf. Haro Hopfl, *The Christian Polity of John Calvin* (Cambridge: Cambridge University Press, 1982), 84–85.

26. William Sherlock, *A Vindication of the Rights of Ecclesiastical Authority: Being an Answer to the First Part of the Protestant Reconciler* (London, 1685), 426.

27. Brett, *Account of Church Government,* 7. Hickes, *Two Treatises,* 1:295–97. Kettlewell, "Practical Believer," 665–66.

28. Beveridge, "Sermon VII," 1:132, 135–36. Bull, *Vindication of the Church of England,* 156–58. Thomas Wilson, *The Principles and Duties of Christianity* (1707; reprinted, Menston, Yorkshire: The Scholar Press, 1972), 53. Wilson (1663–1755), a High Churchman, educated at Trinity College, Dublin, was deeply revered by the members of his diocese of Sodor and Man, which he served for fifty-seven years, turning down several offers of preferment.

29. Henry Broxap, *The Later Non-Jurors* (Cambridge: Cambridge University Press, 1924), 30–34. Henry R. Sefton, "The Scottish Bishops and Archbishop Arsenius," in *Studies in Church History,* Derek Baker, ed. (Oxford: Basil Blackwell, 1976), 239–46. Steve Runciman, "The British Non-Jurors and the Russian Church," in *The Ecumenical World of Orthodox Civilization: Russia and Orthodoxy,* Andrew Blane and Thomas E. Bird, eds. (The Hague: Mouton and Co., N.V. Publishers, 1974), 155–61. John Spurr, "The Church of England, Comprehension and the Toleration Act of 1689," *English Historical Review* 104 (October 1989); 927–46. Sykes, *William Wake,* 1:252–314, 2:178–80.

30. Hickes, *Two Treatises,* 1:297. Sherlock, *Vindication of the Rights of Ecclesiastical Authority,* 412.

31. [Henry Dodwel], *A Defense of the Vindication of the Deprived Bishops* (London, 1695), 19. Cf. Hickes, *Two Treatises,* 2:325–26. Kettlewell, "Christian Communion," 2:468, 568. Kettlewell, "Practical Believer," 1:679.

32. Brett, *Account of Church Government,* 6–7. Cf. Beveridge, "*Ecclesia Anglicana,*" 7:359. Bull, Vindication of the Church of England, 162. Hill, *Catholic Balance,* 45. On Cyprian see G. W. H. Lampe, "Christian Theology in the Patristic Period," in *A History of Christian Doctrine,* Hubert Cunliffe-Jones and Benjamin Drewery, eds. (Philadelphia: Fortress Press, 1980), 172–73.

33. [Dodwell], *Doctrine of the Church of England,* V. Hughes, "Preliminary Dissertations," 3:311–12. Kettlewell, "Practical Believer," 1:669, 678. Cf. Findon, "Non-Jurors and the Church of England, 170–72. John Spurr, "Schism and the Restoration Church," *Journal of Ecclesiastical History* 41 (July 1990): 408–24.

34. Potter, *Discourse on Church Government,* 3–4, 6–7. Sharp, "Sermon V," 5:78–79, 86. Henry Stebbing, *A Rational Enquiry into the Proper Methods of Supporting Christianity, So Far as it Concerns the Governors of the Church* (London, 1720), 57–58. Wake, *Principles of the Christian Religion,* 62–63.

35. Henry Sacheverell, *The Rights of the Church of England Asserted and Prov'd: In an Answer to a late pamphlet, intitl'd, The Rights of the Protestant Dissenters, in a Review of their Case,* 2 parts (London, 1705), 2:60. Cf. Frank Dillistone, "The Anti-Donatist Writings," in *A Companion to the Study of St. Augustine,* Roy Battenhouse, ed. (New York: Oxford University Press, 1955), 186.

36. [Thomas Ken], *An Exposition of the Church-Catechism, or the Practice of Divine Love, Revised* (London, 1696), 26. Ken (1637–1711), an Oxford graduate, was chaplain to Princess Mary and then to Charles II before his consecration as

Bishop of Bath and Wells in 1684. He was deprived in 1690, but in 1710 he relinquished his claim to his see and returned to the established church with Henry Dodwell and Robert Nelson.

37. Beveridge, "Sermon IX," 1:158. Wake, *Principles of the Christian Religion,* 65.

38. Nathaniel Marshall, *The Penitential Discipline of the Primitive Church, for the First Four Hundred Years After Christ; Together with its Declension from the Fifth Century, Downwards to its Present State: Impartially Represented* (Oxford: John Henry Parker, 1844), 2. Marshall (d. 1730), was both a High Churchman and an ardent defender of the established church. Educated at Emmanuel College, Oxford, he received his Doctor of Divinity degree from Cambridge in 1717. He served as curate of Kentish Town, rector of the united parishes of St. Veast, Foster Lane, and St. Michael-le-Querne, London, and as Canon of Windsor.

39. Beveridge, *"Ecclesia Angicana,"* 7:364–65. John Sharp, "Sermon III: A Sermon on I Peter ii.15,: in *The Theological Works of the Most Reverend John Sharp,* 5 vols. (Oxford: Oxford University Press, 1829), 5:40, 46–47.

40. Marshall, *Penitential Discipline,* x.

41. [Francis Atterbury and Benjamin Shower], *Letter to a Convocation Man* (London, 1697), 2–3. Hickes, *Two Treatises,* 1:301. Thomas Wilson, "Sermon LXXXIX: Reciprocal Obligations of Christian Ministers and Their People," in *The Works of the Right Reverend Father in God, Thomas Wilson, D.D.,* 7 vols. (Oxford: John Henry Parker, 1847), 3:427–28. Cf. Eamon Duffy, "Primitive Christianity Revived; Religious Renewal in Augustan England," in *Studies in Church History,* Derek Baker, ed. (Oxford: Basil Blackwell, 1977), 292–98. Holmes, *Trial of Doctor Sacheverell,* 34. Tina Isaacs, "The Anglican Hierarchy and the Reformation of Manners 1688–409. Kenyon, *Revolution Principles,* 87.

42. Beveridge, "Sermon VI," 1:64. Gilbert Burnet distinguished between things necessary for salvation, faith, and repentance, and those things required to preserve order in the body of Christ. The institutional church and its ministry, for him, were not necessary for salvation, rather they were *adiaphora*. Burnet, *Exposition of the Thirty-nine Articles,* 258. Cf. Findon, "Non-Jurors and the Church of England," 174.

43. Potter, *Discourse on Church Government,* 10–11.

44. Beveridge, "Sermon IV," 1:62–63. Law, "Three Letters to the Bishop of Bangor," 1:175. Cf. Hoadly, *Preservative against the Non-Jurors,* 89–91. Sykes, *Authority of the Clergy,* 70–71.

45. Chapters 5 and 6 describe in detail the High Church and Non-Juror doctrines of the ministry and the sacraments. It is important to stress that for these two movements, not only doctrine but the visible practices of the church were deemed essential to salvation.

46. Kettlewell, "Practical Believer," 1:664. Cf. Beveridge, "Sermon IV," 1:65, 83. Francis Brokesby, *An History of the Government of the Primitive Church for the First Three Centuries and the Beginning of the Fourth* (London, 1712), xxxvi–xxxvii. Hickes, *Constitution of the Church,* 173–81. Potter, *Discourse on Church Government,* 10–11, 14–15. The sacraments and their relationship to the church and to salvation will be discussed in more depth in chapter 6.

## CHAPTER 4. THE INDEPENDENCE OF THE CHURCH FROM THE STATE

1. J. H. Overton, *The Non-Jurors: Their Lives, Principles and Writings* (New York: Thomas Whittaker, 1903), 6–7. Gordon Rupp, *Religion in England 1688–1791* (Oxford: Clarendon Press, 1986), 6–28.

2. John Findon, "The Non-Jurors and the Church of England 1689–1716," (D.Phil. Diss., Oxford University, 1978), 3. Norman Sykes, *Church and State in England in the XVIIIth Century* (Cambridge: Cambridge University Press, 1934; reprinted, New York: Archon Books, 1962), 286. Cf. L. M. Hawkins, *Allegiance in Church and State* (London: George Routledge & Sons, Ltd., 1928), 47–55, 124–26. Margaret Jacob, *The Newtonians and the English Revolution 1689–1720* (Ithaca: Cornell University Press, 1976), 27–71. Guy Martin Yould, "The Origins and Transformation of the Non-Juror Schism, 1670–1715" (Ph.D. Diss., University of Hull, 1979), 208, 306.

3. Mark Goldie, "The Nonjurors, Episcopacy, and the Origins of the Convocation Controversy," *Ideology and Conspiracy: Aspects of Jacobitism 1689–1759,* Eveline Cruickshanks, ed. (Edinburgh: John Donald, 1982), 18, 20. Gerald Straka has also taken note of the religious dimension of the Anglican response to the Revolution. His interest, however, is with the adaptations made to divine right theory. Gerald M. Straka, *Anglican Reaction to the Revolution of 1688* (Madison: University of Wisconsin Press, 1962), 7, 15–17, 38–46. Gerard M. Straka, "The Final Phase of Divine Right Theory in England, 1688–1702," *English Historical Review* 77 (October 1962): 638–58.

4. On the political theology of the English Reformers and of Richard Hooker, see: J. W. Allen, *History of Political Thought in the Sixteenth Century* (London: Methuen and Co., Ltd., 1928), 196. Robert Faulkner, *Richard Hooker and the Politics of a Christian England* (Berkeley: University of California Press, 1981), 145–66. John S. Marshall, "Hooker's Theory of Church and State," *Anglican Theological Review* 27 (1945): 151–60. Leo Stoll, *Church and State in Early Modern England, 1509–1640* (New York: Oxford University Press, 1990), 173, 204–5. W. D. J. Cargill Thompson, "The Philosopher of the 'Politic Society', Richard Hooker as a Political Thinker," in *Studies in Richard Hooker* (Cleveland: Case Western Reserve University Press, 1972), 58–60. H. F. Woodhouse, *The Doctrine of the Church in Anglican Theology, 1547–1603* (London: S.P.C.K., 1954), 132.

5. Cecilia M. Ady, "The Post-Reformation Episcopate (ii) From the Restoration to the Present Day," in *The Apostolic Ministry,* 2nd ed., Kenneth E. Kirk, ed. (London: Hodder and Stoughten Ltd., 1957), 439. G. V. Bennett, *The Tory Crisis in Church and State 1688–1730* (Oxford: Oxford University Press, 1975), 9–10. J. C. D. Clark, *English Society 1688–1832* (Cambridge: Cambridge University Press, 1985), 125–26. Howard Erskine-Hill, "Literature and the Jacobite Cause: Was there a Rhetoric of Jacobitism?" in *Ideology and Conspiracy: Aspects of Jacobitism, 1689–1759,* Eveline Cruickshanks, ed. (Edinburgh: John Donald Publishers, Ltd., 1982), 50. George Every, *The High Church Party, 1688–1718* (London: S.P.C.K., 1956), 61–74. Christopher Hill, *The Century of Revolution 1603–1714,* 2nd ed. (New York: W. W. Norton and Company, 1980), 216. J. R. Jones, *The Revolution of 1688 in England* (New York: W. W. Norton and Company, 1972), 122–25, 127, 313. Paul Kleber Monod, *Jacobitism and the English People 1688–1788* (Cambridge: Cambridge University Press, 1989) 17–19. Straka, *Anglican Reaction to the Revolution of 1688,* 25–36, 38–46. Straka, "The Final Phase of Divine Right Theory," 638–58. Daniel Szechi, *Jacobitism and Tory Politics 1710–1714* (Edinburgh: John Donald Pubishers, Ltd., 1984), 42–43. Yould, "Origins of the Non-Juror Schism," 114–15.

6. Simon Lowth (1630–1720), a Non-Juror and a Cambridge graduate, served as rector of St. Michael, Harbledown and vicar of St. Kosius and Damian on the Bleen, before being deprived in 1690.

7. Findon, "Non-Jurors and the Church of England," 158–59, 170–72. John Kettlewell, *The Measures of Christian Obedience* (London, 1681), 135–36. Simon

Lowth, *Of the Subject of Church Power, In Whom it Resides* (London, 1685), 6, 162–63. Findon joins Harold Laski and Norman Sykes in attributing the Non-Juror separation primarily to political causes. Paul Monod has noted that earlier church historians, such as J. H. Overton, denied that the Non-Jurors had any interests in politics. Monod states, truthfully, that while not all Non-Jurors were Jacobite agents, simply the refusal of the oaths was considered a "strong political statement." Thus, it is important to take a balanced position, recognizing both the political and the theological aspects of the movement. Cf. Hawkins, *Allegiance in Church and State,* 124–26. Harold J. Laski, *Political Thought in England From Locke to Bentham* (New York: Henry Holt and Company, 1920; reprint, Westport, CT: Greenwood Press, 1973), 82–83. John Marshall, "The Ecclesiology of the Latitude-men 1660–1689: Stillingfleet, Tillotson and 'Hobbism'," *Journal of Ecclesiastical History* 36 (July 1985): 408. Monod, *Jacobitism and the English People,* 138–39. Sykes, *Church and State in England,* 286–87.

8. Goldie, "Origins of the Convocation Controversy," 18–19. Cf. Thomas Brett, *An Account of Church-Government and Governours,* 2nd ed. (London, 1710), 14–16, [note: this document predates Brett's conversion to the Non-Juror movement]. Thomas Brett, *The Independency of the Church Upon the State as to its Pure Spiritual Powers* (London, 1717), 10–12, 38–41. [Jeremy Collier], *Brief Essay Concerning the Independency of Church Power* (London, 1692), 2–7, 11–12. George Hickes, *The Constitution of the Catholic Church, and the Nature and Consequences of Schism* (London, 1716), 118–20. John Hughes, "Preliminary Dissertation to St. Chrysostom's *De Sacerdotio,"* in George Hickes, *Two Treatises on the Christian Priesthood, and on the Dignity of the Episcopal Order,* 4th ed., 3 vols. (Oxford: John Henry Parker, 1847), 3:363–65. [Charles Leslie], *The Case of the Regale and the Pontificate stated, in the Relation of a Conference concerning the Independency of the Church, as to her purely Spiritual Power and Authority,* (London, 1700), 14. Cf. Overton, *Nonjurors,* 6–7. Straka, *Anglican Reaction to the Revolution,* 44.

9. Straka, *Anglican Reaction to the Revolution,* 56. Straka, "Final Phase of Divine Right Theory," 646–47. J. P. Kenyon, *Revolution Principles: The Politics of Party 1689–1720* (Cambridge: Cambridge University Press, 1990), 26–29.

10. John Potter, *A Discourse on Church Government: Wherein the Rights of the Church and the Supremacy of Christian Bishops are Vindicated and Adjusted,* 5th ed. (London: Samuel Bagster, 1839), 17–20. Edmund Gibson, *Codex Juris Ecclesiastici Anglicani,* 2 vols. (London, 1713), 1:xvii–xviii, xxix. William Beveridge, *"Ecclesia Anglicana Ecclesia Catholica;* or the Doctrine of the Church of England Consonant to Scripture Reason, and Fathers: in a Discourse upon the Thirty-nine Articles Agreed upon in the Convocation Held at London MDLXII," in *The Theological Works of William Beveridge, D.D.,* 12 vols. (Oxford: John Henry Parker, 1845), 7:556–57. A contrasting view of the complete separation of church and state from the Dissenting side is provided by Daniel Defoe in his *Christianity No Creature of the State: or, if it be made One, Reasons why it should be Abolished* (London, 1717). Cf. Ady, "Post-Reformation Episcopate," 443. Every, *High Church Party,* 156–58. Paul Langford, "Convocation and the Tory Clergy, 1717–61," in *The Jacobite Challenge,* Eveline Cruickshanks and Jeremy Black, eds. (Edinburgh: John Donald Publishers, Ltd., 1988), 111. Pedro Thomas Meza, "The Question of Authority in the Church of England, 1689–1717," *Historical Magazine of the Protestant Episcopal Church* 42 (March, 1973): 77–80.

11. William Warburton, *Alliance Between Church and State* (London, 1736),

55, 68–69. R. W. Greaves, "The Working of the Alliance, A Comment on Warburton," in *Essays in Modern Church History*, G. V. Bennett and J. D. Walsh, eds.
(London: A. and C. Black Ltd., 1966), 163–64. Sykes, *Church and State in England*, 316–24.

12. [Atterbury and Shower], *Letter to a Convocation-man*, 17–19. Francis Atterbury, *The Rights, Powers, and Privileges of an English Convocation*, 2nd ed.
(London, 1701), 128–30. Henry Sacheverell, *Political Union* (London, 1710), 6–
7, 20. The tract *The Mitre and the Crown, or a Real Distinction between them*,
(London, 1711), which has been attributed to Atterbury, takes a firm position in
favor of an independent church. Mark Goldie sees this as evidence of Atterbury's
belief in the "two societies" doctrine. G. V. Bennett, however, states that the
Non-Juror flavor of the tract is sufficient proof against Atterbury's authorship,
since Atterbury's program was to reform the church in partnership with the state.
Bennett, *Tory Crisis in Church and State*, 152. Goldie, "Origins of the Convocation Controversy," 19. Cf. Hawkins, *Allegiance in Church and State*, 169. Geoffrey Holmes, *Trial of Doctor Sacheverell* (London: Eyre Methuen, Ltd., 1973),
33, 42–43.

13. Monod, *Jacobitism and the English People*, 144–45.

14. Brett, *Independency of the Church*, 11–12. [Henry Dodwell], *A Defense of
the Vindication of the Deprived Bishops* (London, 1695), 13. [Henry Dodwell],
*Vindication of the deprived Bishops* (London, 1692), 17, 30, 75–76. Hickes, *Constitution of the Catholic Church*, 103–10.

15. Brett, *Independency of the Church*, 38. [Collier], *Brief Essay*, 3. [Dodwell],
*Defense of the Deprived Bishops*, 85–87. [Leslie], *Case of the Regale*, 14–15.
George Hickes, *Two Treatises on the Christian Priesthood, and on the Dignity
of the Episcopal Order*, 4th ed., 3 vols. (Oxford: John Henry Parker, 1847), 1:249–
250, 294–95. Lowth, *Subject of Church Power*, 65–66. [Matthew Tindal], *The
Rights of the Christian Church Asserted, against the Romish, and all other Priests
who claim an Independent Power over it*, 3rd ed. (London, 1707), 29, 35.

16. [Collier], *Brief Essay*, 11–12. Hickes, *Two Treatises*, 1:192, 249–50;
2:381–82.

17. Hickes, *Two Treatises*, 1:190. [Dodwell], *Defence of the Deprived Bishops*,
82–86. Hughes, "Preliminary Dissertations," 3:292, 314–15, 356. Cf. George H.
Tavard, *The Quest for Catholicity: A Study in Anglicanism* (New York: Herder
and Herder, 1964), 84–85. Warburton, *Alliance in Church and State*, 48–49, 53.

18. Brett, *Account of Church Government*, 16–18. Brett, *Independency of the
Church*, 9–10. [Dodwell], *Vindication of the Deprived Bishops*, 27–30. Matthias
Earbery, *A Historical Essay Upon the Power of the Prince in Calling, Proroguing
and Dissolving Councils, Synods and Convocations* (London, 1717), 29–30.
Hickes, *Two Treatises*, 1:192–93. Hughes, "Preliminary Dissertations," 3:363–65.
John Kettlewell, "The Duty of Allegiance," in *The Compleat Collection of the
Works of the Reverend and Learned John Kettlewell, B.D.*, 2 vols. (London, 1719),
2:259. John Kettlewell, "Of Christian Communion to be Kept in the Unity of
Christ's Church, and among the Professors of Truth and Holiness," in *The Com-
pleat Collection of the Works of the Reverend and Learned John Kettlewell, B.D.*,
2 vols. (London, 1719), 2:489. Roger Laurence, *The Bishop of Oxford's Charge,
Considered* (London, 1712), 8–9. Laurence (1670–1736) was Dissenter who had
been re-baptized in the Anglican Church in 1708. He later was received into the
Non-Juror communion by George Hickes, who ordained him in 1714. In 1733 he
was consecrated a bishop, along with Thomas Deacon, by Archibald Campbell,
Lowth, *Subject of Church Power*, 90–94. Potter, *Discourse on Church-govern-*

*ment,* 191. Cf. Goldie, "Origins of the Convocation Controversy," 26–27. Meza, "Question of Authority," 77–84.

19. [Leslie], *Case of the Regale,* 14–15.

20. [Leslie], *Case of the Regale,* 15–16.

21. Lowth, *Of the Subject of Church Power,* 64. Cf. Brett, *Independency of the Church,* 40–44. [Dodwell], *Defence of the Deprived Bishops,* 87–93. [Leslie], *Case of the Regale,* 18–19.

22. [Leslie], *Case of the Regale,* 6–10.

23. [Dodwell], *Defence of the Deprived Bishops,* 83.

24. Hickes, *Two Treatises,* 1:196. [Dodwell], *Defence of the Deprived Bishops,* 76–77. Goldie, "Origins of the Convocation Controversy," 26.

25. Thomas Brett, *Dr. Brett's Vindication of Himself from the Calumnies thrown upon Him in some late Newspapers, wherein He is falsely Charged with Turning Papist* (London, 1715) 23–25. Brett, *Independency of the Church,* 90. Earbery, *Historical Essay,* 25. Laurence, *Bishop of Oxford's Charge,* 6–7. [Leslie], *Case of the Regale,* 15–16, 69, 111–12. Cf. Henry Broxap, *The Later Non-Jurors* (Cambridge: Cambridge University Press, 1924), 28, 323.

26. [Dodwell], *Defence of the Deprived Bishops,* 83–86. Cf. Monod, *Jacobitism and the English People,* 17–19. Yould, "Origins of the Non-Juror Schism," 114–15.

27. G. V. Bennett, "Conflict in the Church," in *Britain After the Glorious Revolution, 1689–1714,* Geoffrey Holmes, ed. (New York: St. Martins Press, 1969), 159. J. R. Jones, *The Revolution of 1688 in England* (New York: W. W. Norton and Company, 1972), 122–27.

28. Sacheverell, *Political Union,* 6–7, 19–20. Cf. Holmes, *Trial of Doctor Sacheverell,* 32–33.

29. John Spurr has noted that, for the Restoration church, the national church increasingly was equated with an episcopal church. Thus, even prior to the Non-Juror separation, bishops were seen as indispensable to the church. John Spurr, "Schism and the Restoration Church," *Journal of Ecclesiastical History,* 41 (September 1990): 413–14. See chapter 5 for a more detailed discussion of the high-church view of the episcopate.

30. [Dodwell], *Defence of the Deprived Bishops,* 75, 92–93. Peter Newman Brooks, *Cranmer in Context* (Minneapolis: Fortress Press, 1989), 25–26.

31. Gilbert Burnet, *An Exposition of the Thirty-nine Articles of the Church of England,* 3rd ed. (London, 1705), 258.

32. Straka, *Anglican Reaction to the Revolution,* 100–102. Sykes, *Church and State in England,* 288–90.

33. Brett, *Independency of the Church,* 7–12. [Collier], *Brief Essay,* 2–3. Jeremy Collier, *An Ecclesiastical History of Great Britain, Chiefly of England from the First Planting of Christianity, to the End of the Reign of Charles the Second,* new ed., 9 vols. (London: William Straker, 1845), 2:47. [Leslie], *Case of the Regale,* 144–45. Lowth, *Subject of Church Power,* 94. See chapter 5 for a more complete discussion of episcopal and ministerial authority.

34. [Atterbury], *Mitre and the Crown,* 17–18. Brett, *Independency of the Church,* 43–44. [Leslie], *Case of the Regale,* 94–97, 107. Potter, *Discourse on Church Government,* 416–19. Edward Welchman (1665–1739), a liberal who served successively as rector of Lapworth, Warwickshire, Berkshire, Archdeacon of Cardigan, and rector of Solihull, Warwickshire, agreed that as long as the magistrate was not a Christian the two societies were distinct, but when a nation has become Christian, they become one; [Welchman], *Defence of the Church of*

*England*, 7–9. In contrast to the Non-Juror and High Church perspective of the Constantinian era, Kenneth Scott Latourette, *A History of Christianity*, rev. ed., 2 vols. (New York: Harper and Row, Publishers, 1975), 1:154–55, 184–85, states that the involvement of Constantine at Nicea set a precedent of civil involvement and leadership in ecclesiastical affairs. Though the church was not as subservient as the pagan cults had been, the emperors still had considerable power over the church.

35. Nathaniel Bisbie (1635–95) was educated at Christ Church, Oxford, receiving the Doctor of Divinity degree in 1668. He served as rector of Long Melford, Sudbury, Suffolk, from 1660 to 1690, when he was deprived as a Non-Juror.

36. [Nathaniel Bisbie], *Unity of the Priesthood Necessary to the Unity of the Church* (London, 1692), 5–6. Cf. Joseph Betty, *The Divine Institution of the Ministry and the Absolute Necessity of Church Government: A Sermon preached before the University of Oxford on Sunday the 21st of September, 1729*, 2nd ed. (London, 1729), 10–11. Brett, *Independency of the Church*, 45. [Collier], *Brief Essay*, 3. Apostolic succession will be discussed further in chapter 5.

37. Kettlewell, "Christian Community," 2:490, 531–33, 540–41. Sykes, *Church and State in England*, 289–90. Brett, *Independency of the Church*, 47–49, 115. [Dodwell], *Defence of the Deprived Bishops*, 77. [George Hickes], *An Apology for the New Separation* (London, 1691), 8, 11. Hickes, *Constitution of the Catholic Church*, 78–79. [Leslie], *Case of the Regale*, 65–69. Cf. Samuel Hill, *The Catholic Balance: Or a Discourse Determining Controversies Concerning I. Tradition of Catholic Doctrine, II. The Primacy of S. Peter and the Bishop of Rome. III. The Subjection and Authority of the Church in a Christian State: According to the Suffrages of the Primest Antiquity* (London, 1687), 121.

38. Benjamin Hoadly, *A Preservative Against the Principles and Practices of the Non-Jurors both in Church and State*, 2nd ed. (London, 1716), 80–84. [Welchman], *Defence of the Church of England*, 10–12.

39. Brett, *Independency of the Church*, 75–77, 89–93. [Dodwell], *Doctrine of the Church of England*, LX–LXXI. [Leslie], *Case of the Regale*, 39–43.

40. Brett, *Account of Church Government*, 34–38. Brett, *Independency of the Church*, 60–61. Hoadly, *Preservative Against the Non-Jurors*, 33. [Welchman], *Defence of the Church of England*, 10–12. Cf. Goldie, "Origins of the Convocation Controversy," 25. Sykes, *Church and State in England*, 289–90.

41. Goldie, "Origins of the Convocation Controversy," 25. Cf. [Dodwell], *Defence of the Deprived Bishops*, 11–12, 77. [Dodwell], *Vindication of the Deprived Bishops*, 42–49, 75–76. Earbery, *Historical Essay*, 30. Lowth, *Historical Collections*, 2–7.

42. Brett, *Independency of the Church*, 80–81. Matthias Earbery, *A Serious Admonition to Dr. Kennet* (London, 1717), 6. Hickes, *Constitution of the Catholic Church*, 109–10.

43. [Dodwell], *Defense of the Deprived Bishops*, 77, 80.

44. [Bisbie], *Unity of the Priesthood*, 5–6.

45. [Leslie], *Case of the Regale*, 4–5.

46. [Dodwell], *Defense of the Deprived Bishops*, 10. John Kettlewell, "Appendix Number V: A Letter to John Tillotson, Nominated to the Archbishoprick of Canterbury," in *The Compleat Collection of the Works of the Reverend and Learned John Kettlewell, B.D.*, 2 vols. (London, 1719), 1:v. Kettlewell, "Duty of Allegiance," 2:268. Kettlewell, "Of Christian Communion," 2:529.

47. Francis Brokesby, *The Life of Henry Dodwell* (London, 1715), 454–56, 460, 476. Brokesby summarizes Dodwell's tract published in 1705, *Case in View*,

*Considered* and a second document published in 1710, *Case in View, Now in Fact.* These two documents state Dodwell's views concerning the length of the separation. Cf. [Dodwell], *Doctrine of the Church of England,* 68–71. Broxap, *Later Non-Jurors,* 1. Every, *High Church Party,* 71–74, 127–28. Goldie, "Origins of the Convocation Controversy," 20–21.

48. Hickes, *Constitution of the Catholic Church,* 32–34, 94–101. Brokesby, *Life of Dodwell,* 462, 473. Hickes had been consecrated, along with Thomas Wagstaffe (1645–1712), the deprived rector of St. Gabriel Fenchurch, London, in 1693 by William Lloyd, the deprived Bishop of Norwich, at the behest of William Sancroft, so as to continue the Non-Juror succession. Cf. Broxap, *Later Non-Jurors,* 1, 7–14. Every, *High Church Party,* 69–79, 128. William Hutton, *The English Church From the Accession of Charles I to the Death of Ann (1625–1714)* (New York: Macmillan and Co., 1903, reprinted, New York: AMS Press, 1970), 240. Rupp, *Religion in England,* 11–12, 15–16.

49. Hickes, *Constitution of the Catholic Church,* 173, 212–20, 226–28, 243–47, 256–57. These bishops operated largely in secret, and according to George Every, Henry Dodwell did not even know that the consecrations had occurred until 1701. Every, *High Church Party,* 69. Cf. Rupp, *Religion in England,* 15–16.

50. Monod, *Jacobitism and the English People,* 144.

51. Findon, "Nonjurors and the Church of England," 183. Goldie, "Origins of the Convocation Controversy," 20–21. Hutton, *English Church,* 238–45. For the history of the later Non-Jurors see Broxap, *Later Non-Jurors* and Overton, *Non-jurors,* 309–76.

52. Goldie, "Origins of the Convocation Controversy," 16–18. Bennett, *Tory Crisis in Church and State,* 48–62. G. M. Yould has noted the influence of the Non-Jurors on Atterbury; he believes that the association in the popular mind, though never in fact, of Atterbury with the Non-Jurors did his cause more harm than good. Yould, "Origins of the Non-Jurors," 305. Cf. J. A. W. Gunn, *Beyond Liberty and Property* (Kingston and Montreal: McGill-Queen's University Press, 1983), 137. Hawkins, *Allegiance in Church and State,* 170–74. Rupp, *Religion in England,* 56–64. R. J. Smith, *The Gothic Bequest: Medieval Institutions in British Thought, 1688–1863* (Cambridge: Cambridge University Press, 1987), 31–34. Straka, *Anglican Reaction to the Revolution of 1688,* 19–20. Sykes, *Church and State in England,* 301–2. Norman Sykes, *From Sheldon to Secker: Aspects of English Church History 1660–1768* (Cambridge: Cambridge University Press, 1959), 44–48. Norman Sykes, *William Wake Archbishop of Canterbury, 1657–1737,* 2 vols. (Cambridge: Cambridge University Press, 1957), 1:80–156.

53. Goldie, "Origins of the Convocation Controversy," 17–18. Cf. Hawkins, *Allegiance in Church and State,* 172, for a similar view of Atterbury's intentions.

54. Bennett, *Tory Crisis in Church and State,* 152. Sykes, *William Wake,* 1:84–86.

55. [Atterbury and Shower], *Letter to A Convocation Man,* 17–18; Atterbury, *Rights of Convocation,* 128–130. Samuel Hill, in his response to Wake's answer to Atterbury, took Atterbury to be affirming the divine right of the church to call synods. [Samuel Hill], *Municipium Ecclesiasticum, Or the Rights, Liberties, and Authorities of the Christian Church* (London, 1697), 1. On the other hand, Henry Sacheverell, who was of a similar mind to Atterbury, clearly advocated the view that church and state were one unified society, and that both church and state shared the same fate. One could say that Sacheverell's motivations were the protection of the church from Latitudinarian and Non-conformist encroachment,

rather than Erastian capitulation. Sacheverell, *Political Union*, 6–7, 19–20. Cf. Every, *High Church Party*, 86–88.

56. [Atterbury and Shower], *Letter to a Convocation Man*, 19–20, 30. Atterbury, *Rights of a Convocation*, 4–5. Cf. Smith, *Gothic Bequest*, 31–35.

57. Atterbury, *Rights of Convocation*, 75–76. [Atterbury and Shower], *Letter to a Convocation Man*, 22–23, 29, 50, 63–64. Goldie states that Atterbury's major error was linking Convocation to the *Praemunire* clause, which Wake had shown to be a false interpretation. For Goldie, Henry Dodwell had more cogently argued that the independence of Convocation "flowed naturally from the idea of the Church as a distinct society." Goldie, "Origins of the Convocation Controversy," 28. [Dodwell], *Doctrine of the Church of England*, LI. Cf. [Thomas Brett], *The Authority of Presbyters in Provincial Synods Vindicated* (London, 1712), 66–68. [Leslie], *Case of the Regale*, 128–29. Bennett, *Tory Crisis in Church and State*, 49–54. Every, *High Church Party*, 89. Smith, *Gothic Bequest*, 35–38. Sykes, *Church and State in England*, 298. Sykes, *William Wake*, 1:85–90, 101–2.

58. Francis Atterbury, *The Parliamentary Original and Rights of the Lower House of Convocation Cleared* (London, 1702), 3. [Atterbury and Shower], *Letter to a Convocation Man*, 29; Atterbury, *Rights of Convocation*, [138, page misnumbered or out of place].

59. Atterbury, *Rights of Convocation*, 25–26. Earbery, *Historical Essay*, 66–71.

60. [Atterbury and Shower], *Letter to a Convocation Man*, 44, 66–67. For the definitive discussion of the Convocation Controversy, and Atterbury's involvement in it, see the works of G. V. Bennett. G. V. Bennett, "The Convocation of 1710: An Anglican Attempt at Counter-Revolution," in *Studies in Church History: Councils and Assemblies*, G. J. Cuming and Derek Baker, eds. (Cambridge: University of Cambridge Press, 1971), 7:311–19. Bennett, "Conflict in the Church," 165–75. Bennett, *Tory Crisis in Church and State*, 44–160.

61. [Dodwell], *Defence of the Deprived Bishops*, 11–12, 103. [Dodwell], *Vindication of the Deprived Bishops*, 48–49, 75–76. Cf. Every, *High Church Party*, 68–69. Goldie, "Origins of the Convocation Controversy," 17.

62. [Dodwell], *Defense of the Deprived Bishops*, 13. Hickes, *Constitution of the Church*, 75–76. Goldie, "Origins of the Convocation Controversy," 26–29. Sykes, *William Wake*, 1:90–91. Bennett, "Conflict in the Church," 170–72. Sacheverell, *Political Union*, 24.

63. Brett, *Independency of the Church*, 82–83. Prior to his conversion to the Non-Juror communion, Brett's views were much closer to Atterbury's, than to the one he espoused following his conversion; [Brett], *Authority of Presbyters in Provincial Synod*, 66–68. Atterbury, *Rights of Convocation*, 121–22. Earbery, *Historical Essay*, 27–28, 34–37. Hill, *Catholic Balance*, 122–23. Cf. Bennett, *Tory Crisis in Church and State*, 214–15. Goldie, "Origins of the Convocation Controversy," 28–30. Rupp, *Religion in England*, 64.

64. Bennett, *Tory Crisis in Church and State*, 185–95. Gunn, *Beyond Liberty and Property*, 136, 152–56. Monod, *Jacobitism and the English People*, 145–54. Straka, *Anglican Reaction to the Revolution*, 107–15. Straka, "Final Phase of Divine Right Theory," 638–58.

## CHAPTER 5. THE DOCTRINE OF THE MINISTRY

1. Gilbert Burnet, *An Exposition of the Thirty-nine Articles of the Church of England*, 3rd ed. (London, 1705), 258–59. Samuel Clarke, "Of the Catholic Church of Christ," in *The Sermons of Samuel Clarke*, 6th ed., John Clarke, ed., 6 vols.

(London, 1744), 4:264–66. Benjamin Hoadly, *A Preservative Against the Principles and Practices of the Non-Jurors both in the Church and State*, 2nd ed. (London, 1716), 78–80. John Toland, "The Primitive Constitution of the Christian Church," in *A Collection of Several Pieces of Mr. John Toland*, 2 vols. (London, 1726), 2:122–23.

2. George Every, *The High Church Party 1688–1718* (London: S.P.E.C., 1956), 4–9, 11–12, 15–17. Cf. Cecilia M. Ady, "The Post-Reformation Episcopate: (ii) From the Restoration to the Present day," in *The Apostolic Ministry*, 2nd ed., Kenneth E. Kirk, ed. (London: Hodder and Stoughton, Ltd., 1957), 444. F. C. Mather, "Georgian Churchmanship Reconsidered: Some Variations in Anglican Public Worship 1714–1830," *Journal of Ecclesiastical History* 36 (April 1985): 255. John Potter, *A Discourse on Church Government: Wherein the Rights of the Church and the Supremacy of the Christian Bishops are Vindicated and Adjusted*, 5th ed. (London: Samuel Bagster, 1839), 109–10. Norman Sykes, *Old Priest and New Presbyter* (Cambridge: Cambridge University Press, 1956), 167–70. Norman Sykes, *Church and State in England in the XVIIIth Century* (Cambridge: Cambridge University Press, 1934; reprinted, Hamden, CT: Archon Books, 1962), 412–13. See chapter 3 on the relationship of the church to salvation and chapter 6 on the nature of the sacraments.

3. Peter Virgin, *The Church in an Age of Negligence* (Cambridge: James Clarke and Co., 1989), 3. Although Virgin's analysis covers the period 1700–1840, his focus is on the latter half of the period. Cf. G. F. A. Best, *Temporal Pillars: Queen Anne's Bounty, the Ecclesiastical Commissioners, and the Church of England* (Cambridge: Cambridge University Press, 1964), 13–21. Sykes, *Church and State in England*, 206–21.

4. G. V. Bennett, *The Tory Crisis in Church and State 1688–1730* (Oxford: Clarendon Press, 1975), 15–16. Best, *Temporal Pillars*, 13–16. Virgin, *Church in an Age of Negligence*, 35–36, 193.

5. [Thomas Stackhouse], *The Miseries and Great Hardships of the Inferiour Clergy, in and about London* (London, 1722), 61–74, 101–101. Cf. Best, *Temporal Pillars*, 207. While Peter Virgin claims that the first pamphlets calling for church reform date from the 1820s, he makes no mention of Stackhouse's work. Virgin, *The Church in an Age of Negligence*, 23–24.

6. [Stackhouse], *Miseries of the Clergy*, 17–19. High Churchmen were not alone in complaining of pluralism, as is seen in the work of Gilbert Burnet. Burnet added a chapter on the problem for the third edition of his *Discourse of the Pastoral Care* (London, 1713). This chapter was published separately under the title, *The New Preface and Additional Chapter, to the Third Edition of the Pastoral Care* (London, 1713). Cf. Virgin *Church in an Age of Negligence*, 192–93.

7. [Stackhouse], *Miseries of the Clergy*, 24–25. Cf. Best, *Temporal Pillars*, 207. Virgin, *Church in an Age of Negligence*, 215–16. Virgin's examples come from the early nineteenth century, but they parrallel those of the early eighteenth century.

8. Ady, "Post-Reformation Episcopate," 444–45. Best, *Temporal Pillars*, 3. Sykes, *Church and State in England*, 92–94. To this we might add the deprivation of the Non-Jurors.

9. Sykes, *Old Priest*, 69. Cf. W. H. C. Frend, *The Early Church* (Philadelphia: Fortress Press, 1982), 40–43, 100. Guy Martin Yould, "The Origins and Transformation of the Non-Juror Schism, 1670–1715" (Ph.D. Dissertation, University of Hull, 1979), 273, 300.

10. Women, of course, were not allowed to serve in the ministry of the church

in any meaningful capacity. Joseph Bingham does note that the office of deaconess was an important ministry in the ancient church, but it had been discontinued. Joseph Bingham, *Origines Ecclesiasticae; or, the Antiquities of the Christian Church,* Richard Bingham, ed., 8 vols. (London, 1821), 1:247–48, 255–58. Bingham (1668–1723), a graduate of Oxford and a protégé of William Sherlock, served as rector of Hedbourne Worthy and rector of Havant.

11. Robert Faulkner, *Richard Hooker and the Politics of Christian England* (Berkeley: University of California Press, 1981), 132–33. John Marshall, "The Ecclesiology of the Latitude-men 1660–1689: Stillingfleet, Tillotson, and 'Hobbism'," *Journal of Ecclesiastical History* 36 (July 1985): 411–12. W. D. J. Cargill Thompson, "The Philosopher of the 'Politic Society': Richard Hooker as a Political Thinker," in *Studies in Richard Hooker* (Cleveland: The Press of Case Western Reserve University, 1972), 54.

12. Thomas Brett, *The Christian Altar and Sacrifice: A Sermon shewing that the Lord's Table is a Proper Altar and the Sacrament of the Eucharist a Proper Sacrifice* (London, 1713), 31. Thomas Brett, *The Divine Right of Episcopacy, and the Necessity of an Episcopal Commission for Preaching God's Word, and for the Valid Ministration of the Christian Sacraments, proved from the Scriptures, and the Doctrine and Practice of the Primitive Church* (London, 1718), 60, 62. Thomas Brett, *The Extent of Christ's Commission to Baptize: A Sermon shewing the Capacity of Infants to Receive and the Utter Incapacity of Our Dissenting Teachers to Administer Christian Baptism* (London, 1712), vii. [Jeremy Collier], *Brief Essay concerning the Independency of Church Power* (London, 1692), 4, 12. Potter, *Discourse on Church Government,* 208–9. See chapter 4 for a discussion of the Non-Juror denial of the validity of lay deprivations.

13. [Stackhouse], *Miseries and Great Hardships,* 11. Thomas Wilson, "Sermon XC: The Duties of Ministers and People," in *The Works of the Right Reverend Father in God, Thomas Wilson, D.D.,* 7 vols. (Oxford: John Henry Parker, 1847), 3:434–35. Gilbert Burnet, *A Discourse of the Pastoral Care* (London, 1692), 12–13.

14. Joseph Betty, *The Divine Institution of the Ministry and the Absolute Necessity of Church Government: A Sermon preached before the University of Oxford on Sunday the 21st of September, 1729,* 2nd ed. (London, 1729), 16–17. [Roger Laurence], *Dissenters and Other Unauthorized Baptisms Null and Void, by the Articles and Canons and Rubricks of the Church of England* (London, 1712), 39–40. Potter, *Discourse on Church Government,* 194–95. Matthias Symson, *The Necessity of a Lawful Ministry* (London, 1708), 2. Thomas Wilson, "Sermon LXXXVIII: The Great Blessings of a Standing Ministry," in *The Works of the Most Reverend Father in God, Thomas Wilson, D.D.,* 7 vols. (Oxford: John Henry Parker, 1847), 3:416. Wilson, "Sermon XC," 3:435.

15. Robert Nelson, *A Companion for the Festivals and Fasts of the Church of England with Collects and Prayers for Each Solemnity* (London, 1704; reprinted, London: S.P.C.K., 1841), 504.

16. A. G. Dickens, *The English Reformation* (New York: Schocken Books, 1968), 83–108. Faulkner, *Richard Hooker,* 142–43. John Findon, "The Non-Jurors and the Church of England 1689–1716" (D.Phil. Dissertation, Oxford University, 1978), 160, 170. Mark Goldie, "The Non-Jurors, Episcopacy, and the Origins of the Convocation Controversy," in *Ideology and Conspiracy: Aspects of Jacobitism 1689–1759,* Eveline Cruickshanks, ed. (Edinburgh: John Donald, 1982), 16. William P. Haugaard, "Toward an Anglican Doctrine of Ministry: Richard Hooker and the Elizabeth Church," *Anglican and Episcopal History* 56 (September1987):

269–70, 279–80. Marshall, "Ecclesiology of the Latitude-men," 412–13. Marshall notes that Stillingfleet based his views, in part, on Thomas Cranmer's episcopal doctrines, which he found republished in Gilbert Burnet's *History of the Reformation* (1679–81). Sykes, *Old Priest,* 58–69. Matthias Symson, a High Church divine, noted that while the Presbyterians agreed on the need for a divinely authorized ministry, the two churches differed on the method by which the authorization was given; Symson, *Lawful Ministry,* 11. Yould, "Origins of the Non-Jurors," 271–73, 300.

17. Bingham, *Origines Ecclesiasticae,* 1:116. Thomas Brett, *An Account of Church Government and Governours,* 2nd ed (London, 1710), 386–87. Thomas Brett, *The Independency of the Church from the State as to Its Pure Spiritual Powers* (London, 1717), 10–12. [Collier], *Brief Essay,* 2–3. Hoadly, *Preservative against the Non-Jurors,* 55–61. Potter, *Discourse on Church Government,* 256–60. William Sclater, *An Original Draught of the Primitive Church,* 1st American ed. (Columbus, Ohio, 1833), 144. Sclater (1638–1717), had been vicar of Bramford Speke, Devonshire, prior to his ejection for refusing the oaths. His work was written in response to Peter King's defense of presbyterian orders, *Enquiry into the Constitution, Discipline, Unity and Worship of the Primitive Church* (London, 1691; 2nd ed., 1713).

18. Betty, *Divine Institution of the Ministry,* 10–11. William Beveridge, "Sermon I: Christ's Presence with His Ministers," in *The Theological Works of William Beveridge, D.D.,* 12 vols. (Oxford: John Henry Parker, 1842), 1:6. Nelson, *Companion to the Festivals,* 506. Potter, *Discourse on Church Government,* 121. Wilson, "Sermon LXXXVIII," 3:413–14.

19. Beveridge, "Sermon I," 1:8–9.

20. Beveridge, "Sermon I," 1:10–11, 16–17. Brett, *Account of Church Government,* 65. Potter, *Discourse on Church Government,* 111–13.

21. Symson, *Lawful Ministry,* 12. Cf. William Beveridge, "Sermon IX: The Preparatory Duties For Holy Orders," in *The Theological Works of William Beveridge, D.D.,* 12 vols. (Oxford: John Henry Parker, 1842), 1:159. John Hughes, "Preliminary Dissertations to St. Chrysostom's *De Sacerdotio,*" in George Hickes, *Two Treatises on the Christian Priesthood, and on the Dignity of the Episcopal Order,* 4th ed., 3 vols. (Oxford: John Henry Parker, 1847), 3:324. Charles Leslie, "A Discourse Shewing who they are that are Now Qualify'd to Administer Baptism and the Lord's Supper: Wherein the Cause of Episcopacy is Briefy Stated," in *The Theological Works of the Rev. Mr. Charles Leslie,* 2 vols. (London, 1721), 2:721.

22. William Beveridge, "Sermon II: The Institution of Ministers," in *The Theological Works of William Beveridge, D.D.,* 12 vols. (Oxford: John Henry Parker, 1842), 1:27. William Beveridge, "Sermon XI: Ministers of the Gospel, Christ's Ambassadors," in *The Theological Works of William Beveridge, D.D.* (Oxford: John Henry Parker, 1842), 1:200. William Roberts, *The Divine Institution of the Gospel Ministry, and the necessity of Episcopal Ordination, Asserted by Proofs from Scripture, and the Practice of the Primitive and Purest Ages of the Church,* 4th ed. (London, 1753), 2.

23. Bingham, *Origines Ecclesiasticae,* 1:116. Brett, *Divine Right of Episcopacy,* 8. Nelson, *Companion for Festivals,* 477–78, 487–88. Roberts, *Divine Institution of the Ministry,* 10–11, 20. Sclater, *Original Draught of the Primitive Church,* 144, 177–78, 218. Symson, *Lawson Ministry,* 10. Charles Wheatly, *A Rational Illustration of the Book of Common Prayer of the Church of England* (London: Wm. Tegg and Co., 1853), 94. Wheatly (1686–1742), an Oxford graduate, served

as vicar of the parishes of Brent, Pelham and of Furneaux, Pelham. His views resembled those of John Johnson, a High Churchman with a Non-Juror flavor. Cf. Henry Broxap, *The Later Non-Jurors* (Cambridge: Cambridge University Press, 1924), 185–87.

24. Burnet, *Exposition of the Thirty-nine Articles*, 259. Haugaard, "Anglican Doctrine of the Ministry," 282. Symson, Lawful Ministry, 10–11.

25. Beveridge, "Sermon IX," 1:174. Bingham, *Origines Ecclesiasticae*, 1:64– 65. Hughes, "Preliminary Dissertations," 3:337, 339. Wheatly, *Rational Illustration*, 96. Cf. Every, *High Church Party*, 53–56. Marshall, "Ecclesiology of the Latitude-men," 416–17. Sykes, *Old Priest*, 132–38.

26. Brett, *Church Government*, 81–82. Cf. Bingham, *Origines Ecclesiasticae*, 1:66. Every, *High Church Party*, 4–5.

27. Roberts, *Divine Institution of the Ministry*, 3. Symson, *Lawful Ministry*, 4–5.

28. [George Hickes], *An Apology for the New Separation*, (London, 1691), 8.

29. [Stackhouse], *Miseries of the Clergy*, 16. Stackhouse appealed to John Chrysostom in support of his views. Roberts, *Divine Institution of the Ministry*, 3. Cf. Frend, *Early Church*, 235–36.

30. [Stackhouse], *Miseries of the Clergy*, 20–21.

31. Beveridge, "Sermon I," 1:20.

32. George Hickes, *The Constitution of the Catholic Church, and the Nature and Consequences of Schism* (London, 1716), 32–33, 211–12. [Nathaniel Bisbie], *Unity of the Priesthood Necessary to the Unity of the Church* (London, 1692), 5. [Charles Leslie], *The Case of the Regale and the Pontificate Stated. In the Relation of a Conference Concerning the Independency of the Church as to her Purely Spiritual Power and Authority* (London, 1700), 87–88.

33. See Burnet, *Discourse of the Pastoral Care*, 142–44, 169–70, for a similar discussion of qualifications and training for ministry. The decription of qualifications tends to transcend party lines.

34. Roberts, *Divine Institution of the Ministry*, 3. Cf. Brett, *Divine Right of Episcopacy*, 5, 8, 60. Symson, *Lawful Ministry*, 7–8.

35. George Bull, *A Companion for the Candidates of Holy Orders. Or the Great Importance and Principle Duties of the Priestly Office* (London, 1714), 20–21. Charles Leslie, "A Dissertation Concerning the Use and Authority of Ecclesiastical History," in *The Theological Works of the Rev. Mr. Charles Leslie*, 2 vols. (London, 1721), 729. Cf. Symson, *Lawful Ministry*, 5–6.

36. Every, *High Church Party*, 173–74. Findon, "Nonjurors and the Church of England," 51–52. Paul Monod, *Jacobitism and the English People 1688–1788* (Cambridge: Cambridge University Press, 1989), 152, 275–78. Norman Sykes, *From Sheldon to Secker, Aspects of English Church History 1660–1768* (Cambridge: Cambridge University Press, 1959), 200–201. Virgin, *Church in an Age of Negligence*, 132. Although Findon notes the even distribution of Cambridge and Oxford students among the Non-Jurors, Monod states that there was a strong Jacobite tradition among Oxford students following the Glorious Revolution. Monod also asserts that there were few ejections of Non-Jurors and Jacobites at Oxford, while Jacobites were treated harshly at the more whiggish Cambridge.

37. Bull, *Companion for Candidates*, 23.

38. Bull, *Companion for Candidates*, 26–28. Symson, *Lawful Ministry*, 6. While Bull placed greater emphasis on one's theological training, Gilbert Burnet emphasized character; Burnet, *Discourse of the Pastoral Care*, 142–44.

39. The Anglican, even high church, understandings of the call and preparation

for ministry were well within the mainstream of Christian thought. For a similar modern view, see Thomas Oden, *Pastoral Theology* (San Francisco: Harper and Row, Publishers, 1983), 18–25.

40. [Leslie], *Case of the Regale,* 219–22. J. C. D. Clark, *English Society 1688– 1832* (Cambridge: Cambridge University Press, 1985), 93. Every, *High Church Party,* 6–12. Haugaard, "Anglican Doctrine of the Ministry," 268, 280–81. John W. Packer, *The Transformation of Anglicanism 1643–1660* (Manchester: Manchester University Press, 1969), 104–28. Sykes, *Old Priest,* 168–69.

41. Bingham, *Origines Ecclesiasticae,* 1:41–43. Brett, *Account of Church Government,* 48–50. Brett, *Divine Right of Episcopacy,* 11–19. Francis Brokesby, *An History of the Government of the Primitive Church for the First Three Centuries and the Beginning of the Fourth* (London, 1712), 48. Thomas Comber, *A Discourse upon the Form and Manner of Making, Ordaining, and Consecrating Bishops, Priests, and Deacons, According to the Order of the Church of England* (London, 1699), 3–4. Comber (1645–99) a Cambridge graduate and a strong supporter of William and Mary, was Dean of Durham from 1689. Comber's work, however, demonstrates high-church leanings. Hughes, "Preliminary Dissertations," 3:324–25. Roberts, *Divine Institution of the Ministry,* 8. Thomas Stackhouse, *A Compleat Body of Speculative and Practical Divinity,* 3rd ed. (London, 1743), 736–39. Wheatly, *Rational Ilustration,* 94. Cf. Frend, *Early Church,* 39–41.

42. Bennett, *Tory Crisis in Church and State,* 48–49, 57–60. J. A. W. Gunn, *Beyond Liberty and Property* (Kingston and Montreal: McGill-Queen's University Press), 137–38.

43. Findon, "Non-Jurors and the Church of England," 182–83. Cf. Ady, "Post-Reformation Episcopate," 442. Packer, *Transformation of Anglicanism,* 105–28. John Potter, "A Charge Delivered to the Clergy of the Diocese of Oxford, in July 1725," in *The Theological Works of the Most Reverend Dr. John Potter, Late Lord Archbishop of Canterbury,* 3 vols. (Oxford, 1753), 1:406–8. Sykes, *Old Priest,* 66–68.

44. Bingham, *Origines Ecclesiasticae;* Brokeby, *History of the Government of the Primitive Church;* Potter, *Discourse on Church Government;* Sclater, *Original Draught of the Primitive Church.* Brett, *Divine Right of the Episcopacy;* Hickes, *Constitution of the Catholic Church;* George Hickes, *Two Treatises: One of the Christian Priesthood, the Other of the Dignity of the Episcopal Order,* 3 vols. (Oxford: John Henry Parker, 1845).

45. Beveridge, "Sermon I," 1:6–7, 11. Brett, *Account of Church Government,* 59, 65, 76. Brett, *Divine Right of Episcopacy,* 18–19, 25–27. Leslie, "Discourse Shewing who are now Qualify'd," 2:721. Roberts, *Divine Institution of the Ministry,* 17, 25.

46. [Thomas Ken], *Lacrymae Ecclesiae Anglicanae: Or a Serious and Passionate Address of the Church of England, to her Sons, especially those of the clergy* (London, 1689), 6.

47. Comber, *Discourse Upon the Form,* 28–29. Hickes, *Two Treatises,* 1:267. Hughes, Preliminary Dissertations, 3:331–32. Roberts, *Divine Institution of the Ministry,* 25. Henry Sacheverell, *The Rights of the Church of England Asserted and Prov'd: In an Answer to a late Pamphlet, intitl'd, The Rights of the Protestant Dissenters, in a Review of Their Case* (London, 1705), 1:51–52.

48. Leslie, "Discourse Shewing who are Qualify'd," 2:734.

49. Comber, *Discourse on the Form,* 53–55. [Roger Laurence], *Lay Baptism, Invalid* (London, 1708), 67–69. Cf. G. V. Bennett, "Conflict in the Church," in

*Britain after the Glorious Revolution, 1689–1714,* Geoffrey Holmes, ed. (New York: St. Martins Press, 1969), 172–73.

50. Betty, *Divine Institution of the Ministry,* 34–35. Symson, *Lawful Ministers,* 18–19. Cf. Brett, *Account of Church Government,* 84–85. Brett, *Divine Right of Episcopacy,* 123–27. Hickes, *Two Treatises,* 1:274. Sykes, *Old Priests,* 145–49. Sykes notes that High Churchmen had offered to provide Prussian Protestants with an episcopate during the 1680s. On Calvin's views of the episcopate, see Harro Hopfl, *The Christian Polity of John Calvin* (Cambridge: Cambridge University Press, 1982), 109–12. Calvin did affirm both the existence and the positive nature of an episcopate to oversee the life of the church, but he seems to have been vague as to its necessity.

51. Leslie, "Discourse Shewing who are Qualify'd," 1:721–22. Cf. John Lindsay, "Preface," to Francis Mason's, *Vindication of the Church of England, and the Lawful Ministry thereof* (London, 1734), iii. Lindsay (1686–1768) was the minister for the Non-Juror society at Trinity Chapel, Aldersgate Street. Brett, *Account of Church Government,* 93. J. R. H. Moorman, *A History of the Church in England,* 3rd ed. (London: Adam and Charles Black, Ltd., 1976.), 3–5.

52. Bingham, *Origines Ecclesiasticae,* 1:80. Brett, *Account of Church Government,* 257–62, 274–77, 282. Hickes, *Two Treatises,* 2:374–76. Stackhouse, *Body Divinity,* 743–44. On the advocacy of the primacy of Jerusalem, see Broxap, *Later Non-Jurors,* 30–31. Henry Sefton, "The Scottish Bishops and Archbishop Arsenius," in *Studies in Church History,* Derek Baker, ed. (Oxford: Basil Blackwell, 1976), 241. Cf. J. C. Dickinson, *An Ecclesiastical History of England: The Later Middle Ages* (New York: Harper and Row Publishers, Inc., 1979), 66–68. W. H. C. Frend, *The Rise of Christianity* (Philadelphia: Fortress Press, 1984), 398–405. Frend, *Early Church,* 111–12. Sykes, *Old Priest,* 59–60.

53. Brett, *Account of Church Government,* 247, 251–52. Edmund Gibson, in his program of church reform proposed the revival of suffragans as well as a more equitable division of parishes among the dioceses. Every, *High Church Party,* 151, 162. Sykes, *Church and State in England,* 142. Virgin, *Church in an Age of Negligence,* 158.

54. Broxap, *Later Non-Jurors,* 30–31, 35–36.

55. Symson, *Lawful Ministry,* 9–10.

56. William Beveridge, *"Ecclesia Anglicana, Ecclesia Catholica;* or the Doctrine of the Church of England Consonant to Scripture, Reason, and Fathers in a Discourse upon the Thirty-nine Articles Agreed Upon in the Convocation Held at London MDLXII," 2nd ed., in *The Theological Works of William Beveridge, D.D.,* 12 vols. (Oxford: John Henry Parker, 1845), 8:362–63. Cf. Bingham, *Origines Ecclesiasticae,* 1:60–61.

57. Bingham, *Origines Ecclesiasticae,* 1:189.

58. Brett, *Account of Church Government,* 50–51, 59. Brett, *Divine Right of Episcopacy,* 13, 26–27. Sclater. *Original Draught of the Primitive Church,* 144, 176–77. Cf. Nelson, *Companion to the Festivals,* 483. Stackhouse, *Body Divinity,* 738.

59. Thomas Brett, "A Sermon of the Honour of the Christian Priesthood, and of the Necessity of a Divine Call to that Office," (1712), in *The Curate of Souls,* John R.H. Moorman, ed. (London: S.P.C.K., 1958), 126–27. Hickes, *Two Treatises,* 2:6–8, 11. John Johnson, The Unbloody Sacrifice and Altar Unvailed and Supported" in *The Theological Works of Rev. John Johnson, M.A.,* 4 vols. (Oxford: John Henry Parker, 1847), 1:430.

60. Brett, "Sermon on the Priesthood," 128–130. [George Hickes], *The Case*

*of Infant Baptism* (London, 1685), 10–12. Hickes, *Two Treatises,* 2:13–14, 17–19. Nelson, *Companion to the Festivals,* 496–97. Potter, *Discourse on Church Government,* 238.

61. Hickes, *Two Treatises,* 2:207. Bingham, *Origines Ecclesiasticae,* 1:205–6. Cf. Betty, *Divine Institution of Ministry,* 5–6.

62. Brett, *Extent of Christ's Commission,* 21. Hickes, *Two Treatises,* 2:69–79, 87. Johnson, "Unbloody Sacrifice," 1:428. [Laurence], *Lay Baptism, Invalid,* 44–48, 65–66. Nelson, *Companion for the Festivals,* 504–5. Potter, *Discourse on Church Government,* 238. Daniel Waterland, "Letters on Lay Baptism," in *The Works of the Rev. Daniel Waterland, D.D.,* 3rd ed. (Oxford: Oxford University Press, 1856), 6:77. Wheatly, *Rational Illustration,* 356, 359. Wilson, "Sermon XC," 3:436. See chapter 6 for a more detailed discussion of the sacraments.

63. Beveridge, "Sermon II," 1:199–200. Brett, *Divine Right of Episcopacy,* 83. John Kettlewell, "Of Christian Communion, to be Kept on in the Unity of Christ's Church, and among the Professors of Truth and Holiness, in three parts" *A Compleat Collection of the Works of the Reverend and the Learned John Kettlewell, B.D.,* 2 vols. (London, 1719), 2:518.

64. Bull, *Companion for the Candidates,* 44–46.

65. Kettlewell, "Christian Communion," 2:520–22. Wilson, "Sermon XC," 3:428, 438–39. Cf. John T. McNeill, *A History of the Cure of Souls* (New York: Harper and Brothers, Publishers, 1951), 236–38.

66. Betty, *Divine Institution of Ministers,* 5–6. Brett, *Extent of Christ's Commission,* 22. Hickes, *Two Treatises,* 2:207. Nelson, *Companion to the Festivals,* 430–31, 505. Symson, *Lawful Ministry,* 14.

67. Symson, *Lawful Ministry,* 22. Nelson, *Companion to the Festivals,* 427. Cf. Brett, *Account of Church Government,* 175.

68. Hughes, "Preliminary Dissertations," 3:353. Potter, *Discourse on Church Government,* 92–93.

69. Bingham, *Origines Ecclesiasticae,* 1:216–26. Brett, *Account of Church Government,* 15–17. Hickes, *Two Treatises,* 2:37–39. Hughes, "Preliminary Dissertations," 3:353–54. Nelson, *Companion to the Festivals,* 428.

70. Bingham, *Origines Ecclesiasticae,* 1:247–48, 255–58.

71. Brett, *Account of Church Government,* 175–79.

## CHAPTER 6. HIGH CHURCH AND NON-JUROR SACRAMENTAL THEOLOGY

1. Gerald R. Cragg, *Reason and Authority in the Eighteenth Century* (Cambridge: Cambridge University Press, 1964), 60. Charles J. Abbey and John H. Overton, *The English Church in the Eighteenth Century,* 2 vols. (London: Longmans, Green and Company, 1878), 1:151–52. John H. Overton and Frederick Relton, *The English Church From the Accession of George I to the End of the Eighteenth Century (1714–1800)* (New York: The Macmillan and Company, 1906), 1.

2. Paul Langford, *A Polite and Commercial People, England 1727–1783;* (Oxford: Clarendon Press, 1989), 259. F. C. Mather, "Georgian Churchmanship Reconsidered: Some Variations in Anglican Public Worship 1714–1830," *Journal of Ecclesiastical History* 36 (April 1985): 255, 271–72. Normal Sykes, *Church and State in England in the XVIIIth Century* (Cambridge: Cambridge University Press, 1934; reprint: Hamden, CT: Archon Books, 1962), 250–53. Norman Sykes,

*From Sheldon to Secker: Aspects of English Church History, 1660–1769* (Cambridge: Cambridge University Press, 1959), 25–30.

3. D. E. W. Harrison and Michael C. Sansom, point out that, although Thomas Cranmer desired to establish frequent communion, there were often insufficient communicants at services; D. E. W. Harrison and Michael C. Sansom, *Worship in the Church of England* (London: S.P.C.K., 1982), 79–81. Peter Virgin notes that the number of communicants in the late eighteenth century was still small. Peter Virgin, *The Church in an Age of Negligence* (Cambridge: James Clarke and Co., 1989), 5, 156. Occasional conformity is discussed more fully in chapter one; see Henry Broxap, *The Later Non-Jurors* (Cambridge: Cambridge University Press, 1924) on the usages controversy, G. V. Bennett, *The Tory Crisis in Church and State 1688–1730* (Oxford: Clarendon Press, 1975), 10–11, 101–2, 220–21, and George Every, *The High Church Party, 1688–1718* (London: S.P.C.K., 1956), 128–32, for a discussion of the lay baptism controversy.

4. Of all the aspects of the High Church and Non-Juror ecclesiologies, their eucharistic doctrine and liturgical developments have received the most attention. These works include: Richard Buxton, *Eucharist and Institution Narrative*, Alcuin Club Collections No. 58 (London: S.P.C.K., 1976); Clifford W. Dugmore, *Eucharistic Doctrine in England from Hooker to Waterland* (London: S.P.C.K.; New York: The Macmillan Company, 1942); W. Jardine Grisbrooke, *Anglican Liturgies of the Seventeenth and Eighteenth Centuries*, Alcuin Club Collections No. 40 (London: S.P.C.K., 1958); Charles Hebert, *The Lord's Supper: Uninspired Teaching* 2 vols. (London: Seeley, Jackson and Halliday, 1879), vol. 2; Darwell Stone, *A History of the Doctrine of the Holy Eucharist*, 2 vols. (London: Longmans, Green and Company, 1909), vol. 2; Guy Martin Yould, "The Origins and Transformation of the Non-Juror Schism, 1670–1715" (Ph.D. Diss., University of Hull, 1979), chapter 8. The following outline is loosely based upon the presentation of the sacraments in Thomas Aquinas's *Summa Theologiae* (New York: McGraw-Hill Book Company, 1964) 60: questions 60–65.

5. William Beveridge, "*Ecclesia Anglicana, Ecclesia Catholica;* or the Doctrine of the Church of England Consonant to Scripture, Reason, and Fathers in a Discourse upon the Thirty-nine Articles Agreed upon in the Convocation Held at London MDLXII," in *The Theological Works of William Beveridge, D.D.,* 12 vols. (Oxford: John Henry Parker, 1845), 7:434. Cf. William Beveridge, "The Church Catechism Explained for the Use of the Diocese of St. Asaph," in *The Theological Works of William Beveridge, D.D.,* 12 vols. (Oxford: John Henry Parker, 1846), 8:112. Augustine's sacramental theology is discussed in Reinhold Seeberg, *Textbook of the History of Doctrines*, Charles E. Hay, trans., 2 vols. (Grand Rapids: Baker Book House), 1:321–22.

6. Harrison and Sansom, *Worship in the Church of England,* 102. Thomas Deacon, *Shorter Catechism,* Lesson XXIII, 69–70, quoted in Grisbrooke, *Anglican Liturgies,* 120. Cf. Henry Broxap, *The Biography of Thomas Deacon* (Manchester: Manchester University Press, 1911), 180–81.

7. Thomas Wilson, "Sermon LXXXI: The Ordinances of God Attended with Certain, though Invisible Effects," in *The Works of the Right Reverend Father in God, Thomas Wilson, D.D.,* 7 vols. (Oxford: John Henry Parker, 1847), 3:340. Beveridge, *"Ecclesia Anglicana,"* 7:437–38. Daniel Waterland, "The Nature, Obligation, and Efficacy of the Christian Sacraments Considered," in *The Works of the Rev. Daniel Waterland,* 10 vols. (Oxford: Clarendon Press, 1823), 5:479. Geoffrey Bromiley notes that Cranmer, at least early on, was willing to allow for a broader meaning of Sacrament that would include more than simply baptism and eucha-

rist, although he would not give ordination sacramental status. In his *True and Catholic Doctrine of the Lord's Supper,* Cranmer limited true sacraments to Baptism and Eucharist; Geoffrey Bromiley, *Thomas Cranmer, Theologian* (New York: Oxford University Press, 1956), 49–50, 59.

8. Beveridge, "Church Catechism," 8:112–13. Thomas Wilson, "A Further Instruction for Such as have Learned the Church Catechism," in *The Works of the Right Reverend Father in God, Thomas Wilson, D.D.,* 7 vols. (Oxford: John Henry Parker, 1851), 4:80. Wilson, "Sermon LXXXI," 3:341. Cf. Seeberg, *History of Doctrines,* 2:126.

9. Thomas Brett, *An Account of Church Government and Governors* (London, 1710), 9–10. For a discussion of the sacraments as a mark of the true church, see chapter 3.

10. [Charles Leslie], *A Discourse Proving the Divine Institution of Water Baptism: Wherein the Quaker-Arguments Against it, are Collected and Confuted with as much as needful Concerning the Lord's Supper* (London, 1697), 8.

11. J. P. Ferguson, *Dr. Samuel Clark: An Eighteenth Century Heretic* (Kineton, Warwick: The Roundwood Press, 1976), 167–72. Philip E. Hughes, *The Theology of the English Reformers,* 2nd ed. (Grand Rapids, MI: Baker Book House, 1980), 194–95. The primacy of the word in the eucharist is espoused as well by Martin Luther and the other Reformers; Timothy George, *Theology of the Reformers* (Nashville: Broadman Press, 1988), 92–94, 238–39.

12. Beveridge, *"Ecclesia Anglicana,"* 7:468. Thomas Brett, *The Divine Right of Episcopacy, and the Necessity of an Episcopal Commission for Preaching God's Word, and For the Valid ministration of the Christian Sacraments, Proved from the Scriptures, and the Doctrine and Practice of the Primitive Church* (London, 1718), 56–58. Thomas Brett, *The Christian Altar and Sacrifice: A Sermon, Shewing that the Lord's Table is a Proper Altar and the Sacrament of the Eucharist a Proper Sacrifice* (London, 1713), 27. John Johnson, "The Unbloody Sacrifice and Altar Unvailed and Supported," in *The Theological Works of the Rev. John Johnson, M.A.,* 4 vols. (Oxford: John Henry Parker, 1847), 1:193, 195; 2:127–28. Daniel Waterland, "A Review of the Doctrine of the Eucharist as Laid Down in Scripture and Antiquity," in *The Works of the Rev. Daniel Waterland* (Oxford: Clarendon Press, 1823), 7:211–12.

13. Thomas Brett, *A Discourse Concerning the necessity of Discerning the Lord's Body in the Holy Communion* (London, 1720), 19–20. Johnson, "Unbloody Sacrifice," 1:272–73. Waterland, "Review of the Eucharist," 8:94. Unlike Cranmer, the High Churchmen saw consecration as more than simply setting common elements apart for a spiritual service. Although it did not change the substance of the elements, it did infuse the elements with spiritual power. Cf. Hughes, *Theology of the English Reformers,* 219–20.

14. Johnson, "Unbloody Sacrifice," 1:236, 305, 311–12; 2:4, 13–14. Johnson referred to the Lutheran doctrine of consubstantiation as an "absurd opinion," that ran completely counter to the teachings of the early fathers. On Calvin, see Reinhold Seeberg, *Text-Book of the History of Doctrines,* Charles Hay, trans., 2 vols. (Grand Rapids, MI: Baker Book House, 1977), 2:412–14. Cf. Beveridge, *"Ecclesia Anglicana,"* 7:470–71. Brett, *Discerning the Lord's Body,* x–xi, 13–16. Robert Nelson, *Transubstantiation Contrary to Scripture* (London, 1688), 11–12. Dom Gregory Dix, *The Shape of the Liturgy,* Seabury ed. with additional notes by Paul V. Marshall (New York: Seabury Press, 1982), 630.

15. Brett, *Discerning the Body,* 19–20, 34–35. Johnson, "Unbloody Sacrifice," 1:272, 341–342. Nelson, *Transubstantiation Contrary to Scripture,* 11–12, 15.

Grisbrooke refers to this view as "dynamic virtualism;" Grisbrooke, *Anglican Liturgies*, xv. Seeberg, *History of Doctrines*, 2:412–14. Cf. Buxton, *Eucharist and Institution Narrative*, 170. Dugmore, *Eucharistic Doctrine in England*, 145. Edward P. Echlin, *The Anglican Eucharist in Ecumenical Perspective: Doctrine and Rite from Cranmer to Seabury* (New York: Seabury Press, 1968), 169–70.

16. Johnson, "Unbloody Sacrifice," 1:298. On John Chrysostom see Frances Young, *From Nicaea to Chalcedon* (Philadelphia: Fortress Press, 1983), 152–54.

17. Johnson, "Unbloody Sacrifice," 1:266–67. Cf. Brett, *Christian Altar*, xiii.

18. Brett, *Discerning the Body*, 46–48. William Beveridge, in contrast, rejected the practice of reservation of the elements, especially with regard to the worship of the reserved host. He asserted that the elements were to be eaten and not reserved, a truth that Trent had affirmed. Beveridge, *"Ecclesia Anglicana,"* 7:487–88.

19. Johnson, "Unbloody Sacrifice," 1:342–44. Cf. Buxton, *Eucharist and Institution Narrative*, 170–71.

20. Grisbrooke, *Anglican Liturgies*, 78–79.

21. Beveridge, *"Ecclesia Anglicana,"* 7:459. Thomas Brett, *A Discourse Concerning the Necessity of Discerning the Lord's Body in the Holy Communion* (London, 1720), 19–20. Johnson, "Unbloody Sacrifice," 1:398. Waterland, "Review of the Eucharist," 7:235–36. Thomas Wilson, "Sermon LXXV: The Lord's Supper, The Medicine of the Soul," in *The Works of the Right Reverend Father in God, Thomas Wilson, D.D.*, 7 vols. (Oxford: John Henry Parker, 1847), 3:268.

22. Thomas Brett, *The Extent of Christ's Commission to Baptize: A Sermon Shewing the Capacity of Infants to Receive and the Utter Incapacity of Our Dissenting Teachings to Administer Christian Baptism* (London, 1712), 18–19. Brett, *Divine Right of Episcopacy*, 56–58. Johnson, "Unbloody Sacrifice," 1:431; 2:215–16. Daniel Waterland, "Letters on Lay Baptism," in *The Works of the Rev. Daniel Waterland, D.D.*, 3rd ed., 6 vols. (Oxford: Oxford University Press, 1856), 6:77. Charles Wheatly, *A Rational Illustration of the Book of Common Prayer of the Church of England* (London: William Tegg and Company, 1853), 266–67. Cf. Harrison and Sansom, *Worship in the Church of England*, 48–49. Hughes, *Theology of the English Reformers*, 167–70.

23. Brett, *Divine Right of Episcopacy*, 59–60. Brett, *Extent of Christ's Commission to Baptize*, 14–16, 21.

24. Brett, *Divine Right of Episcopacy*, 18–19. John Potter, *Discourse on Church Government: Wherein the Rights of the Church and the Supremacy of Christian Bishops are Vindicated and Adjusted*, 5th ed. (London: Samuel Bagster, 1839), 225–29. Potter appealed to Ignatius, Tertullian, Cyprian, Firmilian, Athanasius, and even Jerome, who he said was not partial to episcopal powers, to support the contention that only bishops and their assistants could baptize.

25. [Roger Laurence], *Dissenters, and Other Unauthorized Baptisms Null and Void, By the Articles, Canons and Rubricks of the Church of England* (London, 1712), 8–9. [Roger Laurence], *Lay Baptism, Invalid: or an Essay to Prove that such Baptism is Null and Void; when Administered in Opposition to the Divine Right of Apostolic Succession* (London, 1708), 66–69. Brett, *Extent of Christ's Commission to Baptize*, vii, 22–24. Laurence's assertion of the invalidity of lay baptism led to a scholarly response by Joseph Bingham, *A Scholastic History of the Practice of the Church in Reference to the Administration of Baptism by Laymen* (London, 1712). Cf. G. V. Bennett, "Conflict in the Church," in *Britain after the Glorious Revolution, 1689–1714* (New York: St. Martins Press, 1969),

172–73. Every, *High Church Party,* 128–130. See chapter 5 for a discussion of the question of the validity of presbyterian ordination.

26. [Laurence], *Lay Baptism, Invalid,* xviii–xix.

27. [Laurence], *Lay Baptism, Invalid,* iii–v, xix–xxii, 44–48. Brett, *Divine Right of Episcopacy,* 99. George Hickes went further and stated that the deprivation of the Non-Juror bishops had created a schism, and the ministrations of those who supported the deprivations were invalid. George Hickes, *The Constitution of the Catholic Church, and the Nature and Consequences of Schism* (London, 1716), 32–33. Bingham, *Scholastic History,* iii–v. Cf. Every, *High Church Party,* 129–30. Yould, "Origins of the Nonjurors," 319–20.

28. Bennett, "Conflict in the Church," 173. Every, *High Church Party,* 130–31.

29. Laurence is quoted in Broxap, *Later Non-Jurors,* 24; Broxap discusses the coalescing of Brett's religious and political positions, as it became clear that the death of Anne meant that Brett would have to take the oaths to George I; *Later Non-Jurors,* 23–28. Brett, *Divine Right of Episcopacy,* 123–27. Brett, *Extent of Christ's Commission to Baptize,* iv, 22–24. George Hickes, *Two Treatises: One of the Christian Priesthood, the Other of the Dignity of the Episcopal Order,* 3 vols. (Oxford: John Henry Parker, 1845), 1:271. [Laurence], *Lay Baptism, Invalid,* 66–67. Cf. Bennett, *Tory Crisis in Church and State,* 151–56. Paul Kleber Monod, *Jacobitism and the English People 1688–1788* (Cambridge: Cambridge University Press, 1989), 139.

30. Wheatly, *Rational Illustration,* 359. Cf. Waterland, "Lay Baptism," 6:76.

31. Brett, *Christian Altar,* 29–31. Brett, *Divine Right of Episcopacy,* 62. [Laurence], *Lay Baptism, Invalid,* 52–53. G. V. Bennett states that the positions held by Brett and Laurence, as popular as they might have been among parish priests, was simply a clerical dream-world at a time when Erastianism was deeply embedded in the bulk of the Anglican laity. He believes that only a small minority of the higher clergy embraced what appeared to be "too thin a cover for Jacobitism." Bennett, *Tory Crisis in Church and State,* 152.

32. Beveridge, *"Ecclesia Anglicana,"* 7:434–35.

33. Waterland, "Nature of the Christian Sacraments," 5:441–42, 468–73, 477. Waterland, "Review of the Eucharist," 7:393–410.

34. Johnson, "Unbloody Sacrifice," 1:298, 342. Cf. Echlin, *Anglican Eucharist,* 170.

35. Johnson, "Unbloody Sacrifice," 1:520–21.

36. Johnson, "Unbloody Sacrifice," 1:458–60, 514, 520–21. Brett, *Discerning the Body,* x–xi. Thomas Brett, *Some Remarks on Dr. Waterland's Review of the Eucharist* (London, 1738), 4–8. Cf. Grisbrooke, *Anglican Liturgies,* 79. Killian McDonnell, *John Calvin, the Church, and the Eucharist* (Princeton: Princeton University Press, 1967), 65.

37. Wilson, "Sermon LXXV," 3:267.

38. Brett, *Remarks on Waterland's Review of the Eucharist,* 12. Johnson, "Unbloody Sacrifice," 1:516–18. Waterland, "Review of the Eucharist," 7:107–9.

39. Waterland, "Review of the Eucharist," 7:393–410, 412–13. Cf. Mather, "Georgian Churchmanship Reconsidered," 269–72. Sykes, *Church and State in England,* 250–51.

40. William Beveridge, "The Great Necessity and Advantage of Frequent Communion," in *The Theological Works of William Beveridge, D.D.,* 12 vols. (Oxford: John Henry Parker, 1846), 8:568–72.

41. Beveridge, "Frequent Communion," 8:580–81. Johnson, "Unbloody Sacrifice," 2:258–81.

42. Beveridge, "Church Catechism," 1:111–12. William Beveridge, "Sermon XXXV: Admission into the Church of Christ, by Baptism, Necessary to Salvation", in *The Theological Works of William Beveridge, D.D.,* 12 vols. (Oxford: John Henry Parker, 1843), 2:180–82. Brett, *Divine Right of Episcopacy,* 63, 99. Brett, *Extent of Christ's Commission,* 25. Johnson, "Unbloody Sacrifice," 2:118, 139–40. [Laurence], *Lay Baptism, Invalid,* 13. [Leslie], *Water Baptism,* 59. Robert Nelson, *A Companion For the Festivals and Fasts of the Church of England* (London: Society for Promoting Christian Knowledge, 1841), 525–26. John Sharp, *The Duty and Advantages of Frequently Receiving the Holy Sacrament: A Sermon preached before the Queen at St. James's Chapel, on Good Friday, March 26, 1703* (London, 1703), 2–3. Wilson, "Church Catechism," 4:79–80. Waterland, "Lay Baptism," 6:213–14. Cf. Bengt Hagglund, *History of Theology,* Gene J. Lund, trans. (St. Louis: Concordia Publishing House, 1968), 192–93, for a similar understanding of necessity that was taught by Duns Scotus. Richard Muller, *Dictionary of Latin and Greek Theological Terms* (Grand Rapids, MI: Baker Book House, 1985), 199, 200.

43. [Laurence], *Lay Baptism, Invalid,* 67–69.

44. [Leslie], *Water Baptism,* 60–61.

45. Francis Oakley, *Omnipotence, Covenant and Order* (Ithaca: Cornell University Press, 1984), 63–64. Heiko Oberman, *Harvest of Medieval Theology,* 3rd ed. (Durham, NC: The Labyrinth Press, 1983), 37.

46. Beveridge, "Church Catechism," 8:111. Waterland, "Nature of the Christian Sacraments," 5:479.

47. Brett, *Extent of Christ's Commission to Baptize,* 19.

48. [George Hickes], *The Case of Infant Baptism* (London, 1685), 21. Cf. Waterland, "Nature of the Christian Sacraments," 5:493.

49. Beveridge, *"Ecclesia Anglicana,"* 7:461, 464–65. Brett, *Extent of Christ's Commission to Baptize,* 5, 12–13. [Hickes], *Case of Infant Baptism,* 24, 40–43. Wheatly, *Rational Illustration,* 321–24.

50. Beveridge, *"Ecclesia Anglicana,"* 7:462–63. Brett, *Extent of Christ's Commission to Baptize,* 4–6.

51. Samuel Clarke, "Sermon I: Of that Belief which is necessary to Baptism," in *The Sermons of Samuel Clarke,* John Clarke, ed., 6th ed. (London, 1744), 4:7. Samuel Clarke, "Sermon II: Of that Belief which is necessary to Baptism," in *The Sermons of Samuel Clarke,* John Clarke, ed., 6th ed. (London, 1744), 4:30–35.

52. Beveridge, "Church Catechism," 8:116–17. Brett, *Extent of Christ's Commission to Baptize,* 9–10. Cf. Hughes, *Theology of the English Reformers,* 203–8.

53. Wheatly, *Rational Illustration,* 318–19. Cf. Beveridge, "Church Catechism," 8:115. Waterland, "Nature of the Christian Sacrament," 5:474.

54. Brett, *Extent of Christ's Commission to Baptize,* 9–10. [Hickes], *Case of Infant Baptism,* 47.

55. Sykes, *Church and State in England,* 118, 121, 132. Abbey and Overton, *English Church in the Eighteenth Century,* 2:502, whose low view of the eighteenth century English church leads them to conclude that "not one in a hundred was confirmed at all. And often the sacred rite wore the appearance of a 'running ceremony' and 'a game for boys'." Cf. Virgin, *Church in an Age of Negligence,* 158–159; who notes that although there was a great disparity in the size and number of parishes between dioceses nothing was done to alleviate the problem prior to 1840.

56. Grisbrooke, *Anglican Liturgies,* 122. Every, *High Church Party,* 121–22.

57. Brett, *Extent of Christ's Commission to Baptize,* 12. Nelson, *Companion for the Festivals,* 492. Henry Stebbing, *A Defence of the Order of Confirmation As Now Settled in the Church of England In a Discourse on Acts 8:17* (London, 1729), 3–6. Philip Stubbs, *Of Confirmation. A Sermon Preach'd at St. Benedict Grace-Church, March 14th, 1693* (London, 1693), 17–18. Waterland, "Review of the Eucharist," 7:312. Wheatly, *Rational Illustration,* 375–76. Wilson, "Church Catechism," 4:1–2.

58. William Law, "Three Letters to the Bishop of Bangor," in *The Works of the Reverend William Law, M.A.,* 9 vols. (London, 1762; reprint, Setley: G. Moreton, 1892), 1:27–28. Potter, *Discourse on Church-Government,* 245–47. Stebbing, *Confirmation,* 14.

59. Potter, *Discourse on Church-Government,* 249.

60. Wheatly, *Rational Illustration,* 373–74. Stubbs, *Confirmation,* 20–23.

61. Nelson, *Companion to the Festivals,* 492. Stebbing, *Confirmation,* 4–5, 10–12. Thomas Wilson, "Parochialia," in *The Works of the Right Reverend Father in God, Thomas Wilson, D.D.,* 7 vols. (Oxford: John Henry Parker, 1843), 7:8–9, 13–18.

62. Stebbing, *Confirmation,* 10–12. Wilson, "Parochialia," 7:8–9, 18, 31.

63. Stubbs, *Confirmation,* 18. Cf. G. J. Cuming, *A History of Anglican Liturgy,* 2nd ed. (London: MacMillan Press, Ltd., 1984), 142–43. Every, *High Church Party,* 122. Grisbrooke, *Anglican Liturgy,* 122.

64. Grisbrooke, *Anglican Liturgies,* 71. Cf. Buxton, *Eucharist and Institution Narrative,* 161–71. Echlin, *Anglican Eucharist,* 165–66. Every, *High Church Party,* 132. Yould, "Origins of the Non-Juror Schism," 321–24.

65. Beveridge, *"Ecclesia Anglicana,"* 7:504–7. Brett, *Christian Altar,* viii–xi. Johnson, *Propitiatory Oblation,* 8. G. M. Yould has stated that George Hickes revived the doctrine of eucharistic sacrifice in his treatise, *The Christian Priesthood* (1709). After Charles Trimnell, Bishop of Norwich, and Dr. John Hancock, Vicar of St. Margaret's, Lothbury, wrote accusing Hickes of "popery," John Johnson entered the debate in support of Hickes with his anonymous, *Propitiatory Oblation in the Holy Eucharist* (1710). Yould, "Origins of the Non-Juror Schism," 320–30. Cf. Buxton, *Eucharist and Institution Narrative,* 161–72. Dugmore, *Eucharistic Doctrine in England,* 150–52.

66. Beveridge, "Church Catechism," 8:119. Potter, *Discourse on Church Government,* 241–44.

67. Johnson, *Propitiatory Oblation,* 26–27, 33. Johnson, "Unbloody Sacrifice," 2:121–23. Thomas Bowyer, *A True Account of the Nature, End and Efficacy of the Sacrament of the Lord's Supper* (London, 1736), 34. Law, "Demonstration of the Errors," 5:55–56. Nelson, *Companion for the Festivals,* 528. Cf. Yould, "Origins of the Non-Juror Schism," 322. Buxton, *Eucharist and Institution Narrative,* 185–86. See Broxap, *Later Non-Jurors,* 35–65 for a discussion of the Usages Controversy.

68. Johnson, "Unbloody Sacrifice," 1:71. Thomas Brett used Johnson's definition as proof that Daniel Waterland was not that far from Johnson's understanding of sacrifice. Waterland taught that the eucharist was a representative sacrifice that was more spiritual than material. Darwell Stone places Waterland in between Benjamin Hoadly on the left and Brett and Johnson on the right. Brett, *Remarks on Waterland's Review of the Eucharist,* 125–26, 208. Daniel Waterland, "Sermon XXXI: Christ's Sacrifice of Himself Explained; and Man's Duty to Offer Spiritual Sacrifice Inferred and Recommended," in *The Works of the Reverend Daniel*

*Waterland, D.D.,* 3rd ed., 6 vols. (Oxford: Oxford University Press, 1856), 5:745–46. Waterland, "Review of the Eucharist," 7:346. Stone, *History of the Eucharist,* 2:502. Cf. Buxton, *Eucharist and Institution Narrative,* 173–74.

69. Brett, *Christian Altar,* 5–6. Brett, *Remarks on Waterland's Review of the Eucharist,* 125–26. Hickes, *Two Treatises,* 2:110–11, 167. Cf. Grisbrooke, *Anglican Liturgies,* 72–73.

70. Johnson, *Propitiatory Oblation,* 14–15. Johnson, "Unbloody Sacrifice," 1:178–79, 393–99. Brett, *Christian Altar,* 5–6, 27.

71. Hickes, *Two Treatises,* 2:159–60, 175. Johnson, *Propitiatory Oblation,* 14–15, 69. Johnson, "Unbloody Sacrifice," 2:178–79. Cf. Yould, "Origins of the Non-Juror Schism," 322. On the definitions of Trent, see David Power, *The Sacrifice We Offer: The Tridentine Dogma and its Reinterpretation* (Edinburgh: T. & T. Clark, Ltd., 1987), 119–20; Seeberg, *History of Doctrines,* 2:439–42.

72. Brett, *Discerning the Body,* 39–40. Johnson, "Unbloody Sacrifice," 1:122, 144–45. Cf. Bowyer, *True Account,* 49–50.

73. Echlin, *Anglican Eucharist,* 167–68. Power, *Sacrifice We Offer,* 44–45.

74. Johnson, "Unbloody Sacrifice," 1:71.

75. Buxton, *Eucharist and Institution Narrative,* 173.

76. Beveridge, "Church Catechism," 8:120. Bowyer, *True Account,* 9. Hickes, *Two Treatises,* 2:85, 87. Law, "Demonstration of Gross and Fundamental Errors," 5:48. Nelson, *Companion to the Festivals,* 526. Nelson, *Transubstantiation Contrary to Scripture,* 17. Daniel Waterland, "Sermon XXXI," 5:745–46. Thomas Wilson, "Sermon LXXVI: The Lord's Supper Practically Explained," *The Works of the Most Reverend Father in God, Thomas Wilson, D.D.,* 7 vols. (Oxford: John Henry Parker, 1847), 3:276–77. Cf. Yould, "Origins of the Non-Juror Schism," 322.

77. Beveridge, "Church Catechism", 8:119. Sharp, *Duty and Advantages,* 11–13. Waterland, "Nature of the Sacraments," 5:477, 574–75. Waterland, "Review of the Eucharist," 7:244. Wilson, "Sermon LXXV," 3:267–68. Wilson, "Sermon LXXVI," 3:276.

78. Bowyer, *True Account,* 84–86. Johnson, "Unbloody Sacrifice," 1:192; 2:132–33. Sharp, *Duty and Advantages,* 9.

79. Beveridge, "Church Catechism," 8:121. Waterland, "Review of the Eucharist," 7:268–269. Wilson, "Church Catechism," 4:84–85. Wilson, "Sermon LXXV," 3:271.

80. Waterland, "Review of the Eucharist," 7:277. See the previous discussion of the effective causes of the sacraments.

81. Johnson, "Unbloody Sacrifice," 2:192–93. Sharp, *Duties and Advantages,* 17–18.

82. Johnson, "Unbloody Sacrifice," 2:118–19, 140–41, 194. Sharp, *Duty and Advantages,* 13–14, 16–17. Wilson, "Church Catechism," 4:86.

83. Johnson, "Unbloody Sacrifice" 2:130, 174.

84. [Daniel Defoe], *The Case of the Protestant Dissenters in England Fairly Stated* (London, 1716), 8. Bennett, *Tory Crisis in Church and State,* 101–2. Sykes notes Benjamin Hoadly's ongoing effort to secure the repeal of the Test Act; Sykes, *Church and State in England,* 341. Fear of what a non-Anglican parliament would do to the national church led John Keble to call the repeal of the Test Act (1828), Catholic Emancipation (1829), and the Passage of the Reform Bill (1832) a "national apostasy." Keble suggested that, following the shattering of the mutually interdependent relationship of church and state, parliament could no longer legislate for the church. J. H. L. Rowlands, *Church State and Society: The Attitudes*

*of John Keble, Richard Hurrell Froude and John Henry Newman 1827–1845* (Worthing, West Sussex: Churchman Publishing, 1989), 46–52.

85. Thomas Sherlock, "A Vindication of the Corporation and Test Acts, in answer to the Bishop of Bangor's reasons for the repeal of them: to which is added a second part, concerning the religion of oaths," in *The Works of Bishop Sherlock,* 5 vols. (London: A. J. Valpy, 1830), 4:433–35, 439. Henry Sacheverell, *Political Union* (London, 1710), 24. Cf. Bennett, *Tory Crisis in Church and State,* 7, 10–11. Every, *High Church Party,* 165–67. Langford, *Polite and Commercial People,* 294–95.

86. Stone, *History of the Eucharist,* 2:515. Cf. Mather, "Georgian Churchmanship Reconsidered," 282.

## EPILOGUE

1. S. C. Carpenter, *Eighteenth Century Church and People* (London: John Murray, 1959), 2.

2. Owen Chadwick, *The Spirit of the Oxford Movement* (Cambridge: Cambridge University Press, 1990), 14. Robert D. Cornwall, "The Search for the Primitive Church: The Use of Early Church Fathers in the High Church Anglican Tradition, 1680–1745" *Anglican and Episcopal History* 59 (September 1990): 303–29.

3. [Charles Leslie], *The Case of the Regale and of the Pontificate stated, In the Relation of a Conference Concerning the Independency of the Church, as to her Purely Spiritual Power and Authority* (London, 1700), 222.

4. William Jones, *Essay on the Church* (London, 1800), 19–22. William Beveridge, "Sermon IV: Salvation in the Church Only, Under Such a Ministry," in *The Theological Works of William Beveridge, D.D.,* 12 vols. (Oxford: John Henry Parker, 1842), 1:62–64. Thomas Brett, *An Account of Church Government and Governours,* 2nd ed. (London, 1710), 7–11. Cf. Chadwick, *Spirit of the Oxford Movement,* 11–14.

5. Clark, *English Society,* 219–21, 270–73. J. H. L. Rowlands, *Church, State and Society: The Attitudes of John Keble, Richard Hurrell Froude and John Henry Newman 1827–1845* (Worthing, West Sussex: Limited, 1989), 8. Cf. Louis Weil, *Sacraments and Liturgy, the Outward Signs* (Oxford: Basil Blackwell Publisher Limited, 1983), 23–24. The challenge to Clark's thesis concerning the *ancien regime* is seen in the following recent articles: James E. Bradley, "Anglican Pulpit, the Social Order, and the Resurgence of Toryism during the American Revolution," *Albion,* 21 (Fall 1989): 361–88; John Money, "Provincialism and the English 'Ancien Regime': Samuel Pipe-Wolferstan and the 'Confessional State', 1776–1820," *Albion,* 21 (Fall 1989): 389–425; John A. Phillips, "The Social Calculus: Deference and Defiance in Later Georgian England," *Albion* 21 (Fall 1989): 426–49. Clark's response is found in J. C. D. Clark, "England's Ancien Regime as a Confessional State," *Albion* 21 (Fall 1989): 450–74.

6. George Every, *High Church Party 1688–1715* (London: S.P.C.K., 1956), 3–9, 66–73. John W. Packer, *The Transformation of Anglicanism* (Manchester: University of Manchester Press, 1969), 104–28. Weil, *Sacraments and Liturgy,* 23.

7. [W. J. Copeland], "*Life and Times of William III, King of England and Stadtholder of Holland,* by the Hon. Arthur Trevor," *British Critic,* 21 (January 1837): 47.

8. F. C. Mather, "Georgian Churchmanship Reconsidered: Some Variations

in Anglican Public Worship 1714–1830," *Journal of Ecclesiastical History* 36 (April 1985): 255–57.

9. J. C. D. Clark, *English Society 1688–1832* (Cambridge: Cambridge University Press, 1985), 146–47. Chadwick, *Spirit of the Oxford Movement,* 19.

10. Geoffrey Rowell, *The Vision Glorious* (Oxford: Oxford University Press, 1983), 1, 4. J. H. L. Rowlands states that Keble continued to believe in royal supremacy after 1832, but in his 1833 sermon "National Apostasy," he articulated the view that although the bond between church and state was indissoluble, Parliament no longer had legislative authority over the church, and the bishops did not have to submit to their ecclesiastical dictums; Rowlands, *Church, State and Society,* 46–52.

11. Rowell, *Vision Glorious,* 1, 4. Rowlands, *Church, State and Society,* 46–52. W. J. Copeland pointed out the witness of the Non-jurors to the divine origins of the church and its independence from the state; Copeland, *"Life and Times of William III,"* 47. Cf. Chadwick, *Spirit of the Oxford Movement,* 3. Clark, *English Society,* 272–73, 415.

12. The liturgies of Brett and Deacon are reprinted with commentaries in W. Jardine Grisbrooke, *Anglican Liturgies of the Seventeenth Centuries,* Alcuin Club Collections, No. 40 (London, S.P.C.K., 1958), 71–135, 273–316.

13. "Tract 81: *Catena Patrum* No. IV," in *Tracts for the Times,* 6 vols. (New York: AMS Press, 1969), 5:41.

14. G. J. Cuming, *A History of Anglican Liturgy,* 2nd ed. (London: MacMillan Press, Ltd., 1984), 143. On the Usages Controversy and the schism within the Non-juror movement see: Henry Broxap, *The Later Non-Jurors* (Cambridge: Cambridge University Press, 1924), 35–65.

15. Broxap, *Later Non-Jurors,* 174, 184–86. Cuming, *History of Anglican Liturgy,* 143–44. Grisbrooke, *Anglican Liturgies,* 136–38. Henry Sefton, "Revolution to Disruption," in *Studies in the History of Worship in Scotland,* Duncan Forrester and Douglas Murray, eds. (Edinburgh: T. & T. Clark, Ltd., 1984), 66–67.

16. Grisbrooke, *Anglican Liturgies,* 112, 156–59. Edward P. Echlin, *The Anglican Eucharist in Ecumenical Perspective: Doctrine and Rite from Cranmer to Seabury* (New York: Seabury Press, 1968), 198–202. Cf. Cuming, *History of Anglican Liturgy,* 144–45.

17. Marion J. Hatchet, *The Making of the First American Book of Common Prayer* (New York: Seabury Press, 1982), 42–43, 111–12. Cf. James Thayer Addison, *The Episcopal Church in the United States 1789–1931* (New York: Charles Scribner and Sons, 1951; reprinted, Hamden, CT: Archon Books, 1969), 58–62, 70–72. Echlin, *Anglican Eucharist,* 205–207. *Prayer Book Studies IV, The Eucharistic Liturgy* (New York: The Church Pension Fund, 1953), 85–89. Sefton, "Revolution to Disruption," 67.

# Bibliography

## Primary Sources

[Anonymous]. *All the Advertisements and Letters by the Lord Bishop of Bangor, Dr. Snape, the Lord Bishop of Carlisle, Dr. Kennet, &c., As they were inserted in the Publick Prints.* London, 1717.

[Atterbury, Francis, and Benjamin Shower]. *Letter to a Convocation Man.* London, 1697.

[Atterbury, Francis]. *Mitre and the Crown, Or a Real Distinction between Them.* London, 1711.

————. *Parliamentary Original and Rights of the Lower House of Convocation Cleared.* London, 1702.

————. *Rights, Powers and Privileges of an English Convocation, Stated and Vindicated.* Second Edition. London, 1701.

Barclay, Robert. "The Anarchy of the Ranters and other Libertines, the Hierarchy of the Romanists and other Pretended Churches, equally refused and Refuted in a Two-fold Apology for the Church and People of God called in Derision Quakers." In *Truth Triumphant Through the Spiritual Warfare, Christian Labours and Writings of that Able Servant of Jesus Christ, Robert Barclay.* London, 1692.

Baxter, Richard. *Of National Churches.* London, 1691.

————. *The Practical Works of Richard Baxter.* 23 volumes. London, 1830.

Betty, Joseph. *The Divine Institution of the Ministry, and the Absolute Necessity of Church Government: A Sermon Preached before the University of Oxford on Sunday the 21st of September, 1729.* Second corrected edition. London, 1729.

Beveridge, William. *Theological Works of William Beveridge, D.D.* 12 volumes. Oxford: John Henry Parker, 1842–48.

Bingham, Joseph. *Origines Ecclesiasticae; or, the Antiquities of the Christian Church.* Edited by Richard Bingham. 8 volumes. London, 1821.

————. *A Scholastic History of the Practice of the Church in Reference to the Administration of Baptism by Laymen.* London, 1712.

[Bisbie, Nathaniel]. *Unity of the Priesthood Necessary to the Unity of the Church.* London, 1692.

Bowyer, Thomas. *The True Account of the Nature, End and Efficacy of the Sacrament of the Lord's Supper.* London, 1736.

Brett, Thomas. *An Account of Church Government and Governors.* Second edition. London, 1710.

————. *The Authority of Presbyters in Provincial Synods Vindicated.* London, 1712.

————. *The Christian Altar and Sacrifice: A Sermon Shewing that the Lord's Table is a Proper Altar and the Sacrament of the Eucharist a Proper Sacrifice.* London, 1713.

————. *A Collection of the Principle Liturgies, used by the Christian Church in the Celebration of the Holy Eucharist. With a Dissertation upon Them.* London, 1720.

————. *A Discourse Concerning the Necessity of Discerning the Lord's Body in the Holy Communion.* London, 1720.

————. *The Divine Right of Episcopacy, and the Necessity of an Episcopal Commission for Preaching God's Word, and for the Valid Ministration of the Christian Sacraments, Proved from the Scriptures and the Doctrine and Practice of the Primitive Church.* London, 1718.

————. *Dr. Brett's Vindication of Himself from the Calumnies Thrown upon Him in Some Late Newspapers, wherein He is Falsely Charged with Turning Papist.* London, 1715.

————. *An Enquiry into the Judgement and Practice of the Primitive Church in Relation to Persons being Baptized by Laymen.* London, 1712.

————. *The Extent of Christ's Commission to Baptize: A Sermon Shewing the Capacity of Infants to Receive and the Utter Incapacity of our Dissenting Teachers to Administer Christian Baptism.* London, 1712.

————. *Farther Proof of the Necessity of Tradition, to Explain and Interpret the Holy Scriptures.* London, 1720.

————. *The Independency of the Church from the State as to its Pure Spiritual Powers.* London, 1717.

————. *A Review of the Lutheran Principles: Showing how they Differ From the Church of England's.* London, 1714.

————. "A Sermon of the Honour of the Christian Priesthood, and of the Necessity of a Divine Call to that Office" (1712). In *Curate of Souls.* Edited by John H. Moorman. London: S.P.C.K., 1958. 126–45.

————. *Some Remarks on Dr. Waterland's Review of the Doctrine of the Eucharist.* London, 1720.

————. *Tradition Necessary to Explain and Interpret the Holy Scriptures.* London, 1718.

Brokesby, Francis. *An History of the Government of the Primitive Church For the First Three Centuries and the Beginning of the Fourth.* London, 1712.

————. *The Life of Henry Dodwell.* London, 1715.

Bull, George. *A Companion for the Candidates of Holy Orders. Or the Great Importance and Principle Duties of the Priestly Office.* London, 1714.

————. *A Vindication of the Church of England from the Errors and Corruptions of the Church of Rome.* London, 1719. Reprinted, Oxford: John Henry Parker, 1840.

Burnet, Gilbert. *A Discourse of the Pastoral Care.* London, 1692.

————. *The New Preface and Additional Chapter, to the Third Edition of the Pastoral Care.* London, 1713.

————. *An Exposition of the Thirty-nine Articles of the Church of England.* Third edition. London, 1705.

Calvin, John. *Institutes of the Christian Religion.* Library of Christian Classics.

Edited by John T. McNeill. Translated by Ford Lewis Battles. 2 volumes. Philadelphia: Westminster Press, 1960.

Campbell, Archibald. *The Doctrines of a Middle State Between Death and the Resurrection.* London, 1721.

Clarke, Samuel. *Sermons of Samuel Clarke.* Sixth edition. Edited by John Clarke. 6 volumes. London, 1744.

[Collier, Jeremy]. *Brief Essay Concerning the Independency of Church Power.* London, 1692.

——. *Defence of the Reasons For Restoring Some Prayers and Directions of King Edward the Sixth's First Liturgy: Being a Reply to a Book Entituled, No Reason for Restoring Them.* Second edition. London, 1718.

——. *Reasons for Restoring Some Prayers and Directions, as they Stand in the Communion Service of the First English Reform'd Liturgy, Compiled by the Bishops in the 2d and 3d Years of the Reign of King Edward VI.* Fourth edition. London, 1718.

Collier, Jeremy. *An Ecclesiastical History of Great Britain Chiefly of England from the First Planting of Christianity, to the End of the Reign of Charles the Second.* New Edition. 9 volumes. London: William Straker, 1845.

——. *Ecclesiastical History of Great Britain.* Two Volumes. London, 1708–1714.

——, Translator. *A Panegyrick upon the Maccabees, by St. Gregory of Nazianzen: Of Unseasonable Diversions by Salvian: A Description of the Pagan World; A Consolary Discourse to the Christians of Carthage visited by a Mortality; Of the Advantage of Patience; these three by St. Cyprian: Done into English by Jeremy Collier.* London, 1716.

Comber, Thomas. *A Discourse upon the Form and Manner of Making, Ordaining, and Consecrating Bishops, Priests, and Deacons, According to the Order of the Church of England.* London, 1699.

[Copeland, W. J.]. "*Life and Times of William III, King of England and Stadtholder of Holland,* by the Hon. Arthur Trevor." *British Critic* 21 (January 1837): 39–66.

Cranmer, Thomas. *Writings and Disputations of Thomas Cranmer.* Parker Society. Volume 15. Edited by John Edmund Coxe. Cambridge: Cambridge University Press, 1844.

[Deacon, Thomas and Thomas Brett]. *A Communion Office, Taken Partly From Primitive Liturgies and Partly from the First English Reformed Common Prayer-Book.* London, 1718.

Deacon, Thomas. *Compleat Collection of Devotions both Public and Private, Taken from the Apostolic Constitutions, the Ancient Liturgies, and the Common Prayer Book of the Church of England.* London, 1734.

[Defoe, Daniel]. *Case of the Protestant Dissenters in England Fairly Stated.* London, 1716.

——. *Christianity No Creature of the State: Or, if it be made one, Reasons Why it should be Abolished.* London, 1717.

——. *An Enquiry into the Occasional Conformity of Dissenters in Cases of Preferment.* London, 1701.

Doddridge, Philip. *A Course of Lectures.* Second edition. Edited by S. Clark. London, 1776.

———. *Free Thoughts on the Most Probable Means of Reviving the Dissenting Interest*. London, 1730.

Dodwell, Henry. *Dissertationes Cyprianici*. Oxford, 1684.

———. *Dissertationes in Irenaeum*. Oxford, 1689.

[Dodwell, Henry]. *A Defence of the Vindication of the Deprived Bishops*. London, 1695.

———. *The Doctrine of the Church of England, Concerning the Independency of the Clergy on the Lay Power, as to those Rights which are Purely Spiritual, Reconciled with our Oath of Supremacy, and the Lay Deprivation of the Popish Bishops in the Beginning of the Reformation*. London, 1697.

———. *A Vindication of the Deprived Bishops*. London, 1692.

Earbery, Matthias. *An Historical Essay Upon the Power of the Prince in the Calling, Proroguing and Dissolving Councils, Synods and Convocations*. London, 1717.

———. *A Review of the Bishop of Bangor's Sermon and His Answer to the Representation of the Committee of the Lower House of Convocation. In Two Parts*. London, 1718.

———. *A Serious Admonition To Dr. Kennet*. London, 1717.

Ellison, Nathaniel. *Of Confirmation*. London, 1701.

Gibson, Edmund. *Codex Juris Ecclesiastici Anglicani: or the Statutes, Constitutions, Canons, Rubricks, and Articles of the Church of England, Methodically Digested under their Proper Heads*. 2 volumes. London, 1713.

Greenslade, S. L., Editor. *Early Latin Theology*. The Library of Christian Classics: Ichthus edition. Philadelphia: Westminster Press, 1956.

Hare, Francis. *Church Authority Vindicated in a Sermon Preached at Putney, May 5, 1719*. Fourth edition. London, 1720.

[Hickes, George]. *An Apology for the New Separation*. London, 1691.

———. *The Case of Infant Baptism*. London, 1685.

Hickes, George. *The Constitution of the Catholic Church, and the Nature and Consequences of Schism*. London, 1716.

———. *A Second Collection of Controversial Letters Relating to the Church of England, and the Church of Rome, as they Passed Between and Honourable Lady and Dr. George Hickes*. London, 1710.

———. *Two Treatises on the Christian Priesthood, and on the Dignity of the Episcopal Order*. Three Volumes. Fourth Edition. Oxford: John Henry Parker, 1845–1847.

———. *A Vindication of Some Among Ourselves Against the False Principles of Dr. Sherlock*. London, 1692.

Hill, Samuel. *The Catholic Balance: or a Discourse Determining the Controversies Concerning I. Tradition of Catholic Doctrines. II. The Primacy of S. Peter and the Bishop of Rome. III. The Subjection and Authority of the Church in a Christian State: According to the Suffrages of the Primest Antiquity*. London, 1687.

[Hill, Samuel]. *Municipium Ecclesiasticum, or the Rights, Liberties, and Authorities of the Christian Church*. London, 1697.

———. *The Rites of the Christian Church Further Defended in Answer to the Appeal of Dr. Wake*. London, 1698.

Hoadly, Benjamin. *An Answer to the Reverend Dr. Hare's Sermon Intitul'd, Church Authority Vindicated.* London, 1719.

————. *An Answer to the Reverend Dr. Snape's Letter to the Bishop of Bangor.* Tenth edition. London, 1717.

————. *Preservative Against the Principles and Practices of the Non-Jurors both in Church and State.* Second edition. London, 1716.

————. *The Works of Benjamin Hoadly, D.D.* Edited by John Hoadly. 3 Volumes. London, 1773.

Hooker, Richard. *Of the Laws of Ecclesiastical Polity.* Edited by Georges Edelen. 3 Volumes. Cambridge: Belknap Press of Harvard University Press, 1977.

Hughes, John. "Preliminary Dissertations to St. Chrysostom's *De Sacerdotio.*" In George Hickes, *Two Treatises on the Christian Priesthood, and on the Dignity of the Episcopal Order.* Fourth edition. 3 Volumes. Oxford: John Henry Parker, 1845–47. Volume 3.

Johnson, John. *The Propitiary Oblation in the Eucharist Truly Stated and Defended From Scripture, Antiquity and the Communion Service of the Church of England.* London, 1710.

————. *The Theological Works of the Reverend John Johnson, M.A.* 4 volumes. Oxford: John Henry Parker, 1847.

Jones, William. *Essay on the Church.* London, 1800.

[Ken, Thomas]. *An Exposition on the Church-Catechism, or the Practice of Divine Love, Revised.* London, 1696.

————. *Lacrymae Ecclesiae Anglicanae: or A Serious and Passionate Address of the Church of England, to Her Sons, especially those of the Clergy.* London, 1689.

Kettlewell, John. *Compleat Collection of the Works of the Reverend and Learned John Kettlewell, B.D.* Two volumes. London, 1719.

————. *The Measures of Christian Obedience.* London, 1681.

King, Peter. *Enquiry into the Constitution, Discipline, Unity and Worship of the Primitive Church.* Second edition. London, 1713.

[Laurence, Roger]. *The Bishop of Oxford's Charge, Considered.* London, 1712.

————. *Dissenters and Other Unauthorized Baptisms Null and Void, By the Articles, Canons and Rubricks of the Church of England.* London, 1712.

————. *Lay Baptism Invalid: Or An Essay to Prove that such Baptism is Null and Void; when Administered in Opposition to the Divine Right of Apostolic Succession.* London, 1708.

————. *Sacerdotal Powers: Or Necessity of Confession, Penance and Absolution Together with the Nullity of Lay Baptism Asserted in an Essay.* London, 1711.

Law, William. *The Works of the Reverend William Law, M.A.* 9 Volumes. London, 1762. Reprint, Setley: G. Moreton, 1892.

[Leslie, Charles]. *The Case of the Regale and the Pontificate Stated, In the Relation of a Conference Concerning the Independency of the Church as to Her Purely Spiritual Power and Authority.* London, 1700.

————. *A Discourse Proving the Divine Institution of Water Baptism: Wherein the Quaker-Arguments Against it, Are Collected and Confuted With as Much as Needful Concerning the Lord's Supper.* London, 1697.

Leslie, Charles. *The Theological Works of the Rev. Mr. Charles Leslie.* London, 1721.

Lindsay, John. Preface to *A Vindication of the Church of England and of the Lawful Ministry Thereof,* by Francis Mason. Translated by John Lindsay. London, 1734.

Locke, John. *The Reasonableness of Christianity with a Discourse of Miracles and Part of a Third Letter Concerning Toleration.* Edited by I. T. Ramsey. Palo Alto: Stanford University Press, 1958.

————. *The Reasonableness of Christianity.* Edited by George W. Ewing. Washington: Regency Gateway Press, 1965.

————. *The Works of John Locke.* New Edition. 10 volumes. London: Thomas Tegg, W. Sharpe and Son, 1823. Reprinted, Germany: Scientia Verlag Aalen, 1963.

Lowth, Simon. *Of the Subject of Church Power, In Whom It Resides.* London, 1685.

Lowth, William. *Directions for the Profitable Reading of the Holy Scriptures.* Second edition. London, 1712.

Marshall, Nathaniel, Editor and Translator. *The Genuine Works of St. Cyprian.* 2 volumes. London, 1717.

————. *The Penitential Discipline of the Primitive Church, For the First Four Hundred Years after Christ; Together with its Declension from the Fifth Century, Downwards to its Present State: Impartially Represented.* London, 1714. Oxford: John Henry Parker, 1844.

Nelson, Robert. *A Companion For the Festivals and Fasts of the Church of England, with Collects and Prayers for each Solemnity.* Fifth edition. 1708. Reprinted, London: S.P.C.K., 1841.

————. *Transubstantiation Contrary To Scripture.* London, 1688.

Newman, John Henry. *Apologia Pro Vita Sua.* New York: Longmans, Green and Co., 1947.

Owen, John. *The True Nature of a Gospel Church and Its Government (1689).* Abridged and edited by John Huxtable. London: James Clarke and Company, Limited, 1947.

Potter, John. *The Bishop of Oxford's Charge to the Clergy of His Diocese at his Triennial Visitation in July 1719.* London, 1720.

————. *A Discourse on Church Government: Wherein the Rights of the Church and the Supremacy of Christian Bishops are Vindicated and Adjusted.* Fifth edition. London, 1707. London: Samuel Bagster, 1839.

————. *The Theological Works of the Most Reverend Dr. John Potter, Late Lord Archbishop of Canterbury.* 3 volumes. Oxford, 1753.

Roberts, William. *The Divine Institution of the Gospel Ministry and the Necessity of Episcopal Ordination, Asserted by Proofs from Scripture, and the Practice of the Primitive and Purest Ages of the Church.* Fourth edition. London, 1753.

Rogers, John. *A Discourse of the Visible and Invisible Church of Christ.* London, 1719.

Sacheverell, Henry. *Political Union.* London. 1710.

————. *The Rights of the Church of England Asserted and Prov'd: In an Answer to a Late Pamphlet, intitul'd, The Rights of the Protestant Dissenters, in a Review of their Case.* London, 1705.

Sclater, William. *An Original Draught of the Primitive Church.* 1717. First American edition. Columbus, OH. 1733.

[Scot, William]. *No Necessity to Alter the Common-Prayer; or the Unreasonableness of the New Separation.* London, 1718.

Sharp, John. *The Duty and Advantages of Frequently Receiving the Holy Sacrament: A Sermon Preached Before the Queen at St. James's Chappel, On Good Friday, March 26, 1703.* London, 1703.

———. *The Theological Works of the Most Reverend John Sharp, D. D.* 5 volumes. Oxford: Oxford University Press, 1829.

Sherlock, Thomas. *The Works of Bishop Sherlock.* 5 volumes. London: A. J. Valpy, 1830.

Sherlock, William. *An Apology for Writing Against the Socinians, in Defence of the Doctrines of the Holy Trinity and Incarnation.* London, 1693.

———. *The Case of the Allegiance Due to Sovereign Powers.* Third edition. London, 1691.

———. *A Vindication of the Rights of Ecclesiastical Authority: Being an Answer to the First Part of the Protestant Reconciler.* London, 1685.

Smalridge, George. *Sixty Sermons Preached on Several Occasions.* Second edition. London, 1727.

Snape, Andrew. *A Letter to the Bishop of Bangor.* Dublin, 1717.

[Spinckes, Nathaniel], *Mr. Hoadly's Measures of Submission to the Civil Magistrate Enquired into and Disproved.* London, 1711.

———. *No Sufficient Reason for Restoring the Prayers and Directions of King Edward the Sixth's First Liturgy.* London, 1718.

[Stackhouse, Thomas]. *The Miseries and Great Hardships of the Inferiour Clergy, in and about London.* London, 1722.

Stackhouse, Thomas. *A Compleat Body of Speculative and Practical Divinity.* Third edition. London, 1743.

Stebbing, Henry. *A Defence of the Order of Confirmation as Now Settled in the Church of England: In a Discourse on Acts 8:17.* London. 1729.

———. *Polemical Tracts; or a Collection of Papers Written in Defence of the Doctrine and Discipline of the Church of England.* Cambridge: Cambridge University Press, 1727.

———. *A Rational Enquiry into the Proper Methods of Supporting Christianity, in so far as it Concerns the Governors of the Church.* London, 1720.

———. *Remarks Upon a Position of the Right Reverend, Benjamin Hoadly, The Lord Bishop of Bangor Concerning Religious Sincerity.* London, 1718.

Stevens, William. *An Essay on the Nature and Constitution of the Christian Church.* London, 1773.

Stubbs, Philip. *Of Confirmation. A Sermon Preach'd at St. Benedict Grace-Church, March 14th, 1693.* London, 1693.

Sykes, Arthur Ashley. *The Authority of the Clergy and the Liberties of the Laity Stated and Vindicated.* London, 1720.

———. *The Corporation and Test Acts, Shown to be of No Importance to the Church of England.* London, 1736.

———. *Some Remarks on Mr. Marshall's Defense of our Constitution in Church and State.* London, 1717.

Symson, Matthias. *The Necessity of a Lawful Ministry.* London, 1708.

Tillotson, John. *The Works of the Most Reverend Dr. John Tillotson, Late Archbishop of Canterbury.* Fifth edition. 3 Volumes. London, 1735.

Tindal, Matthew. *Christianity as Old as Creation: Or the Gospel, a Republication of the Religion of Nature.* London, 1730. Reprinted, Stuttgard-Bad Cannstatt: Friedrich Frommann Verlag, 1767.

[Tindal Matthew]. *The Rights of the Christian Church, Asserted, Against the Romish, and all other Priests who claim an Independent Power over It.* Third edition. London, 1707.

————. *Four Discourses on the Following Subjects: viz. I Of Obedience to the Supreme Powers, and the Duty of Subjects in all Revolutions. II Of the Laws of Nations, and the Rights of Sovereigns. III Of the Power of the Magistrate, and the Rights of Mankind, in Matters of Religion. IV Of the Liberty of the Press.* London, 1709.

Toland, John. *A Collection of Several Pieces of Mr. John Toland.* 2 volumes. London, 1726.

*Tracts for the Times.* 6 Volumes. Reprinted, New York: AMS Press, 1969.

Trapp, Joseph. *The Real Nature of the Church or the Kingdom of Christ.* Second edition. London, 1717.

[Wagstaffe, Thomas]. *The Necessity of an Alteration.* London, 1718.

Wake, William. *An English Version of the Genuine Epistles of the Apostolic Fathers, with a Preliminary Discourse Concerning the Use of those Fathers.* London, 1693.

————. *The Principles of the Christian Religion Explained: In a Brief Commentary upon the Church Catechism.* Third edition. London, 1700.

Warburton, William. *Alliance Between Church and State.* London, 1736.

Waterland, Daniel. *The Works of the Reverend Daniel Waterland, D. D.* 10 volumes. Oxford: Clarendon Press, 1823.

————. *The Works of the Rev. Daniel Waterland, D. D.* Third edition. 6 volumes. Oxford: Oxford University Press, 1856.

[Welchman, Edward]. *A Defense of the Church of England, From the Charge of Schism and Heresie.* London, 1693.

Wheatly, Charles. *A Rational Illustration of the Book of Common Prayer of the Church of England.* London: Wm. Tegg and Co., 1853.

Wilson, Thomas. *The Principles and Duties of Christianity.* 1707. Reprinted, Menston, Yorkshire: The Scolar Press, 1972.

Wilson, Thomas. *The Works of the Right Reverend Father in God, Thomas Wilson, D. D.* 7 volumes. Oxford: John Henry Parker, 1847–1863.

# Secondary Sources

## ARTICLES

Ady, Cecilia M. "The Post-Reformation Episcopate: (ii) From the Restoration to the Present Day." In *The Apostolic Ministry,* edited by Kenneth E. Kirk, 433–60. Second edition. London: Hodder and Stoughton, Limited, 1957.

Bauckham, Richard. "Tradition in Relation to Scripture and Reason." In *Scrip-*

*ture, Tradition and Reason,* edited by Richard Bauckham and Benjamin Drewery, 117–45. Edinburgh: T. & T. Clark, Ltd., 1988.

Bennett, G. V. "Conflict in the Church." In *Britain After the Glorious Revolution, 1689–1714,* edited by Geoffrey Holmes. New York: St. Martin's Press, 1969.

————. "The Convocation of 1710: An Anglican Attempt at Counter-revolution." In *Studies in Church History: Councils and Assemblies.* Edited by G. J. Cuming and Derek Baker, 7:311–19. Leiden: E. J. Brill, 1971.

————. "King William III and the Episcopate." *Essays in Modern English Church History,* edited by G. V. Bennett and J. D. Walsh, 104–31. New York: Oxford University Press, 1966.

————. "Patristic Tradition in Anglican Thought 1660–1900." *Oecumenia* (1971–72): 65–85.

Bradley, James E. "The Anglican Pulpit, the Social Order, and the Resurgence of Toryism during the American Revolution." *Albion* 21 (Fall 1989): 361–88.

————. "Nonconformity and the Electorate in Eighteenth Century England." *Parliamentary History* 6 (1987): 236–61.

————. "Toleration, Nonconformity, and the Unity of the Spirit: Popular Religion in Eighteenth-Century England." In *Church, Word, and Spirit,* edited by James E. Bradley and Richard Muller, 183–99. Grand Rapids, MI: William B. Eerdmans Publishing Company, 1987.

————. "Whigs and Nonconformists: 'Slumbering Radicalism' in English Politics, 1739–1789." *Eighteenth Century Studies* 9 (Fall 1975): 1–27.

Bruce, F. F. "Scripture in Relation to Tradition and Reason." In *Scripture, Tradition and Reason,* edited by Richard Bauckham and Benjamin Drewery, 36–64. Edinburgh: T. & T. Clark, Ltd., 1988.

Clark, J. C. D. "England's Ancien Regime as a Confessional State." *Albion* 21 (Fall 1989): 450–74.

————. "On Moving the Middle Ground: The Significance of Jacobitism in Historical Studies." In *The Jacobite Challenge,* edited by Eveline Cruickshanks and Jeremy Black, 177–88. Edinburgh: John Donald Publishers, Ltd., 1988.

Clifford, Alan C. "The Christian Mind of Philip Doddridge (1702–1751): The Gospel According to an Evangelical Congregationalist." *Evangelical Quarterly* 56 (October 1984): 227–42.

Cornwall, Robert D. "The Search for the Primitive Church: The Use of Early Church Fathers in the High Church Anglican Tradition." *Anglican and Episcopal History* 59 (September 1990): 303–29.

Duffy, Eamon. "Primitive Christianity Revived; Religious Renewal in Augustan England." In *Studies in Church History,* edited by Derek Baker, 14:287–300. Oxford: Basil Blackwell, 1976.

Emerson, Roger L. "Latitudinarianism and the English Deists." In *Deism, Masonry, and the Enlightenment,* edited by J. A. Leo Lemay, 19–48. Newark: University of Delaware Press, 1987.

Erskine-Hill, Howard. "Literature and the Jacobite Cause: Was there a Rhetoric of Jacobitism?" In *Ideology and Conspiracy: Aspects of Jacobitism, 1689–1759,* edited by Eveline Cruickshanks, 49–69. Edinburgh: John Donald Publishers, Ltd., 1982.

Goldie, Mark. "The Nonjurors, Episcopacy and the Origins of the Convocation

Controversy." In *Ideology and Conspiracy: Aspects of Jacobitism, 1689–1759,* edited by Eveline Cruickshanks, 15–35. Edinburgh: John Donald, 1982.

Greaves, R. W. "The Working of the Alliance, A Comment on Warburton." *In Essays in Modern English Church History,* edited by G. V. Bennett and J. D. Walsh, 163–80. London: A. and C. Black, Ltd., 1966.

Greene, Donald. "Latitudinarianism and Sensibility: The Genealogy of the 'Man of Feeling' Reconsidered." *Modern Philology* 75 (1977): 159–183.

Haugaard, William P. "Towards an Anglican Doctrine of the Ministry: Richard Hooker and the Elizabethan Church." *Anglican and Episcopal History* 56 (September 1987): 265–84.

Hill, Christopher. "Occasional Conformity." In *Reformation, Conformity and Dissent,* edited by R. Buick Knox, 199–220. London: Epworth Press, 1977.

Holeton, David. "Communion of All Baptized and Anglican Tradition." *Anglican Theological Review* 69 (January 1987); 13–28.

Isaacs, Tina. "The Anglican Hierarchy and the Reformation of Manners 1688–1738." *Journal of Ecclesiastical History* 33 (July 1982): 391–411.

Langford, Paul. "Convocation and the Tory Clergy, 1717–1761." In *The Jacobite Challenge,* edited by Eveline Cruickshanks and Jeremy Black. Edinburgh: John Donald Publishers, Ltd., 1988.

Marshall, John. "The Ecclesiology of the Latitude-men 1660–1689: Stillingfleet, Tillotson and 'Hobbism'." *Journal of Ecclesiastical History* 36 (July 1985): 407–27.

Marshall, John S. "Hooker's Theory of Church and State." *Anglican Theological Review* 27 (1945): 151–60.

Mather, F. C. "Georgian Churchmanship Reconsidered: Some Variations in Anglican Public Worship." *Journal of Ecclesiastical History* 36 (April 1985): 255–83.

Meyers, Ruth. "Infant Communion: Reflections on the Case from Tradition." *Anglican and Episcopal History* 57 (June 1988): 159–75.

Meza, Pedro Thomas. "Gilbert Burnet's Concept of Religious Toleration," *Historical Magazine of the Protestant Episcopal Church* 50 (September 1981): 227–42.

———. "The Question of Authority in the Church of England, 1689–1717." *Historical Magazine of the Protestant Episcopal Church* 42 (March 1973): 63–86.

Morrill, John. "The Sensible Revolution." In *The Anglo-Dutch Moment,* edited by Jonathan I. Israel, 73–104. Cambridge: Cambridge University Press, 1991.

Pocock, J. G. A. "Post-Puritan England and the Problem of the Enlightenment." In *Culture and Politics from Puritanism to the Enlightenment,* edited by Perez Zagorin, 91–111. Berkeley: University of California Press, 1980.

Porter, Roy. "The English Enlightenment." In *The Enlightenment in National Context,* edited by Roy Porter and Mikulas Teich, 1–18. Cambridge: Cambridge University Press, 1981.

Rack, Henry. "'Christ's Kingdom Not of the this World:' The Case of Benjamin Hoadly Versus William Law Reconsidered." *Studies in Church History: Church Society and Politics,* 12:275–92. Oxford: Basil Blackwell, 1975.

Reedy, Gerard. "Barrow, Stillingfleet on the Truth of Scripture." In *Greene Centennial Studies,* 22–39. Charlottesville: University Press of Virginia, 1984.

Runciman, Steve. "The British Non-jurors and the Russian Church." In *The Ecu-*

*menical World of Orthodox Civilization, Russian and Orthodoxy,* 155–61. The Hague: Mouton and Co., N. V. Publishers, 1974.

Sefton, Henry. "Revolution to Disruption." in *Studies in the History of Worship in Scotland,* edited by Duncan Forrester and Douglas Murray, 65–78. Edinburgh: T. & T. Clark, Ltd., 1984.

———. "The Scottish Bishops and Archbishop Arsenius." In *Studies in Church History,* edited by Derek Baker, 14:239–76. Oxford: Basil Blackwell, 1976.

Sharp, Richard. "New Perspectives on the High Church Tradition: Historical Background 1730–1780." In *Tradition Renewed,* edited by Geoffrey Rowell, 4–23. Allison Park, PA: Pickwick Publications, 1986.

Short, K. R. M. "The English Indemnity Acts 1726–1867." *Church History* 43 (1973): 366–76.

Spellman, William. "Archbishop John Tillotson and the Meaning of Moralism." *Anglican and Episcopal History* 56 (December 1987): 404–22.

Spurr, John. "The Church of England, Comprehension and the Toleration Act of 1689." *English Historical Review* 104 (October 1989): 927–46.

———. "'Latitudinarianism' and the Restoration Church." *The Historical Journal* 31 (January 1988): 61–82.

———. "Schism and the Restoration Church." *Journal of Ecclesiastical History* 41 (July 1990): 408–20.

Straka, Gerald M. "The Final Phase of Divine Right Theory in England, 1688–1702." *English Historical Review* 77 (October 1962): 638–58.

Sykes, Norman. "Benjamin Hoadly, Bishop of Bangor." In *The Social and Political Ideas of the Augustan Age,* edited by F. J. C. Hearnshaw, 112–55. New York: Barnes and Noble, Inc., 1923.

Thompson, W. D. J. Cargill. "The Philosopher of the 'Politic Society': Richard Hooker as a Political Thinker." In *Studies in Richard Hooker,* edited by W. Speed Hill, 3–76. Cleveland: The Press of Case Western Reserve University, 1972.

## BOOKS

Abbey, Charles J., and John H. Overton. *The English Church in the Eighteenth Century.* 2 volumes. London: Longmans, Green and Co., 1878.

———. *The English Church in the Eighteenth Century.* Second abridged edition. London: Longmans, Green and Company, 1887.

Addison, James Thayer. *The Episcopal Church in the United States 1789–1931.* New York: Charles Scribner and Sons, 1951. Reprinted, Hamden, CT: Archon Books, 1969.

Alan, Kurt. *A History of Christianity.* 2 volumes. Translated by James L. Schaaf. Philadelphia: Fortress Press, 1985.

Allen, J. W. *History of Political Through in the Sixteenth Century.* London: Methuen and Co., Ltd., 1928.

Avis, Paul D. *Anglicanism and the Christian Church.* Minneapolis: Fortress Press, 1989.

———. *The Church in the Theology of the Reformers.* Atlanta: John Knox Press, 1981.

Battenhouse, Roy, editor. *A Companion to the Study of St. Augustine*. New York: Oxford University Press, 1955.

Baker, Frank. *John Wesley and the Church of England*. Nashville: Abingdon Press, 1967.

Bennett, G. V. *The Tory Crisis in Church and State 1688–1730*. Oxford: Clarendon Press, 1975.

Best, G. F. A. *Temporal Pillars: Queen Anne's Bounty, the Ecclesiastical Commissioners, and the Church of England*. Cambridge: Cambridge University Press, 1964.

Bosher, Robert S. *The Making of the Restoration Settlement*. London: Dacre Press, 1957.

Bromiley, Geoffrey. *Thomas Cranmer Theologian*. New York: Oxford University Press, 1956.

Brooks, Philip E. *Cranmer in Context*. Minneapolis: Fortress Press, 1989.

Broxap, Henry. *The Biography of Thomas Deacon*. Manchester: Manchester University Press, 1911.

———. *The Later Non-Jurors*. Cambridge: Cambridge University Press, 1924.

Butterfield, Herbert. *The Whig Interpretation of History*. New York: W. W. Norton and Company, 1965.

Buxton, Richard. *Eucharist and Institution Narrative*. Alcuin Club Collections No. 58. London: S.P.C.K., 1976.

Byrne, Peter. *Natural Religion and the Nature of Religion*. London: Routledge, 1989.

Carpenter, S. C. *The Eighteenth Century Church and People*. London: John Murray Limited, 1959.

Chadwick, Owen. *The Spirit of the Oxford Movement*. Cambridge: Cambridge University Press, 1990.

Clark, J. C. D. *English Society 1688–1832*. Cambridge: Cambridge University Press, 1985.

———. *Revolution and Rebellion*. Cambridge: Cambridge University Press, 1986.

Colley, Linda. *In Defiance of Oligarchy*. Cambridge: Cambridge University Press, 1982.

Cragg, Gerald R. *The Church and the Age of Reason 1648–1789*. Baltimore: Penguin Books, 1970.

———. *Freedom and Authority*. Philadelphia: Westminster Press, 1975.

———. *From Puritanism to the Age of Reason*. Cambridge: Cambridge University Press, 1966.

———. *Reason and Authority in the Eighteenth Century*. Cambridge: Cambridge University Press, 1964.

Cranston, Maurice. *John Locke*. New York: The Macmillan Company, 1957.

Cuming, G. J. *A History of Anglican Liturgy*. Second edition. London: MacMillan Press, Ltd. 1984.

Cunliffe-Jones, Herbert, and Benjamin Drewery, Editors. *A History of Christian Doctrine*. Philadelphia: Fortress Press, 1978.

Dickens, A. G. *The English Reformation*. New York: Schocken Books, 1964.

Dickinson, J. C. *An Ecclesiastical History of England: The Latter Middle Ages*. New York: Harper and Row Publishers, Inc., 1979.

Dickinson, H. T. *Liberty and Property.* New York: Holmes and Meier Publishers, 1977.

Dix, Dom Gregory. *The Shape of the Liturgy.* Additional Notes by Paul V. Marshall. Second edition. New York: Seabury Press, 1982.

Dugmore, Clifford W. *Eucharistic Doctrine in England From Hooker to Waterland.* London: S.P.C.K. New York: Macmillan Company, 1942.

Dunn, John. *John Locke.* Oxford: Oxford University Press, 1984.

Echlin, Edward P. *The Anglican Eucharist in Ecumenical Perspective; Doctrine and Rite From Cranmer to Seabury.* New York: Seabury Press, 1968.

Eisenach, Eldon J. *Two Worlds of Liberalism: Religion and Politics in Hobbes, Locke, and Mill.* Chicago: University of Chicago Press, 1981.

Every, George. *The High Church Party 1688–1718.* London: S.P.C.K., 1956.

Faulkner, Robert. *Richard Hooker and the Politics of a Christian England.* Berkeley: University of California Press, 1981.

Ferguson, J. P. *Dr. Samuel Clarke: An Eighteenth Century Heretic.* Kineton, Warwick: The Roundwood Press, 1976.

Frend, W. H. C. *The Early Church.* Philadelphia: Fortress Press, 1982.

———. *The Rise of Christianity.* Philadelphia: Fortress Press, 1984.

George, Timothy. *Theology of the Reformers.* Nashville: Broadman Press, 1988.

Green, I. M. *The Re-Establishment of the Church of England 1660–1663.* Oxford: Oxford University Press, 1978.

Grisbrooke, W. Jardine. *Anglican Liturgies of the Seventeenth and Eighteenth Centuries.* Alcuin Club Collections No. 40. London: S.P.C.K., 1958.

Gunn, J. A. W. *Beyond Liberty and Property: The Process of Self-Recognition in Eighteenth Century Political Thought.* Kingston and Montreal: McGill-Queen's University, 1983.

Hagglund, Bengt. *History of Theology.* Translated by Gene J. Lund. St. Louis: Concordia Publishing House, 1968.

Harrison, D. E. W. and Michael C. Sansom. *Worship in the Church of England.* London: S.P.C.K., 1982.

Harrison, Peter. *'Religion' and the Religions in the English Enlightenment.* Cambridge: Cambridge University Press, 1990.

Hatchett, Marion J. *The Making of the First American Book of Common Prayer.* New York: Seabury Press, 1982.

Hawkins, L. M. *Allegiance in Church and State.* London: George Routledge and Sons, Ltd., 1928.

Hebert, Charles. *The Lord's Supper: Uninspired Teaching.* 2 volumes. London: Seeley, Jackson and Halliday, 1879.

Hill, Christopher. *The Century of Revolution, 1603–1714.* Second Edition. New York: W. W. Norton & Company, 1980.

Holmes, Geoffrey. *The Trial of Doctor Sacheverell.* London: Eyre Methuen Ltd., 1973.

Hopfl, Harro. *The Christian Polity of John Calvin.* Cambridge: Cambridge University Press, 1982.

Hughes, Philip E. *The Theology of the English Reformers.* Second Edition. Grand Rapids, MI: Baker Book House, 1980.

Hunt, John. *Religious Thought in England.* 3 Volumes. London: Strahan and Co., 1870–1873.

Hutton, William H. *The English Church from the Accession of Charles I to the Death of Anne (1625–1714).* New York: Macmillan and Company. 1903. Reprinted New York: AMS Press, 1970.

Jacob, Margaret C. *The Newtonians and the English Revolution 1689–1720.* Ithaca: Cornell University Press, 1976.

————. *The Radical Englightenment: Pantheists, Free Masons and Republicans.* London: George Allen and Unwin, 1981.

Jones, J. R. *The Revolution of 1688 in England.* New York: W. W. Norton and Company, 1972.

Keeble, N. H. *Richard Baxter: Puritan Man of Letters.* Oxford: Clarendon Press, 1982.

Kenyon, J. P. *Revolution Principles: The Politics of Party 1689–1720.* Cambridge: Cambridge University Press, 1990.

Lacey, Douglas. *Dissent and Parliamentary Politics in England, 1661–1689.* New Brunswick, NJ: Rutgers University Press, 1969.

Lamont, William. *Richard Baxter and the Millennium.* Totowa, NJ: Rowman and Littlefield, 1979.

Langford, Paul. *A Polite and Commercial People: England 1727–1783.* Oxford: Clarendon Press, 1989.

Laski, Harold J. *Political Thought in England From Locke to Bentham.* New York: Henry Holt and Company, 1920. Reprinted, Wesport, CT: Greenwood Press, Inc., 1973.

Lathbury, Thomas. *A History of the Nonjurors.* London: William Pickering, 1845.

Latourette, Kenneth Scott. *A History of Christianity.* Revised Edition. 2 volumes. New York: Harper and Row, Publishers, 1975.

Legg, J. Wickham. *English Church Life: From the Restoration to the Tractarian Movement.* London: Longmans, Green and Company, 1914.

Marshall, John S. *Hooker and the Anglican Tradition.* Sewannee, TN: University of the South Press, 1963.

Marshall, William. *George Hopper 1640–1727, Bishop of Bath and Wells.* Milbourne Port, Great Britain: Dorsett Publishing Company, 1976.

McDonnell, Killian. *John Calvin, the Church, and the Eucharist.* Princeton: Princeton University Press, 1963.

McNeill, John T. *A History of the Cure of Souls.* New York: Harper and Brothers, Publishers, 1951.

Middleton, Robert Dudley. *Newman at Oxford: His Religious Development.* London: Oxford University Press, 1950.

Monod, Paul Kleber. *Jacobitism and the English People 1688–1788.* Cambridge: Cambridge University Press, 1989.

Moorman, J. R. H. *A History of the Church in England.* Third Edition. London: Adam and Charles Black, Ltd., 1976.

More, Paul Elmer, and Frank Leslie Cross, Editors. *Anglicanism.* New York: Macmillan Company, 1957.

Morgan, Irvonwy. *The Nonconformity of Richard Baxter.* London: Epworth Press, 1945.

Muller, Richard. *Dictionary of Latin and Greek Theological Terms.* Grand Rapids, MI: Baker Book House, 1985.

Nuttall, Geoffrey, and Owen Chadwick, Editors. *From Uniformity to Unity.* London: S.P.C.K., 1962.

Oakley, Francis. *Omnipotence, Covenant and Order.* Ithaca: Cornell University Press, 1984.

Oberman, Heiko. *Harvest of Medieval Theology.* Third edition. Durham, NC: Labyrinth Press, 1983.

Oden, Thomas. *Pastoral Theology.* San Francisco: Harper and Row, Publishers, 1983.

Overton, John H. and Relton, Frederick. *The English Church From the Accession of George I to the End of the Century (1714–1800).* London: Macmillan and Company Limited, 1924.

Overton, J. H. *The Non-Jurors: Their Lives, Principles and Writings.* New York: Thomas Whittaker. 1903.

Packer, John W. *The Transformation of Anglicanism 1643–1660.* Manchester: Manchester University Press, 1969.

Power, David N. *The Sacrifice We Offer.* Edinburgh: T. & T. Clark, Ltd., 1987.

*Prayer Book Studies IV, The Eucharistic Liturgy.* New York: The Church Pension Fund, 1953.

Redwood, John. *Reason, Ridicule and Religion: The Age of Enlightenment in England 1660–1750.* Cambridge: Harvard University Press, 1976.

Reedy, Gerard. *The Bible as Reason.* Philadelphia: University of Pennsylvania Press, 1985.

Rivers, Isabel. *Reason, Grace, and Sentiment: A Study of the Language of Religion and Ethics in England, 1660–1780: Volume 1 Whichcote to Wesley.* Cambridge: Cambridge University Press, 1991.

Rowell, Geoffrey. *The Vision Glorious.* Oxford: Oxford University Press, 1983.

Rowlands, J. H. L. *Church, State and Society: The Attitudes of John Keble, Richard Hurrell Froude and John Henry Newman.* Worthing, West Sussex: Churchman Publishing, Ltd., 1989.

Rupp, Gordon. *Religion in England 1688–1791.* Oxford: Clarendon Press, 1986.

Sabine, George H. and Thomas Landon Thorson. *A History of Political Theory.* Fourth edition. Hinsdale, IL: Dryden Press, 1973.

Seeberg, Reinhold. *Textbook of the History of Doctrines.* Translated by Charles E. Hay. 2 volumes in 1. Grand Rapids, MI: Baker Book House, 1977.

Smith, R. J. *The Gothic Bequest: Medieval Institutions in British Thought, 1688–1863.* Cambridge: Cambridge University Press, 1987.

Solt, Leo F. *Church and State in Early Modern England 1509–1640.* New York: Oxford University Press, 1990.

Sommerville, C. John. *Popular Religion in Restoration England.* Gainesville: The University Presses of Florida, 1977.

Speck, W. A. *Reluctant Revolutionaries: Englishmen and the Revolution of 1688.* New York: Oxford University Press, 1988.

———. *Stability and Strife: England 1714–1760.* Cambridge: Harvard University Press, 1977.

Stone, Darwell. *A History of the Doctrine of the Holy Eucharist.* 2 Volumes. London: Longman, Green and Company, 1950.

Straka, Gerald M. *The Anglican Reaction to the Revolution of 1688.* Madison: University of Wisconsin Press, 1962.

Stromberg, Roland. *Religious Liberalism in Eighteenth-Century England.* London: Oxford University Press, 1954.

Sullivan, Robert. *John Toland and the Deist Controversy.* Cambridge: Harvard University Press, 1982.

Sykes, Norman. *Church and State in the XVIIIth Century.* Cambridge: Cambridge University Press, 1934. Reprinted, Hamden, CN: Archon Books, 1962.

——. *Edmund Gibson.* Oxford: Oxford University Press, 1926.

——. *From Sheldon to Secker: Aspects of English Church History 1660–1768.* Cambridge: Cambridge University Press, 1959.

——. *Old Priest and New Presbyter.* Cambridge: Cambridge University Press, 1956.

——. *William Wake, Archbishop of Canterbury.* 2 volumes. Cambridge: Cambridge University Press, 1957.

Szechi, Daniel. *Jacobitism and Tory Politics 1710–14.* Edinburgh: John Donald Publishers, ltd., 1984.

Tavard, George. *The Quest for Catholicity.* New York: Herder and Herder, 1964.

Underwood, A. C. *A History of the English Baptists.* London: The Carey Kingsgate Press, Ltd., 1947.

Virgin, Peter. *The Church in an Age of Negligence.* Cambridge: James Clarke and Co., 1989.

Watts, Michael R. *The Dissenters: From the Reformation to the Revolution.* Oxford: Clarendom Press, 1978.

Weil, Louis. *Sacraments and Liturgy: The Outward Signs.* Oxford: Basil Blackwell, Ltd., 1983.

Woodhouse, H. F. *The Doctrine of the Church in Anglican Theology, 1547–1603.* London: S.P.C.K., 1954.

Young, Frances. *From Nicea to Chalcedon.* Philadelphia: Fortress Press, 1983.

## DISSERTATIONS

Findon, John. "The Non-jurors and the Church of England 1689–1716." D. Phil. Diss., Oxford University, 1978.

Yould, Guy Martin. "The Origins and Transformation of the Non-Juror Schism, 1670–1715." Ph.D. Diss., University of Hull, 1979.

# Index